Albert Eugene Reynolds

Albert Eugene Reynolds

Colorado's Mining King

By Lee Scamehorn

University of Oklahoma Press : Norman and London

By Lee Scamehorn

Balloons to Jets: A Century of Aeronautics in Illinois, 1855–1955 (Chicago, 1957)

The Buckeye Rovers in the Gold Rush: An Edition of Two Diaries (Athens, Ohio, 1965, 1989)

(coauthor) *The University of Colorado, 1876–1976* (New York, 1976)

Pioneer Steelmaker in the West: The Colorado Fuel and Iron Company, 1872– 1903 (Boulder, 1976)

Mine and Mill: The CF&I in the Twentieth Century (Lincoln, Nebr., 1992)

This book is published with the generous assistance of The McCasland Foundation, Duncan, Oklahoma.

Library of Congress Cataloging-in-Publication Data

Scamehorn, H. Lee (Howard Lee), 1926–
    Albert Eugene Reynolds : Colorado's mining king / by Lee Scamehorn.
        p.   cm.
    Includes bibliographical references and index.
    ISBN 0–8061–2767–8 (cloth : alk. paper)
    1. Reynolds, Albert Eugene, 1840–1921. 2. Pioneers—Colorado— Biography. 3. Businessmen—Colorado—Biography. 4. Silver mines and mining—Colorado—History. 5. Gold mines and min- ing—Colorado—History. 6. Colorado—Biography. I. Title.
F781.R49S23   1995
978.8'03'092—dc20
[B]   95-15206
                                                                                CIP

The paper in this book meets the guidelines for permanence and durability of the Committee on Production Guidelines for Book Lon- gevity of the Council on Library Resources, Inc. ⊗

1   2   3   4   5   6   7   8   9   10

To Rosslyn

Contents

	List of Illustrations	ix
	List of Maps	xi
	Preface	xiii
1.	Western Entrepreneur	5
2.	Frontier Trader	38
3.	Ranching on the High Plains	63
4.	Creating a Mining Empire	83
5.	An Abundance of Silver	114
6.	Searching for New Bonanzas	139
7.	Decline of the Mining Industry	164
8.	End of a Career	186
9.	The Legacy	208
	Notes	235
	Bibliography	281
	Index	291

Illustrations

Following page 32
Albert Eugene Reynolds (1840–1921)
Caroline Van Horn Reynolds (Mrs. Henry A. Reynolds)
Albert Eugene Reynolds, trader, Indian Territory
Family portrait: A. E. Reynolds and wife Dora; sisters Fanny
  Reynolds and Alice Reynolds; and brother Charles F.
  Reynolds
Frances Eudorah Reynolds (Mrs. A. E. Reynolds)
Dr. Robert Earll
Family portrait: A. E. Reynolds with daughter and grand-
  children

Following page 107
Revenue Mill, Sneffels, Ouray County, Colorado
Virginius Mine, Ouray County, Colorado
Freight wagons on road from Revenue Mill to Ouray, Colo-
  rado
Commodore Mine, Creede, Mineral County, Colorado
Mines at Summitville, Rio Grande County, Colorado
Frank Hough Mine, Hindsdale County, Colorado
Gold Links Mine and Mill, Gunnison County, Colorado
One of A. E. Reynolds's mines near Pitkin, Gunnison County,
  Colorado
Office personnel, Denver, Colorado: A. E. Reynolds, J. P. M.
  Humphrey, David G. Miller, and Charles F. McKenney

Anna Reynolds Morse Garrey, Carl J. Sigfrid, Ben T. Poxson,
  and George H. Garrey

Following page 161
Cutting wheat on the Reynolds farms, La Junta, Colorado
Thoroughbred Hereford heifers, Reynolds Ranch, Chan-
  ning, Texas
Cutting alfalfa on the Reynolds farms, La Junta, Colorado

Maps

The Southwest, ca. 1880   2

Colorado, ca. 1880   107

Preface

ALBERT Eugene Reynolds was the embodiment of the American dream, the legendary youth who left a humble home in the East to seek success and fortune in the American West. Starting with modest means, he combined ambition, industry, skill, and luck to become a successful entrepreneur, pursuing at one time or another a number of different activities or interests. Through various business opportunities he acquired not only wealth but also recognition and respect from his peers as a merchant, overland freighter, cattle rancher, and owner of gold and silver mines. He was, in fact, Colorado's leading promoter and operator of mines, yet his remarkable exploits were generally unknown outside of a circle of close friends and associates in his day, and he has been virtually unknown since his death in 1921.

This lack of attention can be attributed, at least in part, to Reynolds's habit of keeping information from the public. He lived a quiet, unobtrusive life, and he shunned publicity for himself and for his business enterprises. For that reason, even though he was a mining man of great stature, of greater accomplishments perhaps than most of his better-known contemporaries, he has been largely ignored by historians. It is also true that until recently researchers have not had access to more than meager scraps of information about Reynolds and his achievements as an entrepreneur. His extant papers, an unusually complete set of personal and business records, were known only to family members and a few close friends.

After Reynolds's death in 1921 William N. Beggs, president of the Colorado State Natural History and Historical Society, asked Anna Reynolds Morse for her father's papers. The society had a policy of soliciting the records of organizations and people who had played important roles in shaping the history of the state. When, for some reason, there was no reply, Beggs probably assumed that the documents pertinent to Reynolds's career had been discarded or destroyed.

Perhaps because Morse was preoccupied with the task of putting her father's immense estate in order, she did not respond to Beggs's request. However, Reynolds's papers, including records of numerous business enterprises, remained intact in his daughter's care. It was her wish that the papers be placed in a historical records repository only after her death.

In July 1982, one month before Anna Reynolds Morse Garrey's death (she had remarried after her first husband's death) at the age of ninety-eight, her children, Albert Reynolds Morse, Eudorah Morse Moore, and Ann Morse Tippit, gave the papers of A. E. Reynolds to the Colorado Historical Society, successor to the Colorado State Natural History and Historical Society. The collection is a valuable addition to the society's extensive manuscript holdings pertaining to entrepreneurs and mining in Colorado and elsewhere the West.

The challenge of writing a biography of A. E. Reynolds commenced in 1982, with the preparation of an inventory of his papers. These materials are a record of Reynolds's business activities from 1870 to 1921. The documents, initially in almost complete disarray, were identified topically and arranged chronologically in order to reveal the dimensions of Reynolds the man and the magnitude of his career as an innovative, successful businessman. However, the records contain little insight into his personality or into his activities outside of the business enterprises that he owned or controlled during his lifetime.

Although Albert Eugene Reynolds excelled as a mining entrepreneur, he was more than an owner, operator, and promoter of mining properties. As an individual or in partnership with others, he was at one time or another a military sutler (post trader) at Fort Lyon, Colorado Territory; Fort Supply, Indian Territory; and Fort Elliott in the Texas Panhandle. In addition, he was a licensed trader to the Arapahoe and Cheyenne tribes, and he later operated general merchandise stores in Hinsdale and Ouray Counties, Colorado. He owned ranches in Texas and Colorado and after 1900 developed irrigated farms in Colorado's Arkansas River valley.

Chapter 1 treats A. E. Reynolds's passage through life, from his origins in upstate New York to his death eighty-one years later in Old Hickory, Tennessee. Attention is given to his attributes as an entrepreneur, family man, and civic leader, with emphasis on his unique talent for promoting and managing a wide range of business activities and enterprises and his achievements in merchandising, ranching, and mining in the West. His long and illustrious career as a businessman assured him a place of prominence in the affairs of his adopted city, Denver, where he was for many years a quiet but effective promoter of projects for community betterment.

Separate chapters explore Reynolds's roles as an entrepreneur. Chapter 2 is devoted to his activities as the senior member of the firm of Lee and Reynolds, a partnership that operated stores in Indian Territory and the Texas Panhandle. The traders created the region's largest freighting enterprise to serve their transportation needs, in addition to those of the military at Fort Supply and Fort Elliott and the Cheyenne and Arapahoe Agency. Activities in Indian Territory generated considerable wealth, which allowed Reynolds to acquire a large ranch in Texas, in addition to building a mining empire in Colorado.

Chapter 3 is devoted to Reynolds's career as a rancher. After the close of the Red River War of 1874–1875, Lee and Reynolds purchased a large tract of land in the Canadian

River valley, east of the Texas–New Mexico border, on which to raise cattle. The partnership was dissolved in 1882, after which Reynolds, as the principal owner of the LE Ranch, successfully upgraded native longhorn cattle through cross-breeding with purebred Herefords. After twenty years Reynolds sold the Panhandle ranch to the Scottish-owned Prairie Cattle Company, after which he continued to operate a ranch in the Arkansas River valley near La Junta, Colorado, for several years before developing the land as irrigated farms.

Chapters 4 through 8 examine Reynolds's career as a mining entrepreneur and the development of his extensive properties. These included the celebrated Virginius Mine and the Revenue Tunnel on Mount Sneffels in Ouray County; the Commodore and other large silver producers at Creede in Mineral County; the Argenta, Palmetto, Ocean Wave, and Frank Hough near Lake City in Hinsdale County; the Golconda Gold Mining Company, which held titles to about one-half of the claims in the Summitville Mining District of Rio Grande County; the Platoro and adjacent mines at Platoro in Conejos County; the May Day and adjoining claims near Hesperus in La Plata County; the Tarifa and Etcetera at Highlands, above Aspen, in Pitkin County; and more than three hundred claims near Tin Cup, Pitkin, and Ohio City in Gunnison County. Largely undeveloped properties were located in Boulder, Lake, and San Juan Counties in Colorado and in Arizona, New Mexico, Nevada, Utah, and Canada.

According to his son-in-law, Brad Morse, Reynolds could not resist buying mining properties. Morse compared him to a child with a new toy; there was always a need for another and another until Reynolds owned, by his own estimate, three times more mining property than any other single person in Colorado. During the peak years of mining, from 1880 until shortly after the turn of the century, Reynolds was more than an owner of mines; he was an astute promoter and manager of highly successful silver- and gold-producing properties.

The success that crowned Reynolds's efforts derived, in

part, from his willingness to use advances in technology to tackle the engineering problems of mining and from his ability to reduce costs, during a long downward slide in silver prices. His achievements may also be attributed to a remarkable capacity to mobilize large amounts of investment capital with which to acquire, develop, and operate mining properties. Although he made a business of peddling the stocks of high-risk mining ventures to investors, he maintained a reputation for honest, efficient management of mines and the ability to earn large profits from many of his properties.

Unlike many of his contemporaries who made fortunes in mining, Reynolds never lost faith in the industry. During the first two decades of the twentieth century, while friends redirected their efforts to banking, transportation, and merchandising, Reynolds persisted in the search for still more bonanzas. For nearly two decades he struggled against enormous odds to hold onto his properties, the majority of which were idle for lack of capital to underwrite development. Despite a persistent cash-flow problem, he passed his mining empire, largely intact, to his daughter and heir.

Chapter 9 is devoted to A. E. Reynolds's legacy, the immense mining empire that he left to Anna Reynolds Morse and through her to his grand- and great-grandchildren. Morse inherited equities of uncertain value in farms near La Junta and thousands of mining claims, all of which were encumbered with debts. Their value was questionable until Brad Morse assumed the management of his wife's inheritance and proved that many of Reynolds's mining properties, as the old man had insisted for years before his death, were capable of large-scale silver and gold production.

Eventually two of those properties—Creede and Summitville—became large producers of precious metals. The latter, in the hands of a lessee, gained widespread notoriety as the scene of a massive heap-leaching project in the 1980s and 1990s. When the project went awry, the U.S. Environmental Protection Agency (EPA) was forced to take control of the site in an effort to minimize damage to the region's streams and rivers.

The writer of a business biography incurs numerous debts that require acknowledgments of appreciation. A sincere thank-you is extended to librarians, archivists, and manuscript curators, those indispensable people who preserve and make accessible to researchers the records of the past. Outstanding in this respect were the staffs of the History Research Center at the Kansas State Historical Society, Topeka; the library of Wichita State University; the Oklahoma Historical Collection at the University of Oklahoma, Norman; the Ouray County (Colorado) Historical Society; the Western Historical Collections, Norlin Library, University of Colorado, Boulder; the Arthur Lakes Library, Colorado School of Mines, Golden; and the Western History Department, Denver Public Library.

To the personnel of the Stephen H. Hart Library of the Colorado Historical Society, Denver, a very special thank-you is offered. Without their generous assistance this biography could not have been written. Their consistently cheerful and helpful support made five years of research in the A. E. Reynolds Collection both easy and enjoyable.

Other people contributed in special ways to the research and writing of this biography. Dr. Doris Gregory, of Montrose, Colorado, permitted the author to read her manuscript on Hubbell W. Reed and the Virginius Mine. Historians Ruth and Marvin Gregory shared their knowledge of and insights into Ouray's rich mining history and made available to the author seven of Reed's letterpress books for the years 1883–1897. Ouray resident Roger Henn helped track down missing letters and shared with the author a study of the Caroline Mining Company. David Halaas, historian for the Colorado State Historical Society, provided ongoing encouragement and shared with the author his knowledge of the Cheyennes and Arapahoes. Halaas, Thomas J. Noel, and Duane A. Smith contributed valuable suggestions for improving the historical accuracy of the manuscript.

To the grandchildren of A. E. Reynolds a very special thank-you is given for placing the papers of their illustrious ancestor in a public repository. In addition, Albert Reynolds Morse's "Gold Links Tailings," a series of articles published in the *Gunnison Country Times*, provided valuable insights into the life and legend of his grandfather. John H. Tippit, the husband of A. E. Reynolds's younger granddaughter, expertly guided the author through the recent history of the Reynolds mining empire.

Albert Eugene Reynolds

Map 1

THE SOUTHWEST, ca. 1880

1
Western Entrepreneur

IN the aftermath of the long, bloody war between the Union and the Confederacy, the American West was a magnet that attracted great numbers of restless, ambitious people in search of adventure, fortune, or a different way of life. For some the West was a land of opportunity. For others it was a place of frustration and disappointment. A few accumulated great wealth, social position, and economic power, while most toiled on farms and ranches and in mines and shops, contributing through their labor to the dramatic growth of the region.

The land beyond the 100th meridian was ideally suited to Albert Eugene Reynolds's ambition, drive, and talents. He relocated from New York to Colorado via Leavenworth, Kansas, then moved on to Indian Territory and the Texas Panhandle before returning to Colorado, where he spent the final fifty years of his life. In succession he was a military sutler (post trader), Indian trader, freighter, army contractor, High Plains rancher, mining entrepreneur, farmer, and land developer. A wealthy, respected resident of Denver for nearly forty years, he was one of the founders of the Denver Museum of Natural History, a trustee of Colorado Seminary and the University of Denver, an intimate adviser of prominent politicians, and a supporter of many civic causes.

Born on February 13, 1840, in Newfane, Niagara County, New York, Albert Eugene Reynolds was the second child, and first son, of Henry A. and Caroline Van Horn Reynolds.

Albert grew to manhood in Lockport, where the family had relocated when he was an infant. Henry Reynolds owned and operated a general store in addition to a farm near Newfane. Both sources of income were needed because the size of the family increased at a steady space over a period of more than two decades. Every two to three years Caroline Reynolds gave birth to another child.

Ten children survived infancy and childhood illnesses to reach adulthood. Albert had been preceded by Ellen C. in January 1838 and was followed by George E. in February 1842. Andrew J. was born in July 1844; Elizabeth, in April 1847; Abbie, in March 1849; and Charles F., in January 1852. Alice arrived in January 1854; Harriet, in June 1856; and the last of the Reynolds's children, Fanny, in March 1862.[1]

The Reynolds family was prominent in local affairs. Albert's paternal grandfather had been an officer in the War of 1812. His maternal grandfather was the owner of flour and woolen mills in Niagara County. Uncle Burt Van Horn, his mother's youngest brother, was influential in the Republican Party and served in the U.S. House of Representatives from western New York during and after the Civil War.[2]

The Reynolds siblings were a respectable lot, generally educated according to the standards of the time. The girls may have attended local schools, but it seems likely that they were trained mainly in household or domestic arts by their mother. At least two of the boys were educated beyond the public school system. Albert attended the Fort Edward Collegiate Institute and Madison University (later called Colgate College). After only a year at each school he returned home to work on the land and in his father's mercantile enterprise.[3]

Of the other boys, only Andrew appears to have had an opportunity for higher education. It is not apparent that George and Charles attended other than local schools, which probably ended with the eighth grade. They were, however, well grounded in the basic knowledge essential for careers in merchandising, farming, and ranching. Andrew, the second youngest of the boys, graduated from Yale University, after which he practiced law for a time.[4]

As the eldest of the males, Albert was the natural leader, the achiever, and he invariably succeeded at any task to which he devoted attention and effort. This characteristic not only set him apart from his siblings but also prompted them to look to him for their well-being. Albert was ambitious, self-confident, aggressive, tenacious, and competitive, qualities that his brothers and sisters lacked in varying degrees. He was uneasy when dependent upon people but willingly encouraged others to become dependent upon him. He readily accepted responsibility for the actions of his siblings and supported and looked after them in numerous ways throughout his adult years.[5]

At the close of the Civil War, a national drama in which only Andrew, among Henry Reynolds's boys, participated in a military role, Albert left home with $80 in his pocket, the sum of his savings, to seek his fortune in the region west of the Mississippi River. He located in Junction, Kansas, a community on the Missouri River adjacent to Leavenworth, into which it was eventually absorbed.[6] There he found employment with one of the community's numerous mercantile firms. He remained there long enough to acquire, presumably on credit, a stock of goods with which to establish a store in Richmond, Missouri, a farming community located 20 miles north of Lexington, an important Missouri River port. This was a joint venture with one of his brothers, probably George. After about a year A. E. returned to Leavenworth and almost immediately went to Fort Lyon, Colorado Territory, as an agent for a local merchant, to take charge of a post trader's store.

The position of sutler, a trader who sold goods of great variety to officers and enlisted men, had been abolished by Congress in 1866 for alleged abuses of marketing privileges at military posts. Within less than a year, however, the obvious need for retail merchants at remote military facilities caused

Congress to authorize post traders for frontier garrisons
between the 100th meridian and the Sierra Nevada Mountains. It was this reversal of policy that afforded Reynolds an
opportunity to travel to Fort Lyon to take charge of a trader's
store.[7]

Reynolds bought out his employer and became a sutler in
his own right before the close of 1867. A. E. Reynolds and
Company maintained stores at the fort and in the nearby
town of Las Animas. In fact, Reynolds was one of two merchants at the military post. The other was John A. Thatcher,
later a prominent banker in Pueblo, Colorado. When the post
was relocated from the bottomlands of the Arkansas River to
higher ground east of the original site, Reynolds, as a contractor to the army, furnished the lime used to make mortar for
the construction of buildings at the new Fort Lyon.[8]

In 1869 Reynolds surrendered his sutler's license. After
transferring the management of the town business to his
cousin, D. W. Van Horn, Reynolds followed the Cheyenne and
Arapahoe tribes, which were relocated to a new reservation in
Indian Territory. There he hoped to expand business opportunities by serving as merchant to the Indians as well as to the
army.

For a time that goal seemed unattainable because of a rival
claimant for trading rights. At Camp Supply (later desig-
nated Fort Supply), located approximately 100 miles south of
Fort Dodge and Dodge City, Kansas, Reynolds secured a
sutler's license from the post commander, Colonel A. D. Nelson. While preparing to open a store at the camp, Reynolds
sought a license to trade with the Cheyennes and Arapahoes,
who were temporarily located in the vicinity of the post. In
quest of the second permit he had to apply through the local
agent to the commissioner of Indian affairs. On doing so,
Reynolds discovered that the privilege of trading with the
tribes had been granted to W. M. D. Lee, a former army
quarter master, who also wanted to open a sutler's store at
Camp Supply. Rather than compete with each other, Lee and

Reynolds combined operations, forming a partnership that exercised a monopoly on mercantile operations in the northern section of Indian Territory.[9]

The firm of Lee and Reynolds remained active for more than a dozen years. The Indian trade was immensely profitable as long as the Arapahoe and Cheyenne had buffalo robes and hides to trade for merchandise. After the slaughter of the herd on the southern Plains, completed by 1878, Lee and Reynolds sold the Indian agency store and limited their merchandising effort to retail outlets at Fort Supply, at Fort Elliott in the Texas Panhandle, and at places designed to serve the military during temporary field operations or cattlemen driving herds of longhorns out of Texas to the railroad at Caldwell and other points in Kansas.

The partners were bold, imaginative, and ambitious entrepreneurs. They seized upon opportunities to engage in activities that enhanced their roles as traders to the military and the Indians. They provided whatever goods and services were needed when there was a profit to be made in doing so. They operated saloons and billiard rooms in conjunction with sutler's stores. In the nearby river bottoms they put crews to work cutting and curing hay and chopping and splitting cord wood, for which the Department of the Missouri, with headquarters at Fort Leavenworth, contracted annually to meet the needs of Camp (Fort) Supply, Fort Elliott, and Fort Reno (near the permanent Indian agency headquarters at Darlington). The Indian agent bought large amounts of hay and wood for tribal use.

Lee and Reynolds operated a large freighting business from Dodge City southward into Indian Territory and the Texas Panhandle. They hauled their own goods as well as freight for the military. Later they transported supplies for Texas ranchers and for miners in the Colorado Rockies.

The partners pursued a wide range of additional activities. They grazed cattle on the open range in Indian Territory in order to supply, as private contractors, fresh beef to the

Indian agency and to military posts. They operated slaughterhouses at Fort Supply and Fort Elliott. They transported
U.S. mails and served as postmasters at Supply and Elliott. In
1879 they provided the cedar poles with which the army
linked Forts Supply and Elliott by telegraph.

These ventures generated large profits, which the partners
invested in multiple ventures. They bought and stocked a
large ranch in the Texas Panhandle, invested in Utah and
Colorado mineral lands, and purchased large quantities of
railroad and other securities. A quarrel, the exact cause of
which is unknown, at the Panhandle ranch near Tascosa in
January 1882 led to the termination of the partnership.
Thereafter each man pursued his own entrepreneurial objectives. For a time each operated a large ranch in Texas while
pursuing careers elsewhere that earned them wealth and
recognition as businessmen.

Reynolds continued in merchandising and freighting for
several years before abandoning those activities to concentrate on the mining and processing of precious metal ores. His
ventures were principally in Colorado but also on a small scale
in Arizona, New Mexico, Utah, and Nevada. Unlike many of
his contemporaries, he was not attracted to the mines of
Mexico, but he did acquire on behalf of a friend an interest in
mineral lands in the Thunder Bay district of Ontario, Canada.

Silver mines near Lake City, Colorado, first drew Reynolds
to the extraction of precious metal ores. There he launched
what became a lifelong habit of accumulating properties.
Failure to find a bonanza drove him to seek better opportunities to the west, beyond Engineer Mountain in the vicinity
of Ouray. There, with associates, he struck it rich. The Virginius Mine and the Revenue Tunnel, which eventually opened
the vein at a depth of 3,000 feet, were great successes.

The Virginius Mine revealed Reynolds's unusual talent for
organizing and managing mining operations. Whenever he
acquired a potentially valuable property, he placed the responsibility for day-to-day operations in the hands of a highly

competent superintendent. Hubbell W. Reed, an engineer of wide experience, held that position at the Ouray property for twenty years. Angus Snedaker, Charles F. Palmer, and David G. Miller, managers and mining engineers of unquestioned competence, had charge of other properties. Reynolds required that his managers keep him informed of day-to-day operations. No detail was too technical, or too obscure, not to merit his attention.

Although self-taught, Reynolds was well versed on nearly all aspects of geology and mining engineering and could discuss virtually all features of mining and milling operations with the men he hired to administer his properties. He gave them considerable authority to act upon their own, but he expected them to function within guidelines that he alone defined.[10]

The all-important task of maintaining day-to-day control over wide-ranging business affairs was entrusted to Charles F. McKenney, confidential adviser and Reynolds's friend for thirty-seven years. Starting as a clerk for Lee and Reynolds in Indian Territory, McKenney had accompanied Reynolds to Colorado and assumed charge of the Denver office established in 1884.[11] As office manager he kept track of activities at the Panhandle ranch, an ever-increasing number of mining enterprises, and a large volume of speculative investments in corporate securities and silver futures. Initially Reynolds's headquarters was located in the Hughes Block on Sixteenth Street; later it was relocated to the prestigious Equitable Building on Seventeenth Street. McKenney, eventually with the assistance of J. P. M. Humphrey, who became his successor in 1910, gave careful attention to preparing, filing, and, on demand, retrieving an enormous volume of data in the form of letters and related documents. This made McKenney an indispensable employee and a key contributor to Reynolds's successful administration of a growing volume of mining activities.

Another reason for Reynolds's phenomenal success as a mining entrepreneur was his long association with Mahlon D.

Thatcher. The Pueblo banker was an intimate adviser, a key investor in numerous mines, and, after 1891, the owner of one-third interest in the Texas Panhandle ranch. It was from Thatcher that Reynolds borrowed funds for business ventures in good times and bad. As a matter of business strategy Reynolds consistently borrowed funds with which to start new ventures and to sustain those that were ongoing. The two men and their respective families became very close, often taking vacations together.[12] Thatcher, a conservative banker, may have been attracted to Reynolds because of his capacity for innovation, for he had a remarkable talent for responding to changing conditions, whether as a trader, rancher, or mine-owner and operator.

The decline of silver was a major challenge for Reynolds. He recognized that falling prices required reductions in the cost of producing and processing ore. His mines yielded mostly silver, only small quantities of gold, and large quantities of lead or copper. Silver began to slide in 1873, and by 1883, when the Virginius became a large producer for the first time, the uncertain market value of that metal was clouding prospects for profits. Whenever the price fell, as it did more or less consistently, Reynolds tried to match that decline with reductions in expenditures. The alternative in the long run was to operate at a loss. In theory if he could not lower costs, he could suspend operations until the market recovered. However, he did not see that as a viable option. In fact, the price of silver did not return to pre-1883 level values until World War I and then remained high only for a short time.

The downward spiral was particularly dramatic for the ten years commencing in 1883. In December of that year, when the Virginius Mine began large-scale operations, the average market price of silver was $1.104 per ounce. A long-term trend toward lower prices can be seen in the average value of silver in the final month of each subsequent year: $1.75 in 1884, $1.25 in 1885, $0.996 in 1886, $0.928 in 1887, $0.952 in 1889, $1.043 in 1890, $0.948 in 1891, $0.832 in 1892, and

$0.693 in 1893.[13] The financial panic of 1893, combined with the repeal of the Sherman Silver Purchase Act, further undermined the price of silver, but it was a matter of supply exceeding demand that caused silver to remain in the $0.50 to $0.70 range the balance of the decade. This put a premium on the reduction of operating costs, usually by means of intensive applications of technology.

The key to successful mining in western Colorado, Reynolds believed, was economical transportation, particularly for moving ore in bulk from mine to smelter. For that reason he actively encouraged the men who controlled the narrow-gauge Denver and Rio Grande Railroad to build branch lines to Ouray, Lake City, and other mining camps. Reynolds was also an early advocate of railroad tunnels under the Continental Divide to reduce the cost of freight from one slope of the Rockies to the other. This was important to all large mine operators in western Colorado because the most efficient smelters, with the possible exception of plants at Leadville, were at Pueblo and Denver. Lower freight charges meant larger profits from the mining of ore.[14]

Another way to reduce costs was to end dependence on expensive coal-fired steam plants. At the Caroline Mining Company's Virginius Mine at Ouray steam was used to operate the hoister and pumps and to generate compressed air for machine drills. In 1889, convinced that electricity would cost only a fraction of steam power for operating the Virginius and the Revenue Tunnel, then under construction, Reynolds authorized hydroelectric plants on Canyon Creek. The initial expenditure for buildings, dynamos, wires, and motors for hoisters, pumps, and drills was $18,000, approximately the cost of coal delivered to the mine for one season.[15]

The Revenue Tunnel, which tapped the Virginius vein at a depth of 3,000 feet below the entrance to the mine shaft, was Colorado's first all-electric mine, using that source of power for all phases of mining and milling. Three water-driven turbines provided direct-current electricity. Steam power was used only when the cold of winter or the dryness of summer halted the flow of water. In 1901 a coal-fired steam-generating electric plant was erected in Ouray and transmission lines constructed to the Revenue Mine and Mill. An increase in power-generating capacity was required to sink a shaft beneath the tunnel level and to work the mine at an additional depth of 750 feet.[16]

The Revenue Tunnel introduced a new low-cost method of mining. Reynolds claimed to be the first to see the advantage of tapping mineral deposits at great depth by means of adits (invariably called tunnels) rather than vertical or inclined shafts. The cost of steam or electric power for lifting ore, pumping water from wet underground workings, and lowering everything needed to make a mine function efficiently convinced Reynolds that where terrain permitted, adits could serve as traffic ways as well as drainages for water. Deposits could be worked from below, using gravity to move ore from the point of extraction to cars for transporting it from the mine. In this way Reynolds significantly reduced the cost of mining ore, and his Revenue Tunnel became a model that was replicated by mine operators throughout Colorado and elsewhere the West.[17]

His faith in technology as the key to profitable mining was applied successfully to processing and preparing ore for shipment. Mills that combined techniques of amalgamation and concentration were erected at the entrances to tunnels. The Revenue Mill, which became the model for others, utilized electricity and contained state-of-the art machinery for crushing and concentrating low-grade ores. Reynolds insisted that mill superintendents experiment with jigs, bumping tables, vanners, and concentrating tables until they found the combination of equipment that saved the highest volume of gold, silver, lead, and copper values at the lowest possible cost. When concentration alone was not sufficient to extract values from complex ores, he turned to the highly efficient cyanide method of treatment. When that proved inadequate for handling the iron sulfides in the Emma Mine at Dunton, he adopted an oil flotation system.[18]

Because of success at Ouray, Reynolds was called to Aspen to take charge of the Durant Mining Company's claims, owned largely by Cincinnati lawyer David M. Hyman. By 1884 Hyman was locked in a fierce legal contest for control of the area's richest mines, claiming that the Durant property contained the apex that entitled him to work the vein even when it passed through neighboring properties. One of those so-called sideline claims was the Aspen, owned by wealthy New York City merchant Jerome B. Wheeler, who challenged Hyman's claim to all of the mineral from the Durant vein. The result was a classic court battle, a precedent-setting case in the annals of Colorado mining.[19]

In order to match Wheeler's financial resources, Hyman turned for assistance to Reynolds; Charles D. Arms, an iron maker in Youngstown, Ohio; and Charles Robinson, a New York capitalist. The two easterners put up the money to support the apex suit but insisted that Hyman place the management of the properties as well as the apex suit under the direction of an experienced mining man, namely, A. E. Reynolds. With the best legal talent available in Colorado, including Charles J. Hughes Jr. and U.S. Senator Henry Moore Teller, Reynolds scored a series of stunning court victories, but Hyman, apprehensive of the rising cost of the litigation, decided to seek a compromise with Wheeler and his associates. Disappointed at Hyman's failure to push the case to complete victory, Reynolds resigned from all positions in the Durant Mining Company in order to devote attention to driving the Revenue Tunnel at Ouray.

After the Aspen and Ouray ventures boosted Reynolds's reputation, a group of wealthy New York men eagerly sought stocks in his mining enterprises. They provided the capital he needed to acquire, develop, and operate mines throughout western Colorado. These men became close friends as well as business associates.

The New York merchants who supplied goods for Lee and
Reynolds's retail stores in Indian Territory may have been the
first to introduce Reynolds to potential investors in his Colorado
mines. James H. Bradley, a member of the mercantile house of
Buckley, Willing and Company, and E. H. Garbutt, a partner
in Garbutt, Griggs and Company (succeeded by E. H. Garbutt and Company), recommended the westerner to friends
and acquaintances, many of whom subsequently purchased
mining securities. That circle of investors widened as Reynolds's properties established reputations for paying dividends.

Returns on investments, although uneven, were at times
dramatic enough that Reynolds had little trouble funding
operations in the 1880s and 1890s. Wall Street banker William
C. Sheldon headed investors in New York and Boston who
advanced capital for development of the Caroline Mining
Company's Virginius Mine at Ouray. They were repaid in full
and also earned substantial dividends on the company's stock
while it was under their control.

The success of that venture attracted new investors. One of
J. H. Bradley's friends, William F. Havemeyer, who had inherited a fortune from his father's investments in sugar refineries
and New York financial institutions, underwrote a major part
of Reynolds's mining schemes for about a dozen years. Havemeyer put up the money for the initial acquisition and operation of the Hector Mining Company and Cimarron Mill at
Telluride. He and his son-in-law, William R. Willcox, were the
principal stockholders in the Grand Valley Irrigation and
Development Company and the Willcox Canal Company.
These enterprises, in which Reynolds served for a time as a
director, created a large expanse of irrigated farmland in the
Grand Valley shortly after the turn of the century. At one time
Reynolds hoped to market irrigated farmland he owned in
the Arkansas River valley together with Havemeyer's proper-
ty in western Colorado. That scheme was not implemented.[20]

Another consistent supporter of Reynolds's mining enterprises was Charles A. Starbuck, president of the New York Air

Brake Company. A native of Niagara County, Starbuck was ten years younger than Reynolds. Starbuck relocated to New York City in 1870 to work for a diamond merchant. He soon left that job to take a position with the Eames Vacuum Brake Company, which later merged with the New York Air Brake Company. He was promoted to vice president in 1890 and was named president in 1894. He retained that position until his death in 1925.[21]

Reynolds had a long and sometimes stormy relationship with Starbuck. From 1886 to about 1910 the New Yorker was a large stockholder in several of Reynolds's mines, including those in La Plata and Gunnison Counties. Influenced by access to "insider" information, Reynolds, in turn, invested heavily in the stock of the New York Air Brake Company. Much to his annoyance, its price fluctuated wildly on a downward path, despite Starbuck's assurances that the stock would increase in value. Some investors—but not Reynolds—concluded that Starbuck was manipulating the stock for his own advantage. Over a period of nearly two decades Reynolds lost a substantial amount of money speculating in Air Brake securities.[22]

By far the most colorful of Reynolds's financial backers was Theodore N. Barnsdall, a prominent oilman from Pittsburgh who had large interests in Oklahoma. Barnsdall met Reynolds for the first time on a train as both men were traveling to New York City. On learning that Reynolds was an operator of mines in Colorado, Barnsdall proposed to join him in a number of mineral ventures. He became the principal backer of the May Day venture in La Plata County and the Gold Links Tunnel in Gunnison County. Barnsdall also acquired the Consolidated Gold Mining Company at Summitville with the objective of combining his property with Reynolds's Golconda Gold Mining Company. Eventually that combination, which occurred long after the deaths of both men, gave a single corporation control of most of the potentially rich gold camp.[23]

The men who supported Reynolds's enterprises enjoyed some profitable investments. On occasion their dividends were very large. However, they entered into mining ventures with the knowledge that they were putting money into highly speculative activities and that losses were to be expected. Fortunately for all concerned, these particular investors, unlike most of their eastern contemporaries who invested in Colorado mines, enjoyed more gains than losses until shortly after the turn of the century.[24]

Mining was especially rewarding for Reynolds because he was both the promoter and operator of mines. In the first instance he organized companies whose stock he sold to investors, often at a substantial profit. This allowed him to develop mining properties with other people's money.

Reynolds adopted a standard technique for launching new enterprises. He acquired potentially valuable mining claims at nominal cost, organized a mining company with a large authorized capital, and sold to the company his claims in return for all of its stock. He usually returned to the new company's treasury 20 percent of the capital stock, the sale of which was to provide money for initial development and operation.

The balance of the stock Reynolds disposed of as he deemed appropriate. If the initial development was promising, he sold stocks, usually at discount, mainly to his eastern friends. Invariably Reynolds retained sufficient stock to assure his control of the company. If the mine failed, Reynolds lost little, if anything at all. If the operation was crowned with success, as the largest stockholder he was the principal beneficiary of the enterprise's profits.

One obvious reason for Reynolds's phenomenal success in marketing mining securities was his unquestioned integrity. He was honest, at times almost to a fault, and his word was his bond. Prospective investors understood that mining ventures were risky, and they were, with few exceptions, willing to take the losses along with the gains, confident that Reynolds, unlike many promoters, was not trying to "mine" purchasers of stocks.[25]

Reynolds was a highly successful entrepreneur. The gross profits from all of his mines reached a staggering $60 million during his lifetime. The Virginius Mine, developed in part through the Revenue Tunnel, produced ore worth approximately $15 million over a period of slightly less than twenty years. The Durant and Smuggler, celebrated mines at Aspen, yielded large returns. The Commodore and adjacent properties at Creede were similarly productive, paying substantial dividends to stockholders over a period of about a decade. Highly profitable but less spectacular was the May Day Mine near Hesperus.

Contemporary newspapers and journals created a myth of Reynolds's infallibility. He was said consistently to acquire properties of seemingly little value and make them into highly profitable mines. The secret of his success, according to one editor, was his ability to see "into the ground," meaning that he was unusual in the thoroughness of his understanding of mines and mining practices. According to this view, Reynolds, because of hard work, daring, and determination, became Colorado's greatest mine operator.[26]

By dwelling on the Virginius (Revenue Tunnel), Commodore, and May Day Mines, the media overlooked Reynolds's many failures. The Belle of the West and the Palmetto, near Lake City, did not live up to his estimates of their value. The Etcetera and Tarifa at Highlands, above Aspen, did not pay the expenses of development. The Senate, Forest King, and Platoro in Conejos County were equally disappointing. The Golconda at Summitville, a vast, largely low-grade deposit of gold, silver, lead, and copper, could not be worked at a profit with the technology then available for treating ores. The Emma Mine at Dunton, near Rico, did not fulfill Reynolds's hopes, but he persisted in pushing development of the property until his death in 1921.

His greatest disappointment was in Gunnison County, where

he anticipated large returns from mines in three localities. At Tin Cup he was the victim of a carefully planned scam, paying a large price for a mine that had been gutted by the previous owner. In addition, through the circulation of spurious reports of rich silver contacts at depths of from 300 to 700 feet below the surface, he was hoodwinked into buying up a huge block of nearly worthless mining claims in Chicago Park, near the town of Pitkin. Properties at Ohio City also failed to meet Reynolds's expectations.

Even though the scope of Reynolds's holdings established him as one of Colorado's leading mine operators, he was not widely known outside of the industry. In 1898, according to one observer, fewer than 5 percent of the people in the state knew of him even by name.[27] Unlike most of his contemporaries, Reynolds shunned publicity. He deliberately concealed from the public not only information about his mining operations but also about his personal and family affairs. Even his wife and daughter were unaware of the full extent of his business and civic activities.

It was not widely known, for example, that Reynolds, like many of his wealthy contemporaries, supported a variety of intellectual, social, and charitable institutions in Denver and elsewhere in Colorado. He devoted much of his time and money to advancing those causes. For forty years he was a member of the board of trustees of the University of Denver and the Iliff School of Theology. He was also a trustee of the City Temple Institutional Society, which in 1900 brought under one management a number of religious, educational, and benevolent organizations funded by the Episcopal Church. These included the Haven, an industrial school for girls; the Belle Lennox Nursery; the Young Women's Friendly Club; and the City Temple Institutional Church.[28]

A similar commitment to community betterment led Reynolds to participate in the formation and early development of one of Denver's premier cultural institutions. Some two dozen of the wealthiest men in the community, among them David

H. Moffat, John F. Campion, Walter S. Cheesman, Henry R. Wolcott, William H. James, Eben Smith, James B. Grant, and A. E. Reynolds, met in December 1897 to discuss ways and means for establishing a museum and library of natural history. They agreed to organize the Colorado Museum of Natural History and named the founders, including Reynolds, as lifetime trustees. In addition to contributing $2,000, Reynolds served on the committee that raised funds for the construction of buildings and the installation of exhibits. John Campion was the museum's first president, and Reynolds served as vice president, later first vice president, for more than twenty years.[29]

His role in the creation of what became the Denver Museum of Natural History was not widely acknowledged because of his deep-seated aversion to publicity of any kind. Reynolds avoided newspaper and journal reporters, who were, in his estimation, busybodies who frequently made up stories out of whole cloth. The result was misleading and mischievous trash, which Reynolds seldom missed an opportunity to condemn. Largely as a result of a running fight with the media, he became increasingly secretive about his activities, those of his wife and daughter, and those of the enterprises that he controlled. He even asked managers of his properties to discourage employees from giving out information that could become the basis for falsehoods about mining and milling activities.[30]

The printing of misleading or false information prompted quick responses. In November 1892 Reynolds criticized W. C. Wynkoop, editor of the *Mining Industry and Tradesman,* for publishing as facts what were allegedly complete falsehoods. Responding to a story that he was preparing to hire four hundred men and to ship forty cars of ore daily from the New York and Chance Mine at Creede, Reynolds complained that he had seen wonderful lies in print, but nothing that equaled this report. It caused him, as a mine owner, great inconvenience. By publishing such rubbish, Reynolds insisted, Wynkoop gave people in the East the impression that investments in Colorado mines always yielded large profits, which was not true. "It is exceedingly annoying," Reynolds concluded, "to have to respond to inquiries called forth by such lies as this article contains."[31]

A decade later Reynolds directed similar complaints to one of Denver's leading newspapers. To mining editor Frank Hall, Reynolds wrote, "I wish to call your attention to a lying, false, misleading and mischief making article published in yesterday's *Evening Post*, in regard to a great strike of gold ore in the properties of the Revenue Tunnel Mines Company above Ouray." The vein of ore in question was supposedly worth more than $2,000 per ton. "I am sorry to have to annoy you with this matter," Reynolds continued, "but I do not like to see published such an absolutely rotten, lying article about properties in which I am interested."[32]

In private life Reynolds was conservative. Philosophically he was a Republican, yet he seldom expressed publicly his political views. This allowed him the flexibility to support candidates, even parties, in keeping with his business interests. As the owner of silver mines, for example, he objected to the Republican Party's commitment to monometallism. When the market value of silver declined in the 1890s, he showed little patience with advocates of a gold standard. In Reynolds's view the obvious way to reverse that slide was for Congress to remonetize silver by authorizing the U.S. Mint to buy and coin the metal at the legal ratio of sixteen to one with gold.[33] For that reason Reynolds called upon Democrats as well as Republicans to speak out in favor of bimetallism.

Those who did so earned Reynolds's gratitude. After Representative William Jennings Bryan, a Democrat from Nebraska, championed the cause of a two-metal monetary system in a Denver speech in March 1894, Reynolds gave him, as a token of appreciation, a ring made of an amalgam of silver and gold taken from the Hector Mining Company's Cimarron Mine near Telluride. The quartz setting was from the same property. In a letter thanking the mining entrepreneur for the gift, Bryan reported that he had had the band of the ring engraved, "A. E. Reynolds to W. J. Bryan, March 14, 1894." The ring commemorated, Bryan continued, "one of the most pleasant events in my brief public life." He wanted to know the history of the ring and the cost of mining the metals from which it was made so that he could use the information to further the cause of silver coinage.[34]

Bimetallism remained Reynolds's goal throughout the rest of the 1890s. He joined a close friend, Senator Henry Moore Teller, in encouraging the growth of a Silver Republican Party in Colorado and supported Democrats if they, unlike Republicans, were committed to the two-metal monetary system. Teller, with Reynolds's support, won reelection to the Senate as a Democrat in 1902. Reynolds would not, however, support candidates who ran under the banner of Populism, even when they advocated bimetallism. Reynolds rejected the pro-labor stance of the People's Party and its vaguely defined but potentially dangerous, in the eyes of a mine operator, vision of industrial democracy.[35]

The organization of labor was unacceptable because it threatened to deny employers unrestricted control of their enterprises. Reynolds refused to have anything to do with unions by any name and was adamant in his opposition to the Western Federation of Miners (WFM). Mineowners viewed the WFM as a band of ruffians and murderers who sought the destruction of the private enterprise system and the substitution of socialism for capitalism. Reynolds insisted that he would close his mines rather than submit to the organization of miners in his employ.[36]

He also objected to the unionization of mineowners. When operators at Telluride created an association to respond to the threat of the WFM, Reynolds refused to join. He feared that operators, if organized, would established rules that might deny him complete freedom of action in the management his mining companies.

Unhampered freedom of action was Reynolds's goal. If free of restraints by outside influences, he was confident his properties could be worked at a profit for himself and for investors. Mineral bonanzas remained hidden within the Rocky Mountains, and Reynolds was confident he could find them. Therefore, he committed time, money, and effort to mining long after the industry declined dramatically shortly after the turn of the century.

In that respect Reynolds differed from many of his contemporaries. With few exceptions, Colorado's successful mining entrepreneurs devoted a substantial portion of their profits from the production of gold and silver to nonmining activities. Charles Boettcher, John F. Campion, Eben Smith, and David H. Moffat, to name only a few outstanding examples, put the proceeds of their mining ventures into banking, transportation, and manufacturing.[37] Reynolds, who owned more Colorado mining properties that any other single individual, remained committed to mining long after most people had lost interest in it as a field for investment.

More than a successful businessman, Reynolds was also a devoted family man. He supported his unmarried sisters, most of whom lived together in New York City. He provided them with sufficient means to travel to the West in the summer or to go south to a warmer climate in the winter. After Reynolds's marriage in 1883 the sisters spent their summers in New England. Andrew and Charles, and to a lesser degree George, worked for their brother in one capacity or another most of their adult lives. George, who was inclined to be more independent, eventually struck out on his own, but the other two seemed incapable of making their own way in the world.

At one time or another all three brothers worked in the mercantile operations of Lee and Reynolds in Indian Territory. After the partnership was dissolved, George assumed charge of the Panhandle ranch but quickly gave it up. Charles took over the direction of the cattle-raising operation and, according to A. E., was largely responsible for making it a success. Andrew, with his oldest brothers' assistance, secured a license to trade with Kiowas, Comanches, and Wichitas at Anadarko, Indian Territory, in 1885, a venture that lasted only three years. Heavy drinking, lack of management skills, and mounting unpaid bills forced Andrew to sell the store in 1888. A. E. guaranteed his brother's obligations and eventually paid off all creditors.[38]

Reynolds in effect had more than one family. His sisters and brothers were for many years his primary concern. His attachment to them was unwavering. He shared his successes with them, and they were content to depend upon his judgment and support. Reynolds thrived on giving advice and was flattered when people, including siblings, accepted his recommendations.[39] Eventually this created problems for the woman who became his wife, and the key member of his second family, in 1883.

At the age of forty-one, while residing at Fort Supply, A. E. Reynolds decided that it was time to marry. Eligible non-Indian females were almost nonexistent in Indian Territory, and Reynolds lacked the time and opportunity to search for a prospective bride during frequent business trips to Leavenworth, St. Louis, Chicago, and New York. Probably for that reason he enlisted the aid of his partner's wife, Orlina (Lina) Whitney Lee, who suggested that he correspond with a longtime friend from her hometown of Columbus, Wisconsin. Orlina, who married Lee in 1877, had grown up with the four Earll sisters, the daughters of Dr. Robert W. and Angeline Lawton Earll.[40]

A native of Onandago, New York, Earll became a resident of Lowell, Wisconsin, in 1840. At the time he was seventeen years. Nine years later he began the study of medicine in the office of a local physician. After marrying Angeline Lawton, the adopted daughter of Henry Finney of Lowell, in 1850, Earll continued his preparation for a professional career at Rush Medical College, Chicago, from which he graduated in the class of 1853.[41]

That year Dr. Earll and his wife moved to nearby Columbus, where he opened a medical office. The couple had four children, the first of whom, Frances Eudorah (Dora), was born in 1852. In the next eleven years they had three more daughters—Coie, Hattie, and Anna. When Angeline Earll died in 1872, the responsibility of running the household and looking after the needs of the younger children fell to Dora. At an early age she adopted a protective attitude toward her siblings, and over time these sisters as well as their husbands turned to Dora and her husband for solutions to their problems.

It was Dora with whom Reynolds commenced a courtship by mail in the spring of 1881. In June they met for the first time, a brief encounter in Milwaukee, after which, being formally engaged, they discussed via correspondence the prospect of an early wedding. That hope was shattered in January 1882 when Lee demanded that either one of the partners buy out the other. He was confident that Reynolds, whose funds were largely committed to mining enterprises in Colorado, would have to sell. Reynolds, to Lee's surprise, quickly agreed to purchase his partner's interest and signed a mortgage in April to achieve that end. The wedding was postponed from month to month, eventually for a year, as Reynolds traveled to cities throughout the United States and to the British Isles in search of funds. After a thirty-two-day visit to London in early 1883, followed by tedious negotiations in New York, Reynolds secured the money he needed to pay Lee. In March he wrote Dora that with the signing of papers for a loan, he would be "more free than he had been for a long time past."[42]

A. E. Reynolds and Dora Earll were married in Columbus, Wisconsin, on April 25, 1883. The service was conducted by Pastor W. A. Chamberlain of the Olivet Church. After the ceremony the couple traveled to Chicago and eventually to Colorado. They resided for a time in Lake City but relocated to Denver after their only child, Anna Earll Reynolds, was born in Columbus on January 26, 1884.[43]

The marriage lasted thirty-three years. At the time of the union he was forty-three and she, thirty-one. They were, in fact, quite different in their outlook toward life but not because of the difference in their ages. A. E.'s optimism sharply contrasted with Dora's pessimism. Unlimited faith in his own judgment was seldom tempered by reasonable caution. In mines, corporate stocks, and silver futures he was willing to gamble to the limit of his resources. Of an opposite view, Dora wanted certainty, security, and safety. Gambling in any form, even if called business enterprise, was fraught with extreme danger. She could not enjoy her husband's successes because of her preoccupation with the possibility of failure. For this reason she was content to know little, if anything at all, about his entrepreneurial ventures and pursued interests of her own outside of the Reynolds household.[44]

With servants to assist with domestic duties and the raising of one daughter, Dora had time for community activities. Following the example of growing numbers of middle-class females, Dora joined women's clubs that not only actively promoted self-improvement for members through literary studies but also campaigned at the local and state levels of government for social reforms for the needy. She participated in two clubs that were among the first of their kind in Denver. She was a longtime member of the Denver Fortnightly Club and a charter member of the Women's Club of Denver. She also served on the Board of Control for the State Home for Dependent and Neglected Children from the time it was created by the Colorado General Assembly in 1895 until her death in 1916.[45]

A. E. and Dora were longtime residents of Denver. They rented homes on fashionable Capitol Hill for more than twenty years before deciding to buy in the same area. Initially the family's residences changed almost from year to year. It was not until 1889 that A. E. and Dora stayed in one place for any length of time. That year they rented a large dwelling at 1756 Grant Street, southwest of the Colorado State House, from Dr. Frederick J. Bancroft, a prominent physician. By 1892 they had relocated to 1620 Grant, a residence owned by General Grenville M. Dodge, the builder of the Union Pacific and a key backer of the Denver and Fort Worth Railroad. In 1909 Dodge agreed to make additions to the house to provide more living space, but when the work was not completed by 1913, the Reynolds rented a mansion at 1555 Sherman Street from mine and smelter magnate Simon Guggenheim, who had given up a residence in Denver because of political and business interests in the East. A. E. subsequently agreed to purchase the property in his daughter's name for the sum of $25,000, but because of financial problems, he paid only $5,000. Son-in-law Bradish P. Morse completed the purchase in 1921.[46]

The Reynolds were frequent travelers to New York and other eastern cities and occasionally to Europe. Dora accompanied her husband on numerous business trips, particularly when Anna was a student at the Misses Masters School at Dobbs Ferry, New York, and later at Smith College. Anna often spent school vacations with her parents in New York or Washington, D.C. Trips across the Atlantic appear to have been primarily for the purpose of introducing Anna to the art and culture of the British Isles and the Continent.

Anna was one of the first graduates of the Misses Masters School to gain entrance to a four-year college. That she did so was due largely to A. E. Reynolds's criticism that the Dobbs Ferry institution was not preparing his daughter for the challenge of higher education. Stung by Reynolds's remarks, the faculty was determined to prove him wrong. Anna and classmate Daisy Lewis, after graduation in 1903, were admitted to Smith College. They completed the course of instruction as members of the class of 1907.[47]

Anna Earll Reynolds married Bradish P. Morse in 1913. She was an accomplished musician and, following in her mother's footsteps, committed much of her time to social concerns and to women's clubs. He was a successful businessman, a partner in Morse Brothers Machinery and Supply Company of Denver, a firm that specialized in recycling the machinery and equipment of inactive mines, mills, railroads, and industrial plants.

The Morses had three children. Albert Reynolds Morse, born October 13, 1915, was the apple of his grandfather's eye. Dora, after having experienced poor health for a number of years, died of pneumonia in November 1916 and did not live to see the other grandchildren. Eudorah Goodell Morse was born June 15, 1917, and Ann Morse, May 30, 1919.[48]

By the time his grandchildren were born, A. E. Reynolds was struggling to perpetuate his reputation as Colorado's leading mining entrepreneur. After the exhaustion of the Virginius Mine above the level of the Revenue Tunnel in 1901, and the precipitous decline of the Commodore in 1905, his successes in mining were few and short-lived. The May Day Mine near Hesperus was an outstanding producer of gold, but its large output continued for less than two years. The Frank Hough, on Engineer Mountain between Lake City and Ouray, had the potential of being a big moneymaker, but a fire caused the collapse of the shaft, terminating operations in 1911.

Reynolds's attempts to sell his mines proved disappointing. Prospective buyers were numerous, but the ore appeared to be exhausted in the Revenue Tunnel and in the Commodore, and exploration at that time failed to reveal workable deposits at greater depth. Efforts to sell other properties were equally unsuccessful, with the result that Reynolds, desperately in need of cash, turned his attention to the sale of the agricultural land that he owned in the Arkansas River valley, most of it north of the river and east of La Junta.

After having run cattle on the land for several years, Reynolds, responding to the organization and operation of what became the Fort Lyon Canal Company, divided the property into irrigated farms, which he offered for sale as early as 1910. Efforts as a land developer netted him not profits but additional debts at a time when, because of idle mining properties, his finances were in disarray. Convinced that his farms were too large to attract industrious farmers, he subdivided the land into smaller units and sold them to German farmers, recent immigrants by way of Russia, who had been farming on shares in the vicinity of Rocky Ford.

The promotion of irrigated farms did not solve Reynolds's mounting financial crisis. He had vast assets but could not convert them into cash to meet ongoing needs. The failure to sell mining properties, and the inability to attract capital with which to develop and operate them, placed him in a position where he could not meet the interest payments, let alone the principal, on a large volume of debt. This condition was exacerbated by the need to save his wife's brothers-in-law from business failures, one of which carried with it the threat of imprisonment.

By the turn of the century all of Dora's sisters resided in southwestern Colorado. Coie was married to Charles E. Mc-Connell, who, after working in banks in Gunnison and Montrose, opened the Smelter City State Bank in Durango. Hattie, who had married Charles Fay, lived in Milwaukee until the death of her husband, after which she became part of the McConnell household. Anna and her husband, Richard Keller, lived in Montrose. He owned and operated mining properties in the San Juan Country.[49]

One of Keller's ventures at Dunton, Dolores County, required an investment that eventually exceeded his means, prompting a request for assistance from his brother-in-law in Denver. Reynolds completed the purchase of the enterprise and reorganized it as the Emma Gold Mining Company, with himself as majority stockholder. The property produced silver and gold in combination with iron sulfide, from which precious metals could not be saved in sufficient quantity to meet the expenses of operating the property. Because of an inadequate milling process, a high percentage of the mineral values were washed down the West Dolores River with the tailings.

A far greater burden for Reynolds, one with which he struggled for a number of years, was the settlement of Charles McConnell's debts. When the Smelter City State Bank failed in December 1907, Reynolds, after having shored up that institution for years, accepted responsibility for paying the bank's depositors as well as other creditors. A settlement was a matter of urgency because McConnell faced possible criminal charges on the grounds that he had accepted deposits after he knew that the bank was insolvent.

From 1907 to 1913 Reynolds, with limited help from Richard Keller, paid the bank's debts. All remaining assets, mainly property in and near Farmington, New Mexico, was divided between the two men, with Reynolds taking 85 percent. Since there were no buyers for the real estate, annual taxes were one more burden for Reynolds to carry as his income faltered in the years after 1907. Other reverses, including heavy losses from speculation in the stock market, further weakened Reynolds's financial condition during the closing years of his life.

As the owner of numerous mining properties, he possessed, at least in theory, assets of great value, but because of a stagnating mining industry, he could not convert them into cash. In a desperate effort to enhance his personal fortune and pay off a heavy burden of debts, he proposed a new mining venture, the Lime Shale Mining Company, in 1920. This enterprise sought to tap what Reynolds believed to be an immense deposit of silver and gold ore in a stratum of lime shale in the Emma Mine. A lingering illness that prevented Reynolds from raising money for the project undermined any chance for success. Unable to pay miners and local merchants for supplies, Reynolds ended operations on March 20, 1921. One day later death ended the forty-year career of Colorado's mining king.

Although generally unknown during his lifetime and later, Reynolds was one of the giants in the annals of Colorado's mineral industry. Within mining circles he was admired and respected as an innovator who, by his daring, imagination, and industry, became the model mining man of his day. Thomas F. Walsh, owner of the famous Camp Bird Mine, when interviewed in 1898 conceded that he hoped to be as successful as Reynolds, who was then among the leaders of the industry.[50]

A millionaire by the time he was fifty, Reynolds was one of many Colorado entrepreneurs who gained great wealth from mining gold and silver. He acquired his fortune largely from a few very successful mines. By 1910 he was worth an estimated $3 million. This was, in fact, the high point in the development of his personal wealth. In subsequent years the depreciation of mining properties eroded Reynolds's assets. At the time of his death he was worth, on paper, more than $2 million.[51] In fact, he was approaching insolvency because he could not liquidate his immense holdings—for several years there had been little, if any, demand for mining properties in Colorado or elsewhere in the West.

Albert Eugene Reynolds (1840–1921), sutler, Indian trader, freighter, rancher, and mining entrepreneur. *(Courtesy, Colorado Historical Society, neg. F36937)*

Caroline Van Horn Reynolds (Mrs. Henry A. Reynolds), mother of Albert Eugene Reynolds. *(Courtesy, Colorado Historical Society, neg. F36923)*

Albert Eugene Reynolds when he was a trader in Indian Territory. The Arapahoes and Cheyennes called him "Red Beard." *(Courtesy, Colorado Historical Society, neg. F36921)*

Family portrait of, *left to right,* Mrs. A. E. Reynolds, Fanny Reynolds,
A. E. Reynolds, *standing,* Alice Reynolds, and Charles F. Reynolds.
(Courtesy, Colorado Historical Society, neg. F36922)

Frances Eudorah (Dora)
Earll Reynolds (Mrs. Albert
Eugene Reynolds). *(Courtesy,
Colorado Historical Society,
neg. 36924)*

Dr. Robert W. Earll, father
of Mrs. Albert Eugene
Reynolds. *(Courtesy, Colorado
Historical Society, neg. 36925)*

Family portrait, 1920: A. E. Reynolds is holding granddaughter Ann; daughter Anna Reynolds Morse is standing with grandchildren Eudorah and Albert Reynolds. *(Courtesy, Colorado Historical Society, neg. F36938)*

2
Frontier Trader

AFTER the close of the Civil War settlers pushed westward beyond the 100th meridian into what had been called the Great American Desert. They encountered an environment that, unlike that of the fertile prairies to the east, was characterized by a lack of timber and rainfall. Furthermore, the Great Plains were inhabited by nomadic Indians who were determined to resist encroachment on their hunting lands.

In spite of these obstacles, the westward advance of the American people proceeded at a rapid pace. That advance was aided by the construction of transcontinental railroads and by the federal government's policy of confining Indians on small, well-defined reservations whose land for the most part had little value for agriculture or mining. The army was the instrument by which the tribes were pacified, but it was the destruction of the buffalo that left the Indians with no alternative but to exchange their traditional way for sedentary reservation life and the promise of government annuities of beef and other necessities.

Significant, yet frequently overlooked actors in the final conquest of the Plains were traders who served the army as well as the Indian tribes. Military sutlers bought and transported to remote posts for resale a variety of goods that softened for troops, civilian employees, and dependents at military posts the impact of an environment that was often as bleak as it was dangerous. In addition, traders were suppliers of many goods and services, including fresh beef for mess halls; stacked hay for cattle, draft animals, and cavalry horses; cord wood for heat; and wagon transportation for government supplies and personnel.[1]

Indian traders, sometimes the same men who served as military sutlers, offered the tribes an equally wide range of goods and services. In exchange for buffalo robes, hides, pelts, and other commodities of value found on or near the reservations, Native Americans could acquire store goods, the exchange for which was regulated by the local Indian agent, who as the representative of the Bureau of Indian Affairs was responsible for the administration of the reservation. As a contractor the trader might also supply beef, hay, cord wood, and transportation. For unscrupulous merchants there were opportunities for high profits from illegal sales of rifles, ammunition, and, above all, whiskey.

Two trader-partners, Albert Eugene Reynolds and W. M. D. Lee, served the Cheyenne and Arapahoe Agency and Camp Supply, which had been created to oversee reservation life in northwestern Indian Territory. After the signing of the Medicine Lodge Treaty of 1867, by the terms of which the Cheyenne and Arapahoe surrendered their lands in southeastern Colorado for a reservation in Kansas, later changed to Indian Territory, Reynolds and Lee, among others, sought licenses to operate stores for the military and the Indians at the new post. Camp Supply was the temporary location for the Cheyenne-Arapahoe Agency, then called the Upper Arkansas Indian Agency.

As events turned out, Reynolds secured only one license. Lee, a quartermaster with General William T. Sherman's forces during the Civil War and a civilian employee for the army for a time after the close of the conflict, secured the license for the Indian trade. Realizing that they had more to gain through consolidation than competition, the two men merged their business operations as Lee and Reynolds, a partnership in which Reynolds was the senior partner with five-eighths interest. The new firm had a virtual monopoly on retail merchandising for a vast area south of Fort Dodge, Kansas.[2]

The partners soon learned that they had to defend their merchandising privileges against others who were willing to use unscrupulous methods to deprive them of their license. In 1870 they lost their license to conduct a retail business at Camp Supply when the War Department, operating under a new law that authorized the secretary of war to appoint a single sutler at military posts, awarded the license to Edwin C. Latimer, effective October 20. Determined to fight for the trading privilege, Reynolds traveled to Washington, D.C., to seek redress from the proper authorities. In response to a suggestion from a clerk in the War Department that he seek the aid of General J. M. Hedrick of Ottumwa, Iowa, Reynolds journeyed to that city to confer with the man who could allegedly influence the decisions of Secretary of War William Belknap. Hedrick agreed to assist Reynolds in return for an annual payment of $5,000. Without explanation the War Department issued an order on November 17 naming Reynolds as the only licensed trader at Camp Supply.[3]

Six years later Reynolds was called to Washington to testify before a congressional committee investigating charges of graft and corruption in the War Department, one of several scandals that had surfaced in the final years of President Ulysses S. Grant's second term. Reynolds readily admitted having paid money to General Hedrick, but not the amount that had been agreed upon in 1870. After remitting $4,500 over a period of about three years, Reynolds and his partner decided to end the payments. Asked if he feared at that point that the general would influence Secretary Belknap to cancel the traders' license, Reynolds answered that it was a chance he and Lee were willing to take. A committee member asked if the trading privilege was worth the $5,000 annually requested by Hedrick. Reynolds replied that it was. When asked if Lee and Reynolds's profit was at least $10,000 a year,

Reynolds answered in the affirmative. In fact, the profits were substantially in excess of that amount.[4]

The congressional hearing had surprisingly little impact on the Indian traders. Only at Fort Sill, Indian Territory, was a license revoked because bribes had been paid for the privilege of trading at the post. Reynolds must have feared similar action. Perhaps because of his ready admission of wrongdoing, and the termination of the partial payments to General Hedrick after three years, the firm of Lee and Reynolds avoided punishment. In fact, during 1876 Reynolds and Lee were relicensed as traders, respectively, at Forts Supply and Elliott, and the partnership was relicensed as the only trader at the Cheyenne-Arapahoe Agency.[5]

The Lee and Reynolds partnership grew in size and scope from year to year. Camp Supply was an excellent location for a trader's store since from three to six companies of infantry or cavalry normally constituted the garrison. During the Red River War of 1874–1875 the number of soldiers grew even larger, and it remained so for the balance of the decade. As a supply depot designed to support military operations to control the Indians on the southern Plains, the post employed a large number of civilians, who were in charge of warehouses and the maintenance of inventories of arms, munitions, and various implements of war. The retail establishment catered to officers and enlisted men as well as to nonmilitary employees and their dependents.[6]

The store sold various goods. The demand was brisk for military clothing, accessories, and ornamentation; insignia of grade and rank; bugles; knives; and field glasses. Other items for which there was a large call included civilian clothing (under- and outerwear) for men, women, and children; saddles, harnesses, and accessories; farm equipment and tools; household items and furniture; hardware and tools; fresh fruits and vegetables (in season) and processed foods; patent medicines; tobacco; candy; newspapers, magazines, and books; musical instruments (accordions, banjos, guitars, and violins); and playing cards and other games of amusement. Sales were for cash or short-term credit, payable monthly.

The storekeepers were also bankers, issuing certificates of deposit at prevailing rates of interest. Civilian employees at the post constituted the bulk of the depositors. Lee and Reynolds also made loans to officers from time to time but not to enlisted men.[7]

Attached to the store was a saloon, which did a lively business. The bar dispensed large quantities of ale, beer, wine, and whiskey. Initially Lee and Reynolds bought ale and beer from John B. Fleming and Company, the operator of a brewery in St. Louis and later in Atchison, Kansas. Commencing in 1874, the partners patronized Brandon and Kirmeyer, brewers at Leavenworth, Kansas, of ale and beer that one Camp Supply employee called an "A-1 product." Later some beer was purchased from Voechting Shope and Company of Milwaukee. The latter was not satisfactory, allegedly because the brewer did not properly wash and cork the bottles.[8]

The long journey from St. Louis or Leavenworth often affected the quality of the ale and beer that reached Camp Supply. Barrels were sprung in transit, causing the partners frequently to complain of flat or dead ale and beer. They looked, without success, for ways to restore life to the contents of barrels that had leaked because of rough handling on the railroads and on the wagon journey from the railhead to the military post. The brew often suffered adversely from the effects of the temperature extremes common to the High Plains. It froze in the winter and boiled in the summer. In one instance twenty of fifty barrels ruptured because of freezing by the time the shipment reached Dodge City, and all of it was spoiled by the time it arrived at Camp Supply. In spite of handicaps, Lee and Reynolds maintained ample supplies to satisfy the thirst of troops and civilians at Camp Supply. Officers often preferred wine over ale or beer.[9]

Full and half casks of wine as well as cases of pint and quart bottles were purchased from jobbers in Leavenworth and St.

Louis. Popular varieties were dry and sparkling catawba, cabernet sauvignon, claret, port, and sherry. Orders also included large amounts of nondescript brands simply listed as Angelico, Clinton, Imperial, Silver Wedding, and Virginia Seedling. On request, usually for officers, Lee and Reynolds ordered the products of specific regions or wineries. Except for Spanish sherry, wines from the eastern United States were favored over those of California and foreign countries.[10]

At first only beer and wine were sold legally at Camp Supply. Bootlegging was a highly developed industry in the region, and it is likely that soldiers as well as civilians at the post were frequent patrons of so-called whiskey ranches along the trails or roads leading to and from the post. Eventually Lee and Reynolds obtained permission from the local commander to add whiskey to the saloon's inventory. Good quality Kentucky bourbon and country rye were served over the bar and could be purchased in larger quantities at $2.90 per gallon for consumption elsewhere. Purchases for resale were limited to 4.5 gallons because the partners did not have a wholesaler's license.[11]

The saloon's billiard tables, purchased from S. Brunswick Company, St. Louis, were a popular source of recreation. There was one table for enlisted men and another for officers. Both were heavily used, for the proprietors frequently ordered new covers, replacement cues and tips, and new billiard balls from the manufacturer. When the firm erected a new store building in 1877, the old one was converted into a spacious saloon, with separate sections for billiards.[12]

Another store, without a saloon or billiard tables, served the Cheyennes and Arapahoes, plus agency employees and their dependents. Brinton Darlington, an elderly Quaker who succeeded Colonel Edward W. Wynkoop as agent shortly after the tribes relocated to Indian Territory in 1869, established his headquarters in the valley of the North Canadian River 150 miles southeast of Camp Supply. At what became the community of Darlington, Lee and Reynolds was the only firm licensed for local trade.[13]

Initially the traders were active only part time, from late December until about the close of April. During this short season buffalo robes tanned by the Indian women were the main items of trade. By the mid-1870s the store was open year round to serve the Cheyennes and Arapahoes as well as agency personnel, but the robe trade continued to be restricted to a period of about four months at the start of each calendar year.[14]

To stock the stores at Camp Supply and Darlington, Lee and Reynolds ordered for resale large quantities of goods, which were shipped by rail to points near Indian Territory. Initially the firm made a disproportionate share of its purchases from enterprises in New York City, Chicago, and St. Louis. However, when it could, the partnership obtained what it needed from regional and local wholesale merchants and manufacturers.[15]

From business houses in Leavenworth, a relatively short distance from Indian Territory, Lee and Reynolds secured other goods and services. The partners relied heavily on the services of several merchants. William A. Rose, of W. A. Rose and Company, a wholesaler of stationery and writing materials, acted as the partners' banker until 1874, when the First National Bank of Leavenworth assumed that role. E. H. Durfee marketed, at least initially, the firm's buffalo robes, and W. C. Lobenstein disposed of beef hides, skins, and pelts taken in trade with the Cheyennes and Arapahoes. Durfee was an important source of Indian beads and hair pipes, whereas Lobenstein supplied leather goods, particularly harnesses. Cochran, Bittmann and Taylor and C. A. Morehead Company furnished perishable and processed foods. B. S. Richards manufactured saddles and accessories for the Indian trade; R. F. Richards and Company was a source of machinery, implements, tools, and building supplies; and J. F. Schmeltzer was a wholesaler of revolvers, rifles, ammunition, and powder.[16]

The Camp Supply traders patronized merchants in the new towns that sprang up along the railroads as they built westward across Kansas. At Hays City the agent for Kansas Pacific Railroad arranged for the forwarding of express and freight. Local businessmen sold the partners large amounts of fruits, vegetables, and dairy products. The partners also secured, as needed, building materials and grains, particularly corn, in carload lots for freighters' oxen and mules. Bull teams made the trip from Hays City to Camp Supply and back to the railroad head again in an average of twenty-one days.[17]

The long haul to and from Hays City ended when the Atchison, Topeka and Santa Fe Railroad reached Dodge City in 1873. Then a new set of merchants provided perishables and grains that bull and mule trains hauled southward to Camp Supply. Goods from the East and Middle West arrived by train and were sent southward in freight wagons. Six-yoke ox, or bull, teams, which pulled two wagons loaded with from 3 to 5 tons of merchandise, completed the trip from the railhead to the military post in about seven days, whereas eight-hitch mule teams usually made the passage in no more than five.[18]

The merchants of Dodge City maintained a long and profitable relationship with the traders at Camp Supply. Robert M. Wright, who was at one time the sutler at Fort Dodge; A. C. Myers; Charles Rath; and A. J. Anthony operated stores. Wright, Rath, and Anthony were partners in Charles Rath and Company from 1872 to 1877, the region's leading dealer in buffalo hides. The merchants shipped southward large quantities of fresh fruits and vegetables (in season), processed foods, eggs, and dairy products. They also forwarded grains and chopped feed for livestock.[19]

As owners of large mercantile enterprises, Lee and Reynolds became of necessity one of the leading freighters of the region. They had to haul goods from the railhead to stores at Camp Supply, at the Indian agency, and, after 1874, at Fort Elliott in the Panhandle. From time to time they also set up temporary retail stores at points along the cattle trails that traversed the Indian Territory to serve Texas drovers with herds destined for Kansas railroads or to stock the grasslands of the northern Plains.

Initially the partners relied on contract freighters to move their goods. E. B. Allen and Company, a Leavenworth firm, ran teams regularly from the Kansas Pacific Railroad at Hays City, and later from the Atchison, Topeka and Santa Fe line at Dodge City, to Camp Supply. As early as 1870 Lee and Reynolds hired teamsters to take charge of company-owned teams and wagons. Eventually up to twelve teamsters were employed as a group under the direction of a wagon master and sometimes an assistant wagon master.[20]

The first wagon master was George W. Russell, who had been a teamster on the Santa Fe Trail prior to the Civil War. A native of Fulton, Missouri, Russell returned to his home in 1862 to enlist as a private in the First Missouri Cavalry Regiment. He was in numerous battles and was wounded six times over a period of nearly four years. After the close of hostilities he returned to freighting on the Plains, where he was widely known as "Captain" Russell. He went to work for Lee and Reynolds as a teamster in 1870 and assumed charge of the firm's wagon train the following year. Eventually he was one of several men who commanded the company's wagon trains, transporting a wide range of commodities in support of the trader-partners' numerous enterprises.[21]

The decision to operate ox- and mule-drawn wagon trains may have been prompted in part by Lee and Reynolds's commitment to numerous subsidiary enterprises. As early as 1871 the partners, as individuals and as a firm, successfully bid for contracts to provide the army with large quantities of stacked hay and cord wood. Both products had to be cut and transported from river bottoms where grass and trees abounded, sometimes at great distances from the military camp, to the place where the hay and wood were to be consumed. At times additional teams had to be hired to transport hay and wood to Camp Supply, the Indian agency, and later to other military posts by the dates stipulated in the contracts.[22]

The sale of hay, wood, and other products alleviated a cash-flow problem that habitually troubled the partnership. Lee and Reynolds ordered goods for its stores months in advance of sale, and because purchases were nearly always on short-term credit, the partners were constantly hard-pressed to meet their obligations. The buffalo robe trade—for a time the partnership's most lucrative line of business—was particularly difficult because the firm acquired goods prior to or shortly after the opening of the trading season in late December but did not realize cash from robe sales until late spring or early summer at the earliest. The proceeds from government vouchers for hay and wood were used time and again to meet wholesalers' urgent demands for payment.

The hay and wood contracts yielded sizable amounts of cash, normally a scarce commodity in a frontier setting. During Lee and Reynolds's first five years in business, the partners' average annual gross earnings from wood were $12,862.38 and from hay, $7,853.80. The proceeds were invariably earmarked for the payment of suppliers of goods and services for the stores.[23]

Until about 1878 by far the most lucrative aspect of Lee and Reynolds's operations was the Indian trade. The firm's business with the Cheyennes and Arapahoes largely involved the exchange of store goods for buffalo robes. In addition, the partners acquired from the Indians large numbers of steer hides and the skins or pelts of wild animals killed on or near the reservation. For a short time later in the decade the partners marketed buffalo hides, which were a source of leather for tanneries until the American bison was virtually eliminated from the southern Plains.

The buffalo supported the Indians' nomadic lifestyles. Twice each year tribes roamed over large areas of the Plains in pursuit of the animals, which were a source of food, clothing, coverings for lodges, and utensils fashioned from bones. The best of the hides, determined by the color and abundance of fur, were tanned by the women as robes. These were used by the Indians and were eagerly accepted by traders in exchange for store goods because robes were easily marketed at a profit in the eastern United States and in Europe.[24]

In nine years the partners marketed approximately seventy-nine thousand robes. Most were processed by the Cheyennes and Arapahoes. Some were purchased from traders who may have obtained robes from the Comanches and Kiowas. As long as the buffalo roamed the southern Great Plains, robes were a source of profit for the Indians and for the traders.[25]

Initially Indians received store goods in exchange for robes. In March 1873 employees of Lee and Reynolds at the Darlington store gave "30 cups of sugar and coffee, 16 braces of calico, [or] 12 braces of sheeting, for a robe."[26] George Bent, the son of William Bent and his Cheyenne wife; George's brother-in-law, Ed Gurrier; and Ike Alfrey, as interpreters and clerks, handled most of the transactions.[27] Other popular items given in trade for robes, hides, and pelts were beads, hair pipes, and silver-trimmed saddles.

A variety of trade beads, usually dyed seeds, were favored by the Arapahoe and Cheyenne Indians as ornamentations. Prior to the opening of the trading season in late December of each year, Lee and Reynolds ordered thousands of beads of various colors. The demand was greatest for chalk-colored beads, but also popular were bright colors, especially white, orange, lemon, indigo, and turquoise. Without the chalk color, however, the traders could not sell the other colors. Supplies were purchased from Buckley, Willing and Company of New York City; Dodd, Brown and Company of St. Louis; and E. H. Durfee of Leavenworth, Kansas.[28] The New York and Leavenworth houses were also wholesalers of hair pipes.

Tubular beads one and a half inches or more in length, known as hair pipes, were common trade items with North American Indians over a period of about two centuries. Prior to the 1870s hair pipes were usually made of West Indian conch; after that time they were generally made of animal bones. Plains Indians wore hair pipes as ear pendants, hair ornaments, necklaces, chokers, and breastplates. The Cheyennes and Arapahoes preferred the shell variety, or what Lee and Reynolds called "genuine hair pipes," and were reluctant to accept bone hair pipes unless the others were unavailable. Hair pipe ornaments were widely viewed by Indians as symbols of the wearers' prosperity.[29]

In some years the popularity of hair pipes was so great that Lee and Reynolds was hard-pressed to keep in stock all but very long pieces. Invariably those in short supply were from three to four inches in length. Frequently during a trading season the partners wrote to suppliers urgently asking for express shipments of hair pipes to meet unanticipated demand.[30]

Silver-trimmed saddles were another popular trading item. In 1870 Lee and Reynolds ordered saddles from S. C. Condict, but when it was found that they were inferior in quality, the firm's business was transferred to B. S. Richards of Leavenworth. He made as many as 135 saddles in a trading season at costs to the traders of from $10 to $16. The cheaper models had quilted, rather than leather, seats. All saddles had a silver-mounted horn and silver trim on the back of the seat.[31]

The traders were frequently at odds with the saddle maker. They wanted orders filled on very short notice but insisted on first-class work. They reminded Richards again and again that for the Indian trade saddles had to be the best available for the price. The Cheyennes and Arapahoes, the partners insisted, would accept only an "A. No. 1" saddle.[32]

The volume of trade declined as the Cheyennes and Arapahoes harvested fewer and fewer buffalo, reducing the number of robes available for exchange. White hunters slaughtered the immense herd that roamed throughout western Kansas and the Indian Territory in the early 1870s and by 1874 were encroaching on the Indians' traditional hunting ground in the Texas Panhandle. Aroused by what they saw as a threat to their nomadic way of life, the Comanches, Cheyennes, and Kiowas resisted the hunters' southward movement. The opening clash of what became the Red River War occurred at Adobe Walls, where Dodge City merchants had set up stores to trade guns, ammunition, whiskey, and other commodities for hides.[33]

There is reason to suspect that Lee and Reynolds may have played a role in the events that led to the conflict in 1874. Lee, it has been suggested, sought to prevent rival merchants from infringing on his firm's monopoly on robe trade with the Cheyennes. Accordingly, when Charles Rath, Robert M. Wright, and A. C. Meyers opened trading operations in the Panhandle, Lee may have informed the Cheyennes that they could find at Adobe Walls horses that had been stolen from them. What they found was not horses but hunters who, according to the Indians, had no right to kill buffalo in that area. The Comanche-Cheyenne raid on the settlement marked the start of the Red River War.[34]

After the defeat of the tribes and their return to their respective reservations, merchants and hunters moved quickly into the Texas Panhandle to harvest buffalo hides. Lee and Reynolds was among the participants in the slaughter of the southern herd. In 1876 the firm entered into an agreement with Dodge City merchants Charles Rath and Robert M. Wright, then operating as Charles Rath and Company, to establish a trading store in the Texas Panhandle to supply white hunters with guns, ammunition, food, clothing, and other needs in exchange for hides. Two new enterprises were formed. A. E. Reynolds and Company opened a trading store at Hidetown (later called Sweetwater and then Mobeetie) adjacent to Fort Elliott, a new post in the Texas Panhandle, approximately 100 miles south of Camp Supply. Reynolds, Rath and Company established a similar facility farther south beyond Fort Griffin, Texas.[35]

Using the A. E. Reynolds and Company store at Hidetown as a base of operations, the partners traveled to the Double

Mountain Fork of the Brazos River, where they founded
Reynolds City, sometimes called Camp Reynolds or Rath City,
complete with a general store, saloon, dance hall, brothel, and
all-important hide yard. The partners acquired hides from
professional hunters, giving goods and services in exchange
or, if necessary, paying cash. Thousands of hides were transported by bull and mule trains to Dodge City, from which
point they were shipped by rail to tanneries, mainly in the
East. A relatively small number of robe-quality hides were
hauled to the Cheyenne-Arapahoe Agency to be tanned by
Indian women.[36]

The slaughter of what remained of the southern buffalo
herd took less than three years. In the first season Reynolds
Rath and Company shipped more than one hundred thousand hides to tanneries via Dodge City. Commencing in May
1877, Lee and Reynolds, acting in behalf of A. E. Reynolds
and Company and Reynolds, Rath and Company, marketed
another one hundred thousand hides. Select hides, perhaps
fifteen thousand in all, were routed to Darlington in Indian
Territory.[37]

For a brief time there was a flourishing reservation industry
devoted to the processing of buffalo robes. During the winter
of 1876–1877 the Indians, as the result of their annual hunt,
collected about seven thousand hides, which as tanned robes
brought up to $5 each in Lee and Reynolds's trade tokens. For
another fifteen thousand hides, imported by the traders from
the Panhandle, the women earned $2 for each hide they
transformed into a robe. John D. Miles, the Cheyenne-Arapahoe agent, concluded that the tribespeople appreciated the
opportunity to earn money with which to supplement the
increasingly meager rations issued to them by the federal
government.[38]

A. E. Reynolds delegated responsibility for overseeing robe
preparation to his brother George, to whom he issued, as was
his habit in dealing with subordinates, very specific instructions on how to carry out assigned duties. It was essential, the

elder Reynolds stated, that the hides to be dressed as robes be cleaned out to the edges of the skin and not trimmed as the Arapahoes were inclined to do even with their own hides. By cutting two inches or more all around, they sought to reduce the amount of work required for the preparation of a robe. A. E. warned George that he had to give close attention to the work, for poorly dressed robes would not sell at a price equal to their cost. George was to give the Indian women ample time and insist on a first-class product.[39]

Initially payment for the robes was in trade checks. The metallic tokens, bearing the Lee and Reynolds imprint, were worth $0.50 each in merchandise at the store. The standard price for robes was from four to ten tokens, depending on the quality. By 1877 what the Indians wanted more than merchandise was livestock. That spring Lee purchased fifteen hundred head of cows and heifers, together with some ponies, to exchange for tokens and robes. Trade checks were abandoned as of January 1, 1878, by order of the commissioner of Indian affairs. Thereafter Indians received cash for services to the traders and others. That year the average compensation for a high-grade robe was about $3, but the number of hides available from the hunt and from the merchants' operations in the Panhandle fell to less than one thousand and declined rapidly to almost zero.[40]

In the years from 1877 to 1879 Lee and Reynolds marketed more than forty-three thousand robes. Probably more than half that number were tanned by the women of the Cheyennes and Arapahoes. The remainder, purchased from other traders, were probably prepared by the Comanches and Kiowas. Determined to maximize profits at a time when prices were declining because of short-term excessive supply, the partners decided not to dispose of their robes through the jobbers at Leavenworth, with which they had done business in previous years.[41]

For Lee and Reynolds the robe trade had increased in volume throughout most of the 1870s. From 1871 to 1876 the firm sold almost thirty-five thousand robes in Leavenworth. E. H. Durfee handled most of the sales. On occasion the partners contracted with W. C. Lobenstein or the mercantile firm of Cochran, Bittmann and Taylor. The volume of sales advanced from about three thousand in 1870 to more than twelve thousand in 1874. The collection of robes declined during the Red River War, when the Cheyennes were on the warpath. Although the Arapahoes remained at peace, they would not leave the reservation to hunt. The collection from the tribes remained low in 1876, forcing the partners to buy hides from Rath, and perhaps others, for processing by the Indians.[42]

That liaison with Dodge City hide merchants led to the formation of enterprises to revive the hunting of buffalo in the Texas Panhandle. In the next two years Lee and Reynolds acquired more than forty-three thousand robes. By then supply greatly exceeded demand, making it difficult for the partners to sell robes even at the prevailing low prices. For a time they held their robes off the market, hoping that prices would move upward. When it became apparent that was not likely to happen, they decided to maximize their returns by marketing through outlets of their own in Chicago and New York City.[43]

Two firms founded in 1877 specialized in robe sales. In partnership with Seth J. Arnold, a member of the New York mercantile firm of Buckley Willing and Company, the Indian Territory traders organized Lee, Reynolds and Arnold Company in New York, with stores at 597 Broadway, opposite the Metropolitan Hotel, and at 170 Mercer Street. With G. D. Warren, a Chicago businessman, they formed Lee, Reynolds and Warren Company, which opened for business at 196–198 Monroe Street, Chicago.[44]

Over a period of three years the retail outlets sold nearly 37,000 robes. In September 1877, 11,000 and 12,203 robes, respectively in New York and Chicago, were carried on Lee and Reynolds's books, with an aggregate value of $84,270.50.

Initially sales were brisk. During October 1877 the Chicago outlet marketed 4,001 robes of all grades at an average price of $6.14 per robe. This was unquestionably from one-third to one-half more than the partners would have received from Kansas jobbers. However, the overhead was also substantially higher.[45]

Most of the robes were sold to retailers in a six-state area comprising Illinois, Wisconsin, Minnesota, Michigan, Indiana, and Ohio. The principal buyers were Hansen's Empire Fur Factory, Chicago, and two St. Paul firms, Albrecht Lanphier and Finch and Gordon and Ferguson. Montgomery Ward and Company, the large Chicago mail-order firm, bought seventy-eight robes that month.

By the late summer and early fall of 1879 Lee, Reynolds and Warren had completed its final transactions, selling 3,245 robes to Dyer Taylor and Company at an average price of $4.50, minus an allowance of $650 for damage, and 800 robes to H. K. and F. B. Thurber and Company at an average price of $4.50 per robe, less 5 percent commission. What remained of the inventory was transferred to the New York outlet, which closed at the end of October. That marked the end of the robe trade for the Indian Territory traders.

By 1878 Reynolds and Lee had decided to get out of the Indian trade. The virtual extinction of the buffalo herd on the southern Plains meant that the years of high profits had come to a close. That year the partners refocused their operations, concentrating on military stores, freighting, and contracts to supply cord wood, hay, fresh beef, and other commodities to the Indian reservation and military posts. At the same time both men looked for new business opportunities in Indian Territory and in other states and territories.

They sold the store at the Cheyenne-Arapahoe Agency to George Reynolds in December 1878. He had been active in the business as an employee for a number of years before buying out all of the interest of Lee and Reynolds at a cost of nearly $15,000, in the form of four short-term notes held by the partners. That the business continued to prosper is indicated by the new owner's ability to reduce his debt by more than one-half in a period of only fifteen months. He remained at Darlington until July 1881, when he sold the store to Charles T. Connell.[46]

Lee and Reynolds continued to operate stores at Forts Supply and Elliott and near the latter place in the town of Mobeetie, Texas. The two men agreed to reorganize the partnership in 1879, but that task was not completed until 1881, when each man acquired an equal share of the firm's assets. Until then Reynolds had been the senior partner. Under the new arrangement Reynolds made Charles F. Mc-Kenney, who had been chief clerk for Lee and Reynolds since 1874, a partner and resident trader at the Fort Supply store. Lee, the licensed trader at Fort Elliott, apparently served as the resident trader at that post.[47]

The prosperity of the stores depended upon the continuation of Lee and Reynolds's freighting operations. The partners had been managing their own trains for years, but they limited operations largely to their own needs until the Red River War. When that conflict began, they acted as local agents for the army's freighting contractor, Chick Browne and Company of Grenada, Colorado Territory. When the demand for transportation exceeded the contractor's capacity, officers at Fort Supply asked the local traders to transport military supplies to the new post of Fort Elliott and to troops engaged in the campaign against the Comanches, Cheyennes, and Kiowas elsewhere in the Texas Panhandle. This became a very lucrative enterprise for the partners, one that they sought to expand after the close of hostilities.[48]

Wagon trains emblazoned with the firm's name were almost constantly in movement over a network of roads and trails that ran southward from Dodge City to Fort Supply; to the Cheyenne-Arapahoe Agency at Darlington and nearby Fort Reno, a new military post established during the Red River War; to Fort Elliott; and to other points in Indian Territory and the Texas Panhandle. In addition to the military and the Indian reservation, Lee and Reynolds Freighters, with headquarters and warehouses at the Kansas railroad town, provided transportation services for merchants and ranchers. The firm hauled goods to points throughout much of the Southwest.[49]

Lee and Reynolds Freighters operated six wagon trains in 1879. A train, commanded by a wagon master and sometimes an assistant, usually comprised twelve double wagons (lead and trailer), each in the charge of a teamster. William Gibbs had charge of twelve teams, each composed of five yoke of oxen. Wagon masters T. S. Bryant T. M. Lieperd, and John Ashenfelter were in charge of trains comprising twelve teams of double wagons drawn by three yoke of oxen. George W. Russell, the oldest wagon master in length of service, owned one-half of his outfit, which included ten double wagons, each drawn by four yoke of oxen. Andy Jard, another longtime wagon master, was in charge of the stables at Dodge City. August ("Gus") Miller handled Lee and Reynolds's only mule train, which was made up of ten double wagons, each drawn by eight animals.[50]

The freighting business required a very large investment of capital. The inventory included six ox (bull) trains and 680 head of cattle, 80 mules, forty-four Schutter lead and trail wagons, and seventy-four Kansas and other wagons, the aggregate value of which, according to A. E. Reynolds's calculations, amounted to $27,220. That figure did not, however, include the cost of the stables and warehouses at Dodge City and similar but smaller facilities at Forts Supply and Elliott. Furthermore, Reynolds did not compute the cost of spare wagons and animals and blacksmith shops with requisite inventories of tools, equipment, and spare shoes for animals and parts for wagons.[51]

Having freighting outfits enabled Lee and Reynolds to bid successfully for contracts on jobs where the supplying of goods and services for the army required a large amount of transportation. The firm's lucrative wood and hay contracts were a case in point. Another example was the furnishing of cedar poles for the telegraph wire that linked Fort Supply and Fort Elliott. At the former place that line connected with the telegraph service from Fort Dodge. The partners put men and teams to work cutting poles in July 1879, and by September 20 some two thousand poles had been accepted by the army at Fort Supply. Lee and Reynolds earned an additional $60 for loading the poles and dropping them at proper intervals along the route between Forts Supply and Elliott.[52]

From 1879 to 1882 Lee and Reynolds prospered, but the partners, perhaps sensing that conditions were changing in Indian Territory and that prosperous times could not continue indefinitely, looked to business opportunities elsewhere. Reynolds devoted much of his time to mining interests in Colorado, while Lee became largely absorbed in cattle ranching in the Texas Panhandle. With each man moving in a different direction, it was probably only a question of time before they dissolved the partnership.

In 1882 the partnership ended after a heated dispute, the precise nature of which is uncertain. The breakup was formalized in April of that year, when Reynolds acquired Lee's interest in the stores at Fort Elliott and Mobeetie, where D. W. Van Horn was the resident trader; the LE Ranch west of Tascosa, Texas; mining interests in Colorado; and all freighting teams and equipment employed outside of Indian Territory.[53] Thereafter Reynolds was largely preoccupied with the Panhandle ranch and the Colorado silver mines, but he did not immediately abandon merchandising in the region where he had enjoyed great financial success for a dozen years.

He became a silent partner in two mercantile firms. One was located at the Cheyenne-Arapahoe Agency, Darlington, Indian Territory, and the other at Fort Elliott in the Texas Panhandle. The first venture was in association with Weller N. Hubbell and D. H. Doty, and the second was with D. W. Van Horn.

Hubbell was an experienced Indian trader, a longtime employee of the Lee and Reynolds store at the agency. Doty, a Leavenworth merchant, may have been the brother of W. H. Doty, who had worked as a clerk in the Darlington store for several years. Hubbell and Doty were the on-site managers, while Reynolds provided them with business contacts and capital. He arranged with Dodd, Brown and Company, a St. Louis wholesale house, to supply needed merchandise. Reynolds also shipped from Lake City, Colorado, where he had opened another store, items that were unsuited for the mining community market.[54]

D. W. Van Horn and Company owned two stores, complete with saloons, one at Fort Elliott, the other in the nearby town of Mobeetie. Both establishments were prosperous for a number of years. Reynolds's annual share of the profits, as the investor of capital, was both reliable and sizable until 1889, when the volume of business dropped sharply because the army closed the saloon at the fort. The following year, with the closing of the post and the decision of the region's first railroad to build not to Mobeetie but to the relocated town of Clarendon, the business fell on hard times. Van Horn closed the enterprise in November 1890. Thereafter he became the vice president of Charles Goodnight's Bank of Clarendon, where he remained until his death in a railroad accident in 1899.[55]

The store at Darlington was not a success. Within two years of its opening Reynolds was warning his partners to either relocate or sell the enterprise as quickly as possible. He believed that the federal government's termination of reservation leases to cattlemen, together with diminished rations for the tribes, would lead to a mutiny and massacre at the agency within two years, possibly sooner. For merchants this situation was compounded by the action of the commissioner of Indian affairs, J. D. Atkins, in refusing to renew the licenses of competent traders. Some victims of Atkins's policy charged that he hoped to give the profitable trading privileges to his friends. Andrew J. Reynolds, who had been one of three traders at Anadarko, the headquarters of the Kiowa and Wichita Agency, received a one-year renewal, but only because his brother, A. E., had asked Senator Teller to intervene with the Bureau of Indian Affairs. Reynolds could not obtain an extension of the license at Darlington.[56]

On being denied a renewal of the trader's license, Hubbell and Doty relocated from Indian Territory to Caldwell, Kansas. At about that time A. E. Reynolds attempted to convince Robert M. Wright, the Dodge City merchant, that he should include Hubbell and Doty in a projected mercantile venture in the Texas Panhandle. Unsuccessful in that effort, Reynolds instructed his partners to reduce their stock, worth an estimated $10,000, and at the first opportunity to sell out at any reasonable price.[57]

A partial sale was completed in June 1886. W. H. Doty, who had been a clerk in Andrew Reynolds's store at Anadarko, purchased the firm's inventory of groceries, a delivery wagon with team, some accounts payable, and store fixtures for about $1,000. Payment was to be in installments, of which he made only one. Doty traded the team and wagon for town lots in Caldwell but made no settlement with the firm of Reynolds, Hubbell and Doty. In 1887 after Reynolds had relocated his mercantile operations from Lake City, he brought D. H. Doty and his family to Ouray to manage a retail outlet in that thriving mining community.[58]

The transfer of the Hubbell and Doty store from Darlington to Caldwell and then, in fact if not in name, to Ouray severed A. E. Reynolds's last business link with Indian Territory. Even though he spent most of his time thereafter in Colorado, he did not forget the experience of having lived and worked among the personnel of the frontier army garrisons and the people of the Cheyenne and Arapahoe tribes. Officers frequently asked advice or assistance, usually letters of support for promotions or pensions. Reynolds responded with recommendations to friends in Washington, usually

members of Colorado's delegation to Congress. On one occasion he asked Senator Teller to intervene with the War Department in behalf of former Lieutenant J. Worden Pope,
who sought promotion from colonel to brigadier general
before retiring from the army. At another time Reynolds
endorsed a petition for a pension by Luke Cahill, who as a
civilian scout had participated in campaigns against hostile
Indians. Cahill, a pioneer rancher in Las Animas County, had
served under the command of Lieutenant Pope, who as a
retired general had taken an interest in the matter. Reynolds
also assisted former Lieutenant Frank Baldwin, who had
retired as a general, with land transactions in Nebraska.
During the Philippine insurrection Reynolds's letter to
General Adna R. Chafee recommending a friend for employment in the islands brought a warm response, with
assurances that Chafee remembered well the onetime trader at Fort Supply.[59]

Even more intimate ties with the Native American community continued long after Reynolds left Indian Territory. He
remained very close to some of the mixed bloods, particularly
those who had worked for Lee and Reynolds. Included in this
group were George Bent, who had served as clerk and interpreter; George's sister, Julia; and her husband, Ed Guerrier.
When George Bent published, in collaboration with George
Hyde, a series of controversial articles under the title "Forty
Years with the Cheyennes" in *Frontier Magazine*, Reynolds
temporarily put aside his abhorrence of public statements to
defend his friend.

The crux of the controversy in this instance was Bent's
description of the Battle of Sand Creek of November 1864.
Bent called it a massacre of defenseless women and children.
Responding to that charge, Major Jacob Downing, an officer
of the Third Regiment, Colorado Volunteers, the unit that
had attacked the Cheyenne camp, denounced the author as a
"cutthroat and a thief, a liar and a scoundrel, but worst of all a
half-breed." Downing insisted that he had personally counted

the Indian dead, numbering about fifty, and that there was "only one squaw and only one papoose in the lot."[60]

In a letter published in the *Denver Times* of November 10, 1905, Reynolds insisted that Downing's assault on Bent's character was unwarranted. Carefully avoiding the issue of Sand Creek, which he preferred to leave to others, Reynolds insisted that Bent, as an eyewitness, spoke the truth as he remembered it. In defending his letter to another of Bent's critics, Reynolds elaborated on that point: "Whatever George Bent writes on the subject . . . [is] a perfectly accurate, and truthful statement of the time." He concluded by suggesting that the time had come, while witnesses were still alive, for an accurate accounting of the men, women, and children who had been killed at Sand Creek.[61]

The Reynolds-Bent friendship continued until the latter's death. In letters to Bent, Reynolds frequently asked about his former friends on the reservation and was genuinely concerned about their well-being. Bent not only informed Reynolds of conditions on the reservation, but he also requested help in the form of specific items from time to time. On request Reynolds sent, among other things, a shotgun, a team of horses, and money to buy a wagon. In addition, he annually prepared packages of Christmas gifts to be distributed by Bent among family and friends. When Bent died in May 1918, Reynolds was away from Denver and did not learn of that event until more than a week later. Belatedly he paid the cost of the funeral and asked local officials for information about the condition of his friend's survivors.[62]

In later years Reynolds looked back upon his years in Indian Territory with a sense of deep satisfaction. He believed that he had treated the Cheyennes and Arapahoes with fairness and respect. They, in turn, had extended to him their friendship and trust, admitting him to their councils and, on occasion, turning to him as mediator to resolve differences between the tribes and others. As a partner in the firm of Lee and Reynolds, he had assisted the Cheyennes and Arapahoes in adapting to reservation life. The traders had for a brief time sustained a thriving local industry for tanning buffalo hides to make robes. Later they employed men from the reservation in a variety of jobs for which they were paid cash. These tasks included cutting and stacking cord wood and cutting and stacking or baling hay, large supplies of which were consumed at the Indian agency and military posts. Occasionally Lee and Reynolds hired the Cheyennes and Arapahoes to make bricks and to split and haul rails.[63]

There was, however, a negative side to Lee and Reynolds's activities in Indian Territory. The traders' highly profitable entrepreneurial endeavors were instrumental in altering forever the lives of the Cheyennes and Arapahoes as well as other tribes. In the years after the Civil War post traders in the West, including Lee and Reynolds, sustained the army's efforts to restrict the tribes to reservations. As buyers of a large volume of hides and robes, Reynolds and his partner hastened the slaughter of the animals on which the Indians of the southern Plains were dependent for their nomadic existence. Without the buffalo the tribes had to remain on reservations and to depend on government handouts. The fiercely independent Native Americans suffered a loss of pride and dignity as well as a way of life. They became wards of the state, a status akin to pauperism.[64]

Soon after the Indian trade ceased to be highly profitable, Reynolds and Lee, pursuing roughly parallel careers, left Indian Territory to engage in new ventures that included, among other activities, cattle ranching. In sharp contrast to friends and acquaintances who remained on the reservation, Reynolds enjoyed substantial economic success. He was for more than twenty years the principal owner of a large ranch in the Texas Panhandle, where he raised pedigreed Hereford cattle for breeders and for the beef market a range herd of longhorns that were upgraded though crossbreeding with Herefords until they lost most of the characteristics of the native breed.

3
Ranching on the High Plains

THE partners who operated as Lee and Reynolds were bold, imaginative, and ambitious entrepreneurs. As Indian Territory merchants they engaged in numerous enterprises, all of which were designed to support in one way or another their role as traders serving the military and the Cheyenne and Arapahoe tribes. They offered whatever goods and services were needed when they could make a profit from doing so. Among their various subsidiary activities, they offered beef for sale, initially on the hoof, to the military posts and to the Indian agency at Darlington. In order to provide that service, they were among the first to engage in the raising of livestock in northern Indian Territory. Within a decade their ranching operations expanded to the Texas Panhandle.

Lee and Reynolds ran cattle on the open range in the vicinity of Camp Supply as early as 1873. A herd of Texas Longhorn cattle grazed along Sand and Beaver Creeks, west of the forks of Beaver and Wolfe Creeks. Additional grazing land was located along the North Fork of the Canadian River below Camp Supply. In October of that year the partners informed the Dickinson Brothers of Dodge City, who had a contract to provide Camp (later Fort) Supply with beef, that if they needed cattle, the Lee and Reynolds herd was for sale.[1] There is no evidence that the brothers accepted the offer, but this did suggest that Lee and Reynolds had at that early date ample cattle to supply the needs of the local market.

The following year Lee and Reynolds expanded operations by establishing a ranch on Turkey Creek, within the Arapahoe-Cheyenne reservation. This became the Red Fork Ranch, where the partners maintained a store in addition to running cattle. They sold the retail business to Daniel W. Jones, a resident of Caldwell, Kansas, in 1875 but continued to graze cattle in the area for another five years.[2]

The Red Fork Ranch was the center of Lee and Reynolds's cattle production until 1880. Initially the herd comprised several hundred Texas Longhorns. In 1877 the partners bought another six thousand head of native cattle from Captain Richard King of Nueces, Texas, and upgraded that herd by introducing registered bulls, mainly shorthorns, or, as they were known locally, Durhams. Some of the bulls were from the herd of Frederick William Stone, a well-known breeder at Guelph, Ontario, Canada. The mixed breed yielded an excellent quality of beef.[3]

From the Red Fork Ranch Lee and Reynolds regularly supplied beef to the commissaries at Fort Supply, Fort Elliott, Fort Reno, the Indian agency at Darlington, and small military detachments at stations along the route from Supply to Elliott. They maintained stockades (holding pens) and operated slaughterhouses at Supply and Elliott, where large-volume beef sales complemented Lee and Reynolds's merchandising activities. In 1875, for example, beef on the hoof sold for $0.1266 a pound, and gross sales were about $8,000 for the year.[4] The commissary at Fort Elliott required only about half of the amount sold at Fort Supply, but the trade was unquestionably profitable. Lee and Reynolds sold its contract as well as the stockade and slaughterhouse at Elliott to the firm of Volz and Kiesling in June 1879.[5]

In the following year Lee and Reynolds gave up cattle raising in Indian Territory. What remained of the herd, probably more than four thousand head, was sold to J. L. Driskill and Sons of Austin, Texas. The sellers relinquished all rights to grazing lands below Fort Supply but retained exclusive use of the area on Sand and Beaver Creeks.[6] By then the partners were relocating their cattle-raising operations to the Texas Panhandle.

Sometime in 1879, at the request of Lee, Jordan Edgar McAllister, who was in charge of Lee and Reynolds's cattle business in Indian Territory, traveled to the western section of the Panhandle to look for a site for a ranch. Following instructions, he traveled up the Canadian River west of Tascosa to the Texas border with New Mexico. What he saw were abundant water and ideal grazing land along the main watercourse and its tributaries. Much of that land was occupied by sheepherders who had moved into the area in search of open range in the early 1870s. They resided with their families in a dozen plazas that were scattered along the river for a distance of about 30 miles.[7]

In December 1879 Lee, acting for himself and Reynolds, purchased from Gunter and Munson, land agents at Tascosa, 29,440 acres of land in Oldham and Hartley Counties, the area previously investigated by McAllister. This land, offered by the state of Texas to acquire funds for the survey of the remainder of the Panhandle, was acquired at a cost of $0.50 an acre. Although Lee secured legal title to the land, most of it was then occupied by herders and their flocks. To remedy this situation, Lee allegedly set out one day with a bag full of money to visit with the residents of the many plazas. A handful of bills was all the encouragement needed to start them on a journey to New Mexico Territory, where the range was still open and free.[8]

The purchase of 1879 was the initial acquisition of what eventually became a tract of more than 200,000 acres that stretched eastward from the Texas–New Mexico border, covering both sides of the Canadian River and its numerous tributaries, to within a few miles of Tascosa. Known originally as the Canadian Ranch, the property was managed by McAllister in behalf of the partners. He was in charge of twelve men, who became the ranch's first cowboys. Most, if not all, of

these men had been employed by Lee and Reynolds as teamsters and cattle herders in Indian Territory before they were
transferred to the Texas property.[9]

The owners of the new ranch were breeders and dealers in
pure and graded shorthorn and Hereford cattle. Initially
their range was stocked with cattle purchased in New Mexico.
Subsequently the partners bought several thousand head of
Texas Longhorns from George T. Reynolds, William Reynolds, and Joshua Matthews of Albany, Texas. That herd, and
other cattle under McAllister's care, was identified by one of
two brands: LE, for Lee, or LR, for Lee and Reynolds.[10]

Following the practice first adopted in Indian Territory,
Lee and Reynolds upgraded the herd by turning out on the
closed range only bulls that were pedigreed shorthorns or
Herefords. The shorthorns were superseded within less than
two years because of the Herefords' unrivaled ability to survive in the Texas Panhandle, where at times grass was in short
supply.[11]

It had been mainly on Lee's initiative that the partnership
had acquired a ranch in the Texas Panhandle, and it was on
his recommendation that Reynolds bought a half interest in
the Canadian Ranch without visiting the property. At the time
Reynolds's interests were in Colorado. As early as 1879 Reynolds, in partnership with Henry C. Thatcher, John H.
Maugham, and others, invested heavily in silver mines on
Henson Creek at Lake City, Colorado. Maugham was cashier
of the local branch of the Thatcher brothers' bank. In addition, Reynolds devoted much of his time to freighting operations between the end of construction on the San Luis Valley
branch of the narrow-gauge Denver and Rio Grande Railway,
first at Alamosa and later at Del Norte, and the mines in
Hinsdale County. At about the same time Reynolds and
Thatcher, along with others, acquired potentially valuable
properties on Mount Sneffels at Ouray.[12]

By January 1882 it had become apparent that Lee and
Reynolds, after working closely together for a dozen years,

were moving apart, each pursuing business that was of little interest to the other. It may have been impatience with his partner's preoccupation with precious metal mines that prompted Lee to demand either that Reynolds buy all interest in the partnership or, if Reynolds preferred, that Lee buy him out. Even though Reynolds's funds were largely invested in mines and he did not have either the money or established credit with which to buy all of the Lee and Reynolds assets, he responded, probably to Lee's surprise, that he would some-how raise the money to buy all of the partnership.[13]

In April 1882 Reynolds worked out an agreement with Lee for the acquisition of the Canadian Ranch and other property formerly owned by Lee and Reynolds. With the ranch he gained possession of all the land, horses, buildings and im-provements, and cattle, with the exception of thirty-six Aber-deen Angus bulls and the livestock that worked as ox trains at or near Fort Supply in Indian Territory. Reynolds paid $187,500 in six notes secured by a mortgage on the ranch. These were due at intervals from July 1, 1882, to April 1, 1883.[14]

This agreement, Reynolds was convinced, culminated a deliberate effort by Lee over a period of eighteen months, perhaps two years, to acquire control of all of the partner-ship's assets. The scheme failed only because Reynolds was determined not to permit Lee to have his way. The twelve-year-old joint venture, which had been highly profitable to both men, ended with a division of property. Lee acquired the store at Fort Supply, which he continued to operate for several years in partnership with Joe Ferguson. Reynolds acquired, in addition to the Canadian Ranch, the partners' interest in Colorado and Utah mining properties, the freighting outfits that were employed outside of Indian Territory, and the stores at Fort Elliott and Mobeetie, which he subsequently operated in partnership with D. W. Van Horn.[15]

The breakup of the partnership could not have come at a worse time for Reynolds because most of his money was tied up in mining ventures. In order to raise money on short notice, Reynolds sold a one-third interest in the Canadian Ranch to one of his mining associates, John H. Maugham, for $105,000 and authorized him to sell the property to Robert Tennant of London, England, for $600,000. When the sale was completed, Maugham would receive one-third of the proceeds, approximately $125,000, after payment of all obligations, including the mortgage held by Lee.[16]

Although the English sale failed to materialize, Reynolds and Maugham, with money borrowed in New York against the ranch, paid off Lee in March 1883. Using the property as security, they secured from the Dundee Mortgage and Trust Investment Company of Scotland a five-year loan in the amount of $125,000 with which to buy up short-term notes, the proceeds from which they had paid Lee. One-fifth of the loan was earmarked for improving the quality and quantity of the herd.[17]

The ranch remained in possession of the partners until 1884, when they conveyed their interest to the newly organized Reynolds Land and Cattle Company. Incorporated in New York with an authorized capital of $1.5 million, the firm's board of directors included A. E. Reynolds, John H. Maugham, L. C. Hill, and A. G. Bond. Reynolds owned or controlled two-thirds and Maugham one-third of the stock. The directors elected Reynolds president and treasurer; Maugham, vice president; and Hill, secretary. Hill, who was superintendent of the Brooklyn Children's Aid Society, maintained the requisite New York office for transacting the corporation's official business.[18] Most of the company's affairs were handled by Reynolds and his chief assistant, Charles F. McKenney, at the former's Denver office.

The on-the-scene manager was initially George E. Reynolds, who was quickly succeeded by Charles F. Reynolds. Because one or the other was involved in the operation of the ranch over a period of twenty years, it was widely assumed at the time, and at a later date, that the property was owned by the Reynolds brothers. In fact, George and Charley owned only 7.5 and 4.5 percent, respectively, of the Reynolds Land and Cattle Company stock.[19]

During the first six years of Charley Reynolds's tenure as local manager, the ranch foreman was George W. Russell, a former wagon master for Lee and Reynolds. Russell was in charge of the day-to-day operations, supervising a crew of from ten to twenty cowboys. Both Charley and George Russell were appointed to their positions by A. E. Reynolds and reported to him. This created a problem of divided authority that undermined efficient operation of the property. After Russell resigned in 1889, the foreman was hired by Charley and took orders from him. Under Charley's direction the ranch became one of the best in the Texas Panhandle.[20]

The ranch's work schedule was arduous from spring to fall. A skeleton crew remained during the winter and expanded in late April or early May for the first of two annual roundups. In the spring and fall cows with calves were brought in from the ranch's 200,000 acres, one-fifth of which was leased from the state, and from open ranges. Open ranges disappeared in that part of the Texas Panhandle by 1887. In addition, strays had to be retrieved from the pastures of neighboring ranches.[21]

After each roundup calves were branded and sorted according to their assigned roles on the ranch. Those that were castrated were destined for sale in from two to four years, the younger ones as feeder stock. The bulls and heifers were future breeding stock either on the ranch or for sale to other cattle raisers. After all the cattle had been processed, the older steers and some dry cows that were to be shipped to market were driven northward to the Oklahoma Strip to graze there until time to be sold.[22]

This phase of the ranch routine was coordinated with a related enterprise, the McKenney and Over Cattle Company, which had its headquarters at Cline, Oklahoma Territory, and ran cattle on the open range. This enterprise had been founded by Charles F. McKenney and John Over in 1875 and registered its brand as Bar M (M̲). At that time McKenney was Lee and Reynolds's chief clerk, and Over was employed by the same company as a herder. Initially McKenney and Over grazed their cattle with those of Lee and Reynolds on ranges near Fort Supply and on the Cheyenne-Arapahoe reservation.[23]

When Lee and Reynolds relocated cattle operations to the Texas Panhandle, McKenney and Over established its base of operations at Cline. Activities at the Panhandle ranch, where LE and Bar M cattle grazed on the same pastures and ranges, were closely coordinated with those of the property in the Oklahoma Strip. Cattle were driven northward and held in the vicinity of Cline until time to be sold. Then they were driven relatively short distances to railroads at either Englewood or Liberal, Kansas. With the completion of the Denver and Fort Worth and the Santa Fe lines into the western Panhandle, Charley Reynolds had the option of shipping cattle to market from points near the ranch, but he seldom did so until after the turn of the century, by which time the influx of farmers, popularly called grangers, had blocked portions of the trail and limited access to public ranges in the strip.[24]

When it appeared that the strip would be taken up by farmers in the late 1880s, Reynolds and McKenney looked for ranges elsewhere on which to graze cattle until ready for shipment to market. For a time they thought they had found the ideal location on the lands of the Costilla Grant in Colorado, south of Fort Garland. A. E. Reynolds negotiated a multi-year contract that allowed for the grazing of from 250 to 300 head on the land at a nominal annual charge of $0.25 each. The first herd was relocated from the Panhandle to the San Luis Valley in the spring of 1887. Although the water and the grass were all that could be desired, the flies were so thick that the contract was canceled after a single season.[25]

In 1888 cattle operations centered once again in the Panhandle and the Oklahoma Strip. At the latter place an increasing number of farmers imposed restrictions on open-range grazing, but McKenney and Over remained active until the turn of the century. Not until the Chicago, Rock Island and Pacific Railroad built from Liberal to Dalhart, with a shipping station on the ranch, did LE cattle go to market without the annual drive northward.[26]

At the Panhandle ranch the workforce, when not preoccupied with cattle-related duties, was assigned to a variety of tasks that contributed to the efficient operation of the property. During the growing season, if weather conditions permitted, the cowboys cut hay in the meadows of the Canadian River and its tributaries. Anywhere from 350 to 500 tons could be stacked in good years as an important source of feed for the cattle during the winter months. In addition, ranch hands planted and harvested sorghum and alfalfa on 40 acres of irrigated land and elsewhere when there was sufficient rain to grow the crops. They maintained numerous windmills that provided the all-important water supply when the streams invariably dried up during the summer and during frequent periods of drought. Much time was devoted to building and keeping in repair the fences that enclosed the sprawling ranch. In the summer when streams dried up, fences had to be erected along streams to prevent thirsty cattle from "bogging" in muddy streambeds. During such times the indispensable windmills supplied most, if not all, of the water for the ranch.[27]

Maugham, unlike Reynolds, was reluctant to participate in the administration of the ranch. Rather, he preferred to spend much of his time, after resigning from the bank at Ouray, in the British Isles, where he acted as agent for the sale of American mining and ranching properties. In addition, he devoted much time to arranging a consolidation of the Panhandle property with ranches owned by English and Scottish investors. His immediate goal, which Reynolds opposed, was to bring about a merger of the LE Ranch with its largest neighbor, the XIT.[28]

That company had been organized in Chicago by Abner Taylor, A. C. Babcock, and John V. and Charles B. Farwell, wholesale merchants. In the mid-1880s, when Texas offered 3 million acres of land in exchange for the construction of a new state capitol, Taylor, Babcock and Company acquired on assignment the contract from the original bidder. In order to raise the funds to undertake the construction project, the three men organized with British capitalists the Capitol Freehold Land and Investment Company. With the prospect of Texas land, that company raised from English and Scottish investors money that XIT, an American enterprise, used to build the new state capitol. The British firm leased the lands to XIT, which carried on an extensive ranching business in northwestern Texas.[29]

To XIT the Reynolds ranch was an attractive acquisition because it occupied both sides of the Canadian River and most of its principal tributaries. Reynolds disapproved of Maugham's scheme to make what he called a "cousin jack" property of the ranch and warned that it could be done only if Taylor and the Farwells were willing to buy him out. The owners of the XIT ranch balked at paying the $790,000 that Reynolds demanded for his two-thirds interest in the ranch.[30]

Maugham was equally unsuccessful in raising the money that was desperately needed to support the ranch's operations. In March 1885 Reynolds complained that he had exhausted his resources in an attempt to keep the ranch solvent. Not only did he get no help from Maugham, Reynolds also had not heard from him all winter. The following year relations between the two men were further strained when Maugham negotiated a contract for the sale of 3,000 LE steers to the English-controlled Creswell Land and Cattle Company, with payment to take the form of shares of uncertain value in the company. Three years later Maugham signed a similar contract with Creswell Land and Cattle and deliberately withheld from his partner information about an arrangement by which a personal debt of £1,800 was to be paid off on completion of the sale.[31]

By that date Maugham's urgent need for relief from mounting personal debts prompted an attack on Reynolds's administration of the ranch. He charged that the books had been manipulated by McKenney and Reynolds to hide profits that were used by the latter to support his numerous speculations in mining properties and in the stock market. Because of this, according to Maugham, ranch records indicated that it had always operated at a loss, when, in fact, profits had been misappropriated by the majority stockholder. Maugham wanted an audit of the accounts and the payment of money allegedly due him.[32]

Reynolds was incensed by Maugham's charges. They were, he insisted, completely without foundation. Maugham, who had never been to the ranch, received monthly reports on the financial condition of the Reynolds Land and Cattle Company and had no grounds for complaint. In an effort to initiate action against Reynolds, Maugham surrendered control of his stock to John A. and Mahlon D. Thatcher, whom he asked to investigate the ranch's records. However, the Pueblo bankers had no reason to criticize Reynolds's management of the Panhandle property. Within less than a year Mahlon Thatcher had been elected vice president of Reynolds Land and Cattle, and Maugham had disappeared from the company's affairs.[33]

The Pueblo banker had served as a trustee of the company for several years before his election. Membership on the board allowed him to keep abreast of the ranch's financial affairs at a time when a large amount of its stock was deposited with the First National Bank of Pueblo as collateral for loans to A. E. Reynolds. When Maugham sold his interest in the company as payment for personal debts that were carried on the ranch's books, Thatcher purchased those securities, becoming the second largest stockholder.[34]

It is unlikely that the Reynolds Land and Cattle Company could have survived its formative years if Mahlon D. Thatcher had not come to its rescue on more than one occasion. In 1884, for example, the firm had no funds to pay the annual interest on the mortgage, which was held in Dundee, Scotland. Rather than risk the consequences of default, Thatcher reluctantly advanced the money. Three years later, in exchange for a share in A. E. Reynolds's mining interests at Aspen, he again provided the funds with which to pay the interest in order to avert certain default.[35]

After struggling with what he called a bankrupt enterprise for nearly a decade, Reynolds was gratified to see the ranch finally yield substantial profits, a reflection of the growing reputation of its predominantly Hereford stock. The range herd of graded heifers, cows, and bulls, seven-eighths Hereford, was usually sold to breeders. Young steers were offered as feeder cattle.[36]

At one time Reynolds decided to replace Herefords with polled Angus. He experimented with pedigreed black bulls as early as 1892 but replaced them with Herefords within a few years. The offspring of the graded Hereford cows bred by Angus bulls were culled commencing in 1897, and within three years the herd consisted of only white-faced cattle.

By 1890 higher prices for cattle enabled Reynolds to resume payments on the principal of the mortgage on the ranch. That debt was carried at a burdensome rate of 8 percent interest. At about the same time the Alliance Trust Company, successor to the Dundee Mortgage and Trust Investment Company, asked for the payment of all of the principal, $125,000, plus unpaid interest. Although full payment had been due in 1888, the Scottish firm had extended the loan from year to year with the stipulation that interest payments remain current.[37]

The abrupt change in policy was prompted in part by the adoption of a new Texas law regulating alien ownership of property and also by a sharp decline in the value of British investments in American cattle ranches. William Mackenzie, secretary of the Alliance Trust, informed A. E. Reynolds that the directors feared that the statute would jeopardize their interest in the LE Ranch. Reynolds quickly pointed out that the law could not possibly affect the Scottish firm. Mackenzie agreed but insisted nonetheless that the loan could not be extended beyond another year, and that would be possible only if Reynolds paid all outstanding interest and not less than $25,000 toward reduction of the principal.[38]

Faced with what amounted to an ultimatum, A. E. informed Charley that he had to raise the money by selling cattle. A sale of two-year-old steers to a Kansas cattle feeder netted sufficient funds to pay all interest, plus $20,000 on the principle, reducing it to $105,000. The prospect of further reduction of the Scottish loan vanished temporarily when cattle prices collapsed during the depression that following the Panic of 1893. The Scottish firm recognized that further payments would have to be delayed and extended the loan to 1900 while lowering the interest rate from 8 to 7 percent.[39]

As early as 1896 the cattle company experienced improved economic conditions because of higher prices. That year A. E. Reynolds devoted profits to reducing the mortgage and over four years paid $60,000 to the Alliance Trust Company. By the fall of 1900, when the mortgage stood at $45,000, Reynolds proposed to pay it off in three installments over a period of three years with an interest rate of 6 percent. When the Scottish lenders insisted on 7 percent, Reynolds asked for permission to pay off the debt in one year. The mortgage was officially terminated on July 1, 1901.[40]

By 1900 A. E. Reynolds wanted to retire from the cattle business. If freed of a heavy burden of debt, the ranch, he assumed, was readily marketable and would net a reasonable profit for the investors in the Reynolds Land and Cattle Company. To potential buyers he offered the property for $2 an acre. Thirty-five percent of the purchase price was payable at the time of closing, the balance in two years. The land could be purchased with or without the cattle. The cost of the herd, according to Reynolds's estimate, would be between $40,000 and $50,000. The total price for the ranch with cattle would be approximately $500,000.[41]

The more than 200,000 acres that made up the ranch were divided into a number of pastures. In the northwest was the Mineosa pasture of 48,000 acres, with access to water from a small stream that cut across the southwestern corner. Several windmills and wells assured a supply of water for cattle.[42]

Immediately to the east of Mineosa was the Manilla pasture, which was not owned by the Reynolds Land and Cattle Company. Further east was Punta de Agua pasture, 66,000 acres, which derived its name from the stream that crossed it from east to west. East of Punta de Agua were lands leased from the state of Texas and from the Rock Island Railroad.

South of Punta de Agua was the Romero pasture, which was traversed by Romero Creek. The ranch headquarters at Romero, north of the pasture, included a house and related structures required for the efficient operation of the property. Water from a spring was piped to the headquarters for the consumption of personnel and for irrigation of an orchard of three hundred fruit trees that included peach, pear, apple, apricot, and nectarine trees as well as grapevines. Near Romero alfalfa was grown on 40 acres of irrigated meadowland.

West of the junction of Romero Creek with the Canadian, and along both sides of the river was the Joint pasture, shared by the Reynolds and XIT ranches. The two firms conceded that numerous small parcels that each owned in this area could be used efficiently only as a block. West of the Joint pasture was the Trujillo pasture, which derived its name from the creek that ran through it. A small segment of this pasture was owned by XIT. South of Trujillo was Mojares pasture, containing some 9,000 acres. West of Mojares and Trujillo was Browne pasture, comprising nearly 20,000 acres.[43]

Two separate herds on Reynolds's LE Ranch were for sale. A thoroughbred herd of Herefords included 350 bulls and 300 cows, two years old and upward. About 40 of the bulls had been imported from England. An equal number had been purchased in Canada. They were offered at a special price of $150 each and the bred cows at $50 each. If not sold with the land, these cattle would be moved to another ranch.[44]

The range stock of white-faced cattle, numbering in excess of twenty thousand head, had been bred up to Hereford standards. These were moderately priced: cows with calves at their side, $40; dry cows and two-year-old heifers, $27.50; yearling heifers, $18; and bulls, $75. Steers were offered at the market price at the time of purchase.[45]

Two parties indicated an interest in purchasing the LE Ranch. One was M. F. Beaumont of nearby Hartley, Texas. The other was James C. Johnson, manager of the Prairie Cattle Company, Edinburgh, Scotland. Johnson and the board of directors were looking for rangeland on which to expand operations in the Panhandle.[46]

The Scottish-American Mortgage Company had organized in 1880 the Prairie Cattle Company, one of the largest for-eign-owned cattle enterprises in the American West. It owned the JJ Ranch in southern Colorado and other large properties in New Mexico and Texas. By 1885 it reportedly was grazing 150,000 head of cattle and had a reputation for paying large dividends.[47]

Johnson and the Prairie Cattle Company's board of direc-tors considered the purchase of the LS (Lee-Scott) Ranch before agreeing to buy Reynolds's LE Ranch. A delegation of Scots inspected the two properties in the spring of 1902, and on June 4 Johnson agreed to pay the Reynolds Land and Cattle Company $2 per acre for its land. This offer was accepted without hesitation by the firm's board of trustees.[48] The agreement authorized Reynolds to exchange lands with XIT, allowing each to consolidate what had been widely scattered landholdings. In addition, XIT wanted Reynolds's Texas school lands, where titles could be purchased from the state.[49]

Because of the sale, there was a flurry of land transfers that temporarily swamped the recorders' and treasurers' offices in

Hartley and Oldham Counties in 1902. The Reynolds company purchased at a cost of $1.50 per acre seven individual
claims, each in the amount of 2,560 acres, owned by current
and former employees. These were part of the 202,265 acres
purchased by the Prairie Cattle Company at a cost of
$404,530.20. The Reynolds ranch bought 47,267 acres from
the Capitol Freehold Land and Investment Company and
sold it in return 38,142 acres. Each party paid $2 per acre.
Additional transfers at the same price included 8,288 acres to
Kemary Ritter and 314 acres to the Matadore Land and Cattle
Company, purchaser of XIT's Alamocitas Ranch in 1902.
Another 138 acres were conveyed to the Chicago, Rock Island
and Mexico Railroad for right of way at no cost.[50]

Prairie Cattle Company agreed to pay cash in part and the
balance, without interest, in installments over two years. In
return for the concession on interest, Reynolds gained the
right to retain two-thirds of the property the first year and
one-third the second year. In addition, he retained full possession of the house and other structures until the final
payment, allowing ample time for selling off the range herd
and transferring the thoroughbred cattle to another property.[51]

At the time of the sale the Reynolds ranch had two Hereford herds and a herd of horses. A range herd numbered
almost 22,000 head of cattle. Before the close of the year the
herd had been reduced through sales to 8,191 head. The
thoroughbred herd comprised 697 head, of which 50 bulls (2
English and 48 Canadian imports) had been sold by the end
of the year. The ranch had 232 head of horses, of which 68
were sold that year.[52]

Some of the range herd was purchased by local cattle
feeders and breeders, but most of it was sold to a single ranch
in New Mexico. In September 1902 James J. Hagerman, a
prominent mine and railroad promoter with whom Reynolds
had shared some mining interests almost twenty years earlier,
inquired about the possibility of purchasing LE cattle. Hag-

erman, with his sons, Percy and Arthur, was organizing the Southspring Ranch and Cattle Company, whose range in the upper Pecos valley they hoped to stock with graded Herefords. They agreed to pay one-fourth of the purchase price in cash and the balance in three equal installments over a period of eighteen months. The unpaid balance was to be secured by the ranch company's stock and bonds and a mortgage on the cattle.[53]

In October 1902 Charley Reynolds and ranch foreman Ralph P. Church began shipping LE cattle from Hartley. By July 1903 the Hagermans, through their ranch company, had purchased livestock, including horses, at a cost of $128,326, for which they were obligated to make full payment no later than mid-1904. Prior to that date, however, the market for cattle declined to the point where Hagerman could make only a partial payment and asked for the first of numerous extensions of the mortgage. The final payment was not made until February 1908, at which time A. E. Reynolds was left with 75 shares of the Southspring stock, for which there was no market even at discount prices.[54]

The unsold thoroughbred herd, plus what remained of the range cattle, was relocated to land Reynolds owned near La Junta, Colorado. Across the Arkansas River from that community and extending eastward were approximately 3,000 acres, two-thirds of which were irrigated by the Fort Lyon Canal Company. Reynolds had leased a portion of the property to farmers commencing about 1900 and that year brought from the Panhandle ranch Hereford calves that became the nucleus of a breeding herd.

That herd, augmented by transfers in 1902–1903 from the Panhandle, remained in the Arkansas valley for a number of years. In 1909 it was relocated to the EJM (Edward J. Mathews) Ranch near Delta, Colorado, in which Reynolds had a financial interest. Mathews and Reynolds raised thoroughbred Herefords for sale to breeders. For several years they grazed cattle near Delta and on land leased in the Uncom-

paghre Forest. The removal of the herd from land near La
Junta was necessary because Reynolds decided to subdivide
and sell the irrigated tracts to farmers.[55]

The removal of the unsold herd from the Panhandle to
Colorado brought to a close the operations of the Reynolds
Land and Cattle Company. After the proceeds from the sale
were used to pay off all debts, the remainder was distributed
to shareholders. Twenty-four special dividends distributed a
total of $40.91 per share to the twelve stockholders of record
over a period of almost five years.

A. E. Reynolds, the largest stockholder, with 5,999 of
12,000 outstanding shares, received a total of $245,419.09.
M. D. Thatcher, with 3,950 shares (Maugham's 3949 plus 1),
received $161,594.50. All other investors, with a single excep-
tion, were Reynolds's siblings or their estates. George E.
Reynolds's 900 shares earned $36,819. Charles F. Reynolds's
400 shares earned $16,364. Brother Andrew J. and sisters
Ellen C., Abbie N., Elizabeth, Hattie A., Fanny E., and Alice
M. each owned 100 shares, for which they each received
$4,091. A. E. Reynolds's father-in-law, Dr. Robert W. Earll,
received $2,045.50 for his 50 shares.[56]

The ranch income provided A. E. Reynolds with a temporary respite from heavy debts, the result of his persistent faith
in Colorado's declining precious metals mining industry. However, upon the liquidation of the Texas enterprise, Reynolds,
as he had for twenty years, devoted most of his time to silver-
and gold-producing enterprises. He retained interests in the
Arkansas valley farms, which became a welcome refuge from
the problems of his mining investments, then badly in disarray.

Indeed, troubles seemed to descend on Reynolds from all
directions. The Panhandle ranch, although in the hands of
others, frequently required Reynolds's attention because of
deficiencies in the titles to the land. At the time that the
Prairie Cattle Company purchased the ranch, Reynolds, with
that firm's approval, worked out a sale of land to XIT through

A. G. Boyce, the local manager. Five years later XIT's lawyers reported that recent surveys indicated that two parcels involved in the transaction were short a total of 1,537 acres. XIT had paid $2 an acre for land that allegedly did not exist along the Texas–New Mexico boundary. In fact, the missing acres were in New Mexico and were not part of the land originally conveyed by patents from the state of Texas.[57]

This claim for nonexistent acres must have come as a great surprise, for Reynolds had reason to believe that the question of shortages in the leagues along Texas's western border had been resolved twenty years earlier. In 1883 the firm of Browne and Manzanares acknowledged that its leagues along the line were deficient a strip 1,850 feet wide and assumed that Reynolds's land, purchased from the state of Texas at the same time, had similar shortages. This prompted Reynolds to write to the firm of Gunter and Summerfield, successor to Gunter and Munson, from which the property had been purchased, asking for corrections of land titles. Before the end of the year the patents for the land in question were sent to the Texas Land Office for cancellation and then issuance of corrected ones. Presumably the new patents did not include the missing acres.[58]

However, Reynolds was later warned that this was not correct. In the spring of 1887 W. S. Mabry informed Reynolds that because of "overlapping" of land into New Mexico, he was still short a total of 3,231 acres in four parcels. Apparently Reynolds did not seek remedy for this shortage and may have assumed that Mabry was in error.[59]

This may have been why Reynolds was disinclined to believe that the land sold to XIT was short acres. Furthermore, he argued that any claim for compensation was invalid since the ranch company had been liquidated and no longer existed. XIT countered that the titles had been guaranteed; therefore the stockholders who benefited from the sale of the land were liable for losses incurred by the purchaser. When Reynolds refused to make payment without conducting an investigation of his own, XIT threatened to resolve the matter through the courts.[60]

At the time Reynolds was experiencing a severe cash-flow problem because his mining properties were largely inactive and the plan to sell irrigated farm land in the Arkansas valley was a year or more from fruition. Therefore, he stalled for time. It was not until March 1908 that he reluctantly agreed to pay $2 for each of the missing acres sometime after April 1, 1909. The contract for payment was dated May 1 of that year, but it was not until January 1910 that Reynolds and Thatcher paid their proportionate shares of the shortage, which upon further investigation had been reduced to 1227.5 acres, plus interest for twenty-one months.[61]

A similar shortage was discovered by the Prairie Cattle Company when it sold what it called the Romero pasture (the former Reynolds ranch) to John M. Shelton of Amarillo in 1914. After a survey revealed shortages in 5 leagues along the Texas–New Mexico border, Shelton refused to pay for 2,084 acres. In June 1917 John M. Rusk, the liquidator of the Scottish enterprise, asked Reynolds to compensate the purchaser for the $4,168 it had paid for nonexistent land.[62]

In order to determine his liability in this matter, Reynolds wrote to the Texas Land Commission asking for information about the alleged shortages along the border with New Mexico. Texas officials responded that they knew nothing of any shortages but said they would look into the matter. However, no determination was made on this issue, and Rusk's claim remained unpaid at the time of Reynolds's death.[63]

4
Creating a Mining Empire

In 1877 A. E. Reynolds and W. M. D. Lee, as the firm of Lee and Reynolds, first invested in western mining properties. Initially they committed some of the large profits from their Indian Territory enterprises to a Utah railroad venture that proposed to develop a large tract of metallurgical coal suitable for making coke. By the time that venture failed, the partners were investing heavily in silver mines near Lake City and on Mount Sneffels at Ouray, Colorado. When the partnership was dissolved in 1882, Lee restricted his business interests, at least for a time, to merchandising and cattle raising. Reynolds pursued similar activities but continued to invest heavily in Colorado mining properties.

It is not clear why Lee and Reynolds were attracted to coal land investments in Utah. They may have been drawn into this speculative activity by E. H. Garbutt, a New York City wholesaler from whom they purchased large quantities of tobacco and a variety of other goods for resale in their stores at Forts Supply and Elliott and at the Indian agency. By 1879 they had committed a large amount of time and money to the promotion of the Utah and Pleasant Valley Railroad Company and to an affiliated firm, the Utah Coal and Coke Company, which claimed to own valuable metallurgical coal deposits in Pleasant Valley, about 38 miles southeast of Provo.[1]

In addition to Lee, Reynolds, and Garbutt, the chief investors in both enterprises were C. W. Scofield, H. P. De Graaf,

David B. Prosser, and George Goss. All, with the exception of the Indian Territory traders, were probably residents of New York City. In 1879 Scofield and De Graaf agreed to build a railroad from the coalfield to Provo, with the understanding that Lee and Reynolds would purchase the company's bonds in the amount of $10,000. This was in addition to at least $25,000 they had invested in the coal land venture.[2]

The firm of Lee and Reynolds marketed a substantial volume of the stocks and bonds of the railroad through Sheldon and Wadsworth Company, New York City. In December 1879 Reynolds noted that W. C. Sheldon, a partner in the firm, had sold 100 bonds, for which he received, in behalf of Lee and Reynolds, $40,833 in stock and cash. By the terms of another arrangement, Sheldon was to sell 200 shares of the railroad's stock—80 at $0.60 and 120 at $0.75—and pay Lee and Reynolds $0.50 per share, plus one-half of all proceeds over that amount.[3]

The construction of a narrow-gauge line from coal mines at Scofield, in Pleasant Valley, to Provo was hampered by lack of funds. The first segment of 55 miles was completed from Scofield to Springfield in 1879 and the remaining 5 miles from Springfield to Provo, the following year. The company failed in 1880; its assets, including coal lands, were sold two years later to the Denver and Rio Grande Western Railway Company. That enterprise purchased all rights to the Utah and Pleasant Valley line and related assets. The Pleasant Valley mines became an important source of fuel for the railroad and for the region's expanding urban and industrial centers. Lee and Reynolds, as individuals and as a partnership, probably lost some money on the Utah venture when they disposed of their stock and bonds, presumably at some disadvantage, prior to the railroad's declaration of insolvency.[4]

The firm of Lee and Reynolds was also active in Colorado. In 1880 both partners supervised contracts for hauling freight from the terminus of the Denver and Rio Grande Railway at

Alamosa, in the San Luis Valley, to military posts, Indian agencies, mining towns, and railroad construction camps throughout the San Juan Country. Before the close of that year all teams had returned to Indian Territory to assist in moving troops, equipment, and supplies from Fort Dodge to Fort Supply and Fort Elliott. The following spring Reynolds returned to Alamosa, where he arranged to transport a large volume of freight, including store goods, to Lake City.[5]

The traffic to Lake City may have reflected in some measure the partners' investments in mines near that community. Lee and Reynolds contributed two-fifths of the money for an investors' pool to acquire and operate mines. Henry C. Thatcher and his brothers contributed an equal amount, and John H. Maugham gave the remaining one-fifth. The members agreed that the risk capital should not exceed $100,000. Excluded from this limit were profits, if any, from the pool's properties.[6]

Henry C. Thatcher, the brother of Pueblo's leading bankers, Mahlon D. and John A. Thatcher, preferred a career in law to handling other people's money. He had been appointed U.S. attorney for Colorado in 1869 but resigned after little more than a year to give his attention to private practice in partnership with Pueblo lawyer Charles E. Gast. Thatcher was elected to the Colorado Supreme Court and served as its first chief justice. After a single three-year term he returned to the firm of Thatcher and Gast. His business relationship with Lee and Reynolds and Maugham probably came about not from the practice of law but from the traders' long-standing ties to the Thatchers' First National Bank of Pueblo.[7]

John A. Thatcher and A. E. Reynolds had been post traders at Fort Lyon before the latter relocated to Indian Territory in 1869. They remained friends after John moved to Pueblo to join his brother Mahlon in the banking business. Lee and Reynolds's freighting business brought them to Colorado, where through the influence of the bankers and their brother the traders developed interests in mining activities at Lake City.

At that mining community the cashier of the Thatcher Brothers Bank was John H. Maugham. An Englishman, he had served in a similar position at the Thatcher's branch bank in Las Animas, Colorado, before being transferred to the county seat of Hinsdale County. Responding to opportunities for investments that abounded in a new and growing community, Maugham was active in the organization of mining enterprises, often with Reynolds and Henry Thatcher, but also with others. He was, for example, an incorporator of the Copper Hill Mining Company and the San Juan Railroad and Tramway Company, an ambitious scheme to build and operate a rail line linking Lake City, Silverton, and Ouray.[8]

After the dissolution of Lee and Reynolds in 1882, A. E. Reynolds entrusted the management of his Texas Panhandle ranch to his brother Charles in order to relocate to Lake City, where he opened a general merchandise store and looked after the investment in mines that had once been the assets of the partnership. The community, founded in 1875, boasted of two thousand inhabitants, who were mainly engaged in mining or in the reduction of silver ores.[9]

Potentially profitable mines were located south of Lake City along Henson Creek. Some were between Lake City and Rose's Cabin, at the foot of Engineering Mountain, a distance of 15 miles. These mines included the Ute and Ulay (Ule), Excursion, Little Chief, Ocean Wave, Wave of the Ocean, Rustler, Wyandotte, Pride of America, Young America, Big Casino, Phoenix, and Emperor. There was a cluster of mines in the vicinity of Capitol City, 9 miles from Lake City. On Engineer Mountain were the Palmetto, Annie Wood, Gunnison, Chihuahua, Sonora, and Frank Hough. Along Lake Fork of the Gunnison, which formed Lake San Cristobal, were the Belle of the West, Belle of the East, Belle Vernon, Hotchkiss (later called the Golden Fleece), Plutarch, General Sherman, Emerald Isle, Silver Coin, and many others.[10]

The steady producers of silver ore were the Ute and Ulay, owned by the Crooke Consolidated Mining and Smelting

Company, operator of one of the area's three ore reduction plants, which had a combined capacity of 60 tons per day at the time that Reynolds relocated to Lake City. The small Van Gieson lixiviation (ore-leaching) works had been purchased by and was under the management of Mrs. C. E. Stewart. The Ocean Wave Mining and Smelting Company, operator of roasting furnaces and a small 10-ton blast furnace, was closed at the time, ostensibly because the management was caught up in costly litigation.[11]

Ore reduction was a prerequisite for successful mining. The cost of wagon freight, from $25 to $30 a ton to the Denver and Rio Grande Railway at Gunnison, prohibited shipment of anything but high-grade ore. By treating ore in the area, mineowners could get a fair return on all of their output, and the owners of mills and smelters could ship concentrates or copper- and lead-silver matte from smelters to refineries in the East at nominal costs.

The centerpiece of the local mining industry was the Crooke mines and reduction works. John J. Crooke of Crooke Brothers, an old-line New York ore reduction firm, established a reduction works on the Lake Fork of the Gunnison, where waterpower was available, 1 mile above Lake City in August 1876. Originally the plant consisted of crushers, a fifteen-stamp mill, and concentrators. Later a smelter and a chlorination mill were added. Most of the ore processed was from the firm's Ute and Ulay Mines.[12]

In 1878 eastern financial interests organized the Crooke Mining and Smelting Company. Its capital stock of $1.2 million was used to purchase the Crooke Brothers' mines and reduction works, plus other valuable mining properties in the area. The Crooke brothers continued to run the reduction plant, while Samuel W. Hill, a director of the firm, assumed management of the mines. The firm was reorganized in 1882, at which time control passed to a group of English investors.[13]

Reynolds was attracted by Lake City's prosperity and the likelihood of greater wealth when mines then under development became regular producers of ore. The community, in his judgment, was an idea place for a general merchandise store. The supervision of the retail business, including the wagon trains that hauled goods to and from Alamosa, Del Norte, and Gunnison, was entrusted to Charles F. McKenney, leaving Reynolds time to pursue other business opportunities.

That arrangement allowed Reynolds to devote attention to, among other things, local mining properties. These included the Palmetto above Rose's Cabin along the headwaters of Henson Creek on Engineer Mountain, the Frank Hough on the mountain above the Palmetto, and the Belle of the West on the Lake Fork of the Gunnison River. These claims had been discovered or initially developed by John S. Hough, whom Reynolds probably had known fifteen years earlier when a sutler at Fort Lyon. At that time Hough and his brother-in-law, John Wesley Prowers, had owned a store near the military post.[14]

Hough relocated to Lake City to open a general merchandise store in 1876. He handled wholesale and retail groceries and sold a full line of clothing, dry goods, hardware, and miners' supplies. He took in J. F. Waskey as a partner, then sold the store to him and opened a wholesale and retail grocery.[15]

Speculation in mining properties quickly absorbed most of Hough's attention. By December 1879 he owned all or part of fifteen mines. Ten were along the headwaters of Henson Creek on the north side on Engineer Mountain and the remainder at lower levels along the same watercourse.

The Reynolds-Thatcher-Maugham pool bought interests in the Palmetto from John Hough and in the Belle of the West from eastern parties. Hough gave one-fourth interest in the Frank Hough Mine to the same pool. The mine was developed and sold, largely because of Reynolds's energy and managerial skills. The profits Hough gained from these sales may have been used to erect a business block at the corner of Silver and

Third Streets. It was in that building that McKenney opened for A. E. Reynolds and Company a general merchandise store.[16]

The Palmetto offered, in Reynolds's view, the best hope for a successful mining venture. That mine had been developed in a limited way by John Hough, in partnership with George A. Smith and son, prior to 1880, when the Reynolds-Thatcher-Maugham pool secured an interest in the property. That year the owners organized the Palmetto Consolidated Mining and Milling Company to open the mine on a large scale and to erect and operate a mill to reduce the ore to silver bullion.[17]

As evidence of the new company's intention of making a big producer of the Palmetto, Hubbell W. Reed, a well-known Ouray mining engineer, was named superintendent of the mine. While Reed sank a new shaft and explored for a silver vein, the firm of Malter, Lind and Company of San Francisco was engaged to erect a state-of-the-art reduction mill. The plant, completed at a cost of $80,000, commenced operation in the late summer of 1881. Within a year the mine had closed, and the mill, after briefly experimenting with the reduction of ores from other mines, shut down.[18]

The Palmetto venture was a great disappointment to Reynolds. The mine failed to produce in quantity ore that could be reduced efficiently in the mill, but the main problem was that the reduction process was not suited to the ore from the Palmetto Mine. When the mill was in operation, more than 60 percent of the values in the ores floated away on Henson Creek. Because of those high losses, neither the mine nor the mill could meet expenses.[19]

Accumulated debts of more than $40,000 forced the Palmetto Company to close its mine and mill. On the assumption that the stockholders were responsible for the firm's liabilities, Reynolds tried without success to obtain voluntary assessments on the outstanding shares. After foreclosure by creditors, Reynolds and M. D. Thatcher, in order to protect their investments, purchased the property at a sheriff's sale.

However, the mill remained idle, while the mine was worked sporadically by lessees.[20]

The Palmetto was the first of a series of disappointments for Reynolds at Lake City. The initial development of the Belle of the West Mine revealed the possibility of rich ore, but that did not materialize. After Reynolds and associates committed a large amount of money to the property over a period of nearly five years, the title to the property was assailed in the courts. All work was suspended. The mine remained closed for more than thirty years.[21]

A similar disappointment occurred with the Frank Hough. The mine, discovered in 1879 by John Hough and named for his young son, remained undeveloped until the Reynolds-Thatcher-Maugham pool put money into the venture. The mine was developed by Reynolds and sold for $125,000, but after the payment of only $25,000, the contract was terminated. Thereafter, according to Reynolds, the property was managed by Hough, who, unknown to his partners, ran it for his own benefit. He sold the ore without accounting for the proceeds and without paying for supplies used in working the mine. Operations ended in 1884, with the mining company in debt almost $3,500, including goods purchased from McKenney on credit.[22]

Much to Reynolds's frustration, local creditors looked to him, rather than to Hough, for payment. To meet those demands, Reynolds had Andy Jard and Gus Miller, former Indian Territory wagon masters who had been working in the mine, gather up and transport what ore remained on the dump to the Stoiber Brothers in Silverton. On the basis of their samples the ore was sold to the Boston and Colorado Smelting Company at Denver. The proceeds permitted Reynolds to pay the firm's most pressing debts at the rate of $0.60 on the dollar.[23]

The Lake City store was the final disappointment. As long as the mining industry flourished, the town prospered, and the store enjoyed a large volume of business. A reversal com-

menced with the failure of the Crooke Consolidated Mining
and Smelting Company in April 1883. When the Belle of the
West shut down because of a dispute over the title to the mine,
the local economy stagnated. The Crooke firm owed Reynolds's store and freighting outfit more than $15,000, and
there was little hope for payment in sight. Reynolds's financial
problems were compounded by the recession of 1884 and
1885, which paralyzed much of the nation's economy.[24]

In an effort to survive a dull market, Reynolds asked
Hough to reduce the rent on the two rooms occupied by the
store at Third and Silver Streets. After seemingly agreeing to
an adjustment in June 1884, Hough changed his mind four
months later. Frustrated and disappointed with conditions in
Lake City as well as with Hough, Reynolds instructed McKenney to sell the stock and close the business. Within a year
Reynolds was prepared to leave Lake City and Hinsdale
County.[25]

All of Reynolds's enterprises in Lake City had been marked,
he believed, by disaster. The town was "dead and stagnant,"
and what he identified as "the barnacles of the community"
had robbed him on contracts and beat him in every way. It was
time to get out, while he could afford to do so.[26]

By September 1885 Reynolds had disposed of his mercantile assets. The goods and fixtures from the store were sold at
only a little more than half their value to Buddecke and Diehl,
merchants in Montrose. That firm also bought twenty yoke of
oxen, four freight wagons, and a smaller wagon, promising
some cash and the balance in one year. The merchandise that
could not be sold was shipped to Ouray, where Reynolds
hoped to devote his attention to mining.[27]

Located almost directly west of Lake City on the far side of
Engineer Mountain, the county seat of Ouray County had
become by the mid-1880s an important mining and reduction
center. Reynolds became acquainted with the community and
its mineral industry when the investment pool he had formed
with the Thatcher brothers and Maugham purchased the

Virginius mining claim, located above timberline at an altitude of 12,300 feet on Mount Sneffels. In 1880 they organized the Caroline Mining Company, probably named for Reynolds's mother, and arranged with a group of eastern men to underwrite the cost of the property and its development.[28]

Reynolds and his partners agreed temporarily to surrender one-half interest in the Caroline Mining Company in return for needed financial support. The eastern men invested $150,000, which were to be repaid in full with interest at 6 percent per annum before stock certificates could be issued to stockholders. The financial backers included H. H. Cook, H. G. Bond, W. C. Sheldon, E. A. Dickerson, and H. S. Le Roy of New York City; M. P. Bush of Buffalo; and E. A. Wyeth of Framingham, Massachusetts. The westerners exercised management of the property, which was then delegated by the Thatchers and Maugham to Reynolds, but the easterners held all of the corporate offices and had control of the stock.[29]

Reynolds placed the property under the supervision of Hubbell W. Reed, one of three brothers who were Ouray's leading mining engineers. David R. Reed eventually assumed the management of Terrible Mine, located adjacent to the Virginius. The Terrible was underwritten by the same group of eastern investors. A third brother, Caleb Reed, worked in either or both properties in subordinate management positions until his death from pneumonia, the dreaded affliction among miners in that district, in 1885.[30]

The Virginius was originally opened by an adit that cut the vein at a distance of 300 feet. At that point a shaft was sunk on the vein. At 100-foot intervals levels, or drifts, were driven to expose the vein. The output of ore was insignificant until 1883. Thereafter the mine yielded an increasing volume of rich ore as it descended below the fifth level.[31]

Before A. E. Reynolds could immerse himself in the affairs of the mines on Mount Sneffels, his attention was diverted to one of the principal mining controversies of that day. In 1885

David M. Hyman, a Cincinnati lawyer who owned extensive property at Aspen, the seat of government for Pitkin County, asked Reynolds to put up the money to underwrite litigation to enforce a claim to the apex of the vein that had surfaced on the Durant property. According to mining law, the owner of a vein at the surface had exclusive right to it as it descended to greater depth, even if the vein passed beyond the sidelines of the original claim into properties of others.[32]

At the suggestion of Charles Robinson, a wealthy New York resident who invested in western mining properties, Hyman asked Reynolds for financial assistance. Depending upon the word of Robinson and Hyman, Reynolds, without inspecting the properties at Aspen, agreed to put up $25,000 in return for one-fourth of Hyman's mining interests. Robinson had known and admired Reynolds's practical knowledge about mining because of their common investments in the Carbonate Hill Mine at Leadville. At Robinson's insistence Reynolds assumed the management of all of Hyman's properties at Aspen.[33]

As was his habit, Reynolds had a cash-flow problem and had to borrow the requisite $25,000 from Robinson. When that sum proved inadequate, Reynolds organized with Robinson and Charles D. Arms, a Youngstown, Ohio, iron manufacturer, the "Aspen Pool" with which to underwrite further litigation and acquire mining properties in the vicinity of Aspen. Eventually Robinson, Arms, Reynolds, and others who joined the pool advanced nearly $750,000, most of which was used to finance what became the costliest mining litigation of the time. In return they demanded and received from Hyman 55 percent of his Aspen mining properties. Most of these ended up in the hands of Arms, Robinson, and Reynolds.[34]

The litigation continued for nearly three years, during which time each side was represented by the best legal talent available in Colorado. Charles J. Hughes Jr. and Senator Henry Moore Teller were the principal lawyers for Hyman and associates. Thomas M. Patterson, Charles S. Thomas, and J. W. Downing argued the case for Jerome B. Wheeler, D. R. C. Brown, and others. In addition, both parties, the "apexers," who demanded control of the full length of the Durant vein, and the "sideliners," who insisted that they owned the mineral deposit within the boundaries of their claims, mobilized an army of expert witnesses to support their claims.[35]

The enormous cost of the court cases, as viewed by Hyman, threatened to deny him and his associates the fruits of any victory that they might achieve. After favorable court decisions during the years from 1885 through 1887, Hyman concluded that it was time to seek a compromise in order to head off what appeared to be an endless series of prohibitively expensive legal challenges to the Durant apex. Over the objections of Reynolds, Hyman persuaded the remainder of his associates to support a compromise that ended the litigation.[36]

Although the initiative for the compromise was credited to different people, a key role in the proceedings was played by James J. Hagerman and T. M. Davis, president and vice president, respectively, of the Colorado Midland Railway, whose lucrative traffic in Aspen depended upon full operation of the mines without the threat of interruptions from litigation. The two sets of antagonists in the fight over the apex agreed to withdraw all suits. Jerome B. Wheeler and his Aspen Mining and Smelting Company gave to the Durant Mining Company an undivided one-half interest in five claims lying within the endlines of the Durant apex: the Aspen, Emma, Forest, and Little Giant No. 2. All of the territory under the apex was placed in a new enterprise, the Compromise Mining Company, in which all of the parties to the litigation were stockholders. There was to be no indemnity by Wheeler and associates for ore previously extracted from claims covered by the Durant apex.[37]

As president of the Durant Mining Company, Reynolds reluctantly supported the compromise. He preferred a fight to the finish in the courts. From the beginning he had insisted that the apexers would win over the sideliners, and when they did, the Aspen Mine, with an estimated value of $3 million, would yield profits of $100,000 a month for an indefinite period of time. He was personally unwilling to divide the spoils with those who, in his estimation, had illegally plundered the Durant vein. Reynolds's prediction turned out to be conservative. In fact, the Aspen produced ore worth more than $11 million, the net profits from which exceeded $6 million.[38]

When Hyman and Arms insisted on additional compromises with owners of sideline claims, Reynolds resigned in anger and refused to play any role in the management of the Durant Mining Company. By then his personal finances were in a shambles, and he could not put them in order as long as he was devoting most of his time to the Aspen properties. To his friends he insisted that he had left Aspen because Arms and Hyman had overruled him as manager of the Durant enterprise. It seems unlikely that he would have stayed there for any length of time because to do so would have jeopardized his investments in the Texas Panhandle and at Ouray.[39]

By neglecting his own business affairs, Reynolds had to assume a mounting burden of debt in order to underwrite a portion of the litigation costs. Although he acquired substantial interests in the Durant, Smuggler, Late Acquisition, and One Thousand and One claims, he eventually had to dispose of half of those holdings in order to pay pressing debts. Even then he admitted that he had "a hard row to hoe to hold the balance."[40]

Originally Reynolds had assumed direction of Hyman's mining properties at Aspen on the assumption that his investment would not exceed $25,000 and that the litigation would not continue beyond a year, two at the most. When the legal action dragged on year after year, eventually for nearly four, he took the lead in organizing the Aspen Pool and eventually invested in it $71,576.16, mostly funds that he had borrowed from Charles Robinson and Charles D. Arms. He pledged his stock in the Reynolds Land and Cattle Company to secure those loans. Had he known how long it would take to resolve the apex issue, Reynolds probably would not have taken on the management of the mines at Aspen.[41]

On leaving Aspen, Reynolds focused his attention on business opportunities at Ouray. He hoped to get rid of what he called straggling interests, presumably investments at Lake City and Leadville, and to concentrate on mining activities on Mount Sneffels. "It wears me out too fast," he confided to a friend, "having scattered investments, all of which need looking after to make them pay."[42]

Mining on Mount Sneffels became the focus of Reynolds's attention for the next several years. After a slow start the Virginius, under Hub Reed's close attention, prospered. It produced a mere 3 tons of ore in 1881, the cash return from which was $466.05. Output rose from 183 tons in 1882 to 286 tons in 1884, and in the latter year the mine's income exceeded expenses for the first time, yielding a profit of $25,000. In 1885 the net profit soared to $89,296.24. A total of 586.5 tons of ore shipped during the year averaged 257.1 ounces of silver per ton and 35.2 percent lead. The ore varied in value. The highest lot assayed 406.5 ounces of silver and 37 percent lead, whereas the lowest was 152.5 ounces of silver and 32 percent lead.[43]

By 1885 it was apparent to Reynolds and Reed that in order to operate the Virginius Mine on a large scale, they had to resolve a number of problems. These included an economical method for handling an increasing volume of low-grade ores. Until that year second-class ores had gone to the dump because their silver and lead values were not enough to pay for the cost of transportation and treatment at the smelters. Potentially large values of silver and lead would be lost unless the low-grade ore could be upgraded through processes of concentration to standards that permitted profitable reduction by the smelters.

The smelters were a problem in that they were few in number, distant from Ouray, and charging for the reduction ore to base metals what the owners believed the market would bear. Smelters at Ouray were unreliable, forcing Reynolds and Reed to send ore to plants at Gunnison, Pueblo, and Denver. Similar facilities existed at Canon City and Durango. Because of the distances, plus the volume and weight of ore shipments, economical transportation to the smelters was essential if the Virginius Mine was to be operated on a scale that ensured large profits.

An equally perplexing problem was the high cost and inconvenience of moving freight, including ore, between the mine and Ouray. Everything that went to and from the Virginius was carried on pack animals. For almost six months a year the trail up Mount Sneffels was closed by snow, during which time the ore that was mined was stored on-site for shipment at a later date. The shipping season was from late spring to early fall, depending upon the weather and the condition of the trail. Needed was a road that would permit economical transportation over a longer period of each year.

Another problem was economical energy with which to operate the mine. Steam power was used to run the hoisting equipment, the compressor for air drills, the crusher and rollers in the concentrating mill, and the all-important pumps that prevented the mine from filling with water. The operation of coal-fired boilers to produce steam was very expensive because of the difficulty of transporting fuel to the mine. Delivered to the Virginius, coal cost $23 per ton. A lack of coal had precluded any extra underground development work during the winter of 1884–1885.[44]

There were cost-effective solutions to the problems of concentration, transportation, and power for operating the mine and mill. Electricity generated by waterpower was a potential source of cheap, reliable energy with which to operate the mine and mill. A water wheel in Canyon Creek could, Reed concluded, supply the mine with at least part of its electrical power at a reasonable cost. Reynolds concurred and strongly recommended the equipment manufactured by the Daft Electric Company. That firm's electric light plant had been installed at the Virginius in 1885. A dynamo driven by steam provided power for the incandescent bulbs that lighted the concentrating mill.[45]

Construction of a waterpower plant commenced in 1888, and electricity was used to supplement steam power the following year. A Pelton water wheel, dynamo, poles, transmission line, and motors for the hoister and pumps cost approximately $18,000. This figure, Reynolds assured the eastern investors, was approximately equal to the saving in the cost of coal in 1889. Eventually three water-driven dynamos were installed on Canyon Creek to supply all needed power, except during the cold winter and hot, dry summer months when the absence of running water forced the mine and mill to rely on steam power.[46]

Economical power was a prerequisite for profitably processing large amounts of low-grade ore. In 1885 hand-powered jigs were used for experiments with concentrating second-class (low-grade) ore. Machinery was installed at the mine in July to crush the ore to permit treatment with the jigs. That year concentrates made up approximately half of all shipments, clearly indicating that an investment in a mill and mechanical methods of concentration, although necessarily large, would greatly enhance the Virginius Mine's shipments and profits.[47]

A concentrating mill was erected and began operation in 1888. Equipped with a crusher and rolls, revolving screens, double and single jigs, driers, and a slime table, the mill treated 1,649.5 tons the first year to produce 263 tons of concentrates. The mine-run ore contained about 35 ounces of silver to the ton, whereas the concentrates averaged 181 ounces of silver to the ton. Water for the jigs and table was plentiful only about three months of the year. At other times water was pumped from the mine and recycled within the mill. Whenever extremely cold weather caused the freezing of the water supply, the mill shut down and the Virginius dump was overrun with second-class ore.[48]

Concentrates, along with high-grade ore, were shipped to smelters for treatment. In 1885 all ore was sold to the Pueblo Smelting and Refining Company. The following year after the Pueblo company refused to bid on Virginius ore, Reynolds negotiated a contract with the Tomichi Valley Smelting Company, southeast of Gunnison. However, after spending a day at the plant, Reynolds was skeptical about its future.[49]

Capacity was severely limited because only one of three projected furnaces was in operation. The plant treated only 30 tons of ore daily, and with a payroll of seventy men, its profit margin was indeed thin. Before the close of July 1886 B. W. Lewis, the manager, informed Reynolds that for the time being the smelter could not accept any more Virginius ore. That action, Reynolds complained, placed him at a disadvantage because he had to commence negotiations with other smelters in the middle of the shipping season.[50] Shipments were resumed to the Tomichi Valley in 1887, but only for a short time before the plant was permanently closed.[51]

Thereafter most of the Virginius ore was shipped to the Omaha and Grant Smelting Company in Denver. This was an excellent choice, according to Hub Reed, for the smelter had a record of giving accurate assays and weights, more so than its competitors. Furthermore, payments were always prompt. The Pueblo smelter, Reed suspected, often delayed returns on ore in anticipation of a decline in the New York price for silver.[52]

Most argentiferous smelters paid for ore according to a standard formula. Mine operators received a portion of the silver, usually from 93 to 95 percent, based on New York prices for precious metals on the date a statement was issued. Penalties were imposed if the ore did not have a minimum content of lead, normally 30 percent, and a bonus was paid for each percentage point above that level. All smelters charged for treatment, usually from $4 to $12 dollars per ton, depending upon the lead content of the ore.[53]

If Reynolds had a choice of smelters, transportation charges more often than not dictated the plant to which Virginius ore was shipped. The Tomichi Valley smelter had higher treatment charges than its Pueblo or Denver rivals, but this cost was offset by lower freight costs. Rail transportation from Ouray to the Tomichi Valley was $4 a ton and to Pueblo and Denver, from $10 to $30, depending upon the willingness of railroad officials to make concessions in return for a large volume of shipments. Transportation costs were a major part of the expense of producing precious metals.[54]

For that reason Reynolds was a consistent promoter of improved transportation throughout Colorado, particularly the state's western slope. For the Virginius Mine the ability to move ore 10 tons at a time in narrow-gauge railroad cars to the Tomichi Valley, Pueblo, or Denver meant a significant reduction in costs. Until the close of 1887 the nearest railroad was 37 miles from Ouray. A line from that community to distant points was needed. The Denver and Rio Grande Railway Company projected a branchline from Montrose, but the location of the southern terminus was a matter of controversy that delayed completion of construction. Some people in Ouray, particularly banker Jack Jardine and editor of the *Solid Muldoon* David Day, wanted to halt the line at a new town, called Chipeta or Romona, 4 miles north of Ouray.[55]

Reynolds was one of many people who actively campaigned for an extension of the line, and after some delay it was continued to the mining community. Denver banker David H. Moffat, on assuming control of the reorganized Denver and Rio Grande Railroad Company in 1887, put a stop to the Jardine-Day real estate promotion by ordering completion of the line to Ouray. The final segment of track was laid, in part, with money raised locally for that purpose. Reynolds, in behalf of the Caroline Mining Company, contributed $2,000.[56]

The Virginius Mine commenced ore shipments by rail from Ouray on December 24, 1887. The saving over shipments by wagon to the railroad at Montrose was initially $3.50 per ton, and it increased in following years. The saving on all shipments in and out of Ouray, including coal, was approximately $10,000 a year. The Caroline Mining Company, with related enterprises owned or controlled by Reynolds, erected an office and warehouse alongside the tracks in Ouray to reduce the cost of moving goods, particularly coal and ore, in and out of the town.[57]

With the completion of the rail line to Ouray, the lack of economical transportation between that community and the mine became a major concern. In this instance the problem rested with a private enterprise, the Ouray and Mount Sneffels Toll Road Company, owned by railroad entrepreneur Otto Mears. The toll, according to Reynolds, was exorbitant, and Mears refused to rebuild the road up Canyon Creek to Porter's store, a distance of 9 miles from Ouray, with reasonable grades negotiable in both directions by wagons loaded with freight and ore.[58]

Without access to wagon transportation, the Virginius, and neighboring mines, relied on pack trains to move freight up the mountain and to carry ore, at the rate of 300 pounds per animal, to Ouray. John Ashenfelter, a former wagon master with Lee and Reynolds in Indian Territory, provided this crucial service. In 1885, because snowed block the trail, his pack train did not reach the Virginius until June 1. However, this was two months earlier than in 1884. Because of the terrain and weather, Ashenfelter moved freight only about half of the year, and transportation was very costly as long as it was restricted to pack trains.[59]

A public road was belatedly completed up Mount Sneffels in 1889. The voters of Ouray County, recognizing the importance of the area's mines to the local economy, approved $10,000 in bonds to construct the thoroughfare. The mine-owners agreed to pay any costs that exceeded that amount.

After the new road was completed, the county bought out the toll road company's claim to the right-of-way.[60]

The new road easily handled wagon transportation from Ouray to Porter's store, later the site of the hamlet of Sneffels. Beyond Porter's store, at an altitude of about 10,000 feet, pack trains continued to move freight and ore to the Virginius Mine, which was above timberline at 12,300 feet. Even before completion of the new road, the Reed brothers, Hub and Dave, erected at Porter's a large warehouse for the temporary storage of ore carried there by pack trains until such time as it could be forwarded to Ouray by wagons. On the trip up the mountain the wagons carried food, equipment, fuel, and other commodities, which were stored in the warehouse until they could be forwarded by pack animals. In this way the movement of goods between the mines and Ouray was expedited at significantly lower costs.[61]

The warehouse was owned jointly by three companies that had common stockholders. The principal investors in the Caroline Mining Company also owned or controlled the Mount Sneffels Terrible Mining Company and the Monarch Mining Company, all located in close proximity to one another on the slope of Mount Sneffels. A. E. Reynolds was in charge of all three, and the local supervisor for the Monarch as well as the Virginius was H. W. Reed; his brother, David, was in charge of the Terrible Mine.

The Terrible Mine was a large producer of silver ore for a brief time. The Mount Sneffels Terrible Mining Company, incorporated in New York in July 1883, worked a vein that crossed the Virginius claim. Superintendent David R. Reed opened the mine at three levels with drifts that followed the vein into the side of the mountain. A shaft was later sunk to follow the vein to greater depth. An increasing volume of low-grade ores forced Reed to experiment with hand-powered jigs, which pointed to the need, as in the case of the Virginius Mine, to erect a mill with power tables and other equipment for processing a large volume of second-class ore.[62]

When operations in the Virginius and Terrible Mines revealed potentially valuable veins of ore that extended into the adjacent Monarch claim, Reynolds and M. D. Thatcher bought the controlling interest of the property and organized the Monarch Mining Company, under the laws of the state of Colorado, on August 29, 1887. Access to the Monarch was through the underground workings of the Terrible Mine. Shipments of high-grade ore commenced in November 1887.[63]

Of the three properties for which Reynolds acted as manager, the Terrible Mine proved to be the least productive. It earned profits for its investors only in 1887. Even before the close of that year pyrite reduced the value of the ore to the point that smelter returns barely covered the cost of mining and concentration. After heavy losses in 1888 eastern stockholders, headed by J. B. Reynolds, a New York City businessman, appointed A. E. Reynolds as agent to dispose of the company's assets and to pay off insofar as possible debts that then exceeded $25,000. The two men were not related. In 1894 all assets were sold to satisfy unpaid creditors.[64]

The Monarch remained an active producer for almost a decade. The chief beneficiaries of its brief prosperity were Reynolds and M. D. Thatcher, who together owned more than two-thirds of the company's securities. In June 1892 Reed observed that the decline in silver prices made it impossible to meet expenses even if the quality of the ore improved. Operations were suspended, and the company remained dormant until sold at auction to pay debts in 1898. It was bought by J. P. M. Humphrey for Reynolds and others.[65]

The Virginius Mine was the big moneymaker. From substantial earnings year after year the Caroline Mining Company paid all expenses and devoted surpluses to paying back, with interest, the original subscribers who had underwritten the cost of the development in the mine. From 1886 to 1890 the output of ore rose steadily from 839 to 3,230 tons and gross income, from $168,786.13 to $549,518.65.[66]

In 1890, with future earnings assured, the eastern sub-scribers accepted a $60,000 mortgage on the mine for the remaining debt. This allowed the Caroline Mining Company finally to distribute its corporate securities to share-holders. A. E. Reynolds, who had systemically bought out the interest of most of the New York subscribers, with the exception of W. C. Sheldon, was the largest single share-holder, and he and M. D. Thatcher, acting together, con-trolled the enterprise.[67]

Over the years Reynolds had become increasingly impa-tient with the eastern subscribers who controlled the compa-ny. They insisted that all available funds be used to pay off the original subscribers, whereas Reynolds, Thatcher, and Hub Reed preferred to devote available money to opening new ground in the Virginius Mine as a way of earning long-term profits. In order to weaken the influence of the eastern group, Reynolds bought up its interests one by one and in 1890 gave Sheldon a bonus of 25,000 shares in the Caroline Mining Company on condition that he approve the mortgage that paid off the subscribers and permitted issuance of the firm's capital shares.[68]

This move allowed Reynolds, with the support of Thatcher, to use the income of the Caroline Mining Company to under-write the excavation of the Revenue Tunnel designed to tap the Virginius vein at a distance of 5,280 feet or more from the entrance to the tunnel and a depth of 3,000 feet below the surface entrance to the mine. The tunnel was widely ac-claimed as a model of mining efficiency in the West.

The Revenue Tunnel had its origin in Reynolds's decision to buy the Revenue group of claims located on the mountain opposite George R. Porter's store in 1888. That summer he authorized, as a personal venture unrelated to the Caroline Mining Company, a crosscut tunnel to a maximum depth of 1,000 feet to intersect the Revenue vein and any others that might be located within the boundaries of the property. Hub Reed, the local supervisor of the project, aligned the first set of timbers in the tunnel on October 2, and it moved forward at a rate of from 30 to 40 feet a week.[69]

Initially Reynolds hoped to place the Revenue group of claims—the Revenue, Myrtle, Black Hawk, Protection, and Anglo-Saxon—in a corporation whose capital stock could be sold to eastern investors in western mining properties. These claims, on the first 1,500 feet of the tunnel, were to be the principal assets of the Ruby Mountain Mining Company. In anticipation of that event Reynolds sold stock worth $2,000 to Alvan Marble in 1890. However, the organization was not completed because other parties had appropriated the name. Ten years later Reynolds put the Revenue group into another company and sent an appropriate number of shares to Marble, who had never inquired about his investment.[70]

In spite of Reynolds's announced intention of developing the Revenue group, from the first his goal was to continue the adit until it tapped the Virginius vein. However, when he received little support from the eastern subscribers of the Caroline Mining Company, he was prepared to halt work at 1,000 feet. W. C. Sheldon and his associates were unwilling to subscribe to the tunnel venture on the assumption that Reynolds would go ahead with it anyway. The project reached the 1,000-foot mark in early August 1889, and much to the surprise of Reynolds and Reed, there was no Revenue vein. Presumably a geological fault had caused it to "play out" prior to that point.[71]

By that date the heavy expense of working the Virginius Mine at a depth of more than 1,000 feet convinced most the Caroline Mining Company's stockholders as well as those of other enterprises that owned claims in the vicinity that a tunnel offered the only hope of gaining control over soaring operating expenses. For the Virginius Mine the cost of hoisting ore and pumping water with steam was prohibitive because of the high cost of coal delivered to the mine. Reynolds and Thatcher concluded that the Caroline Mining Company had to provide the funds needed to complete the tunnel.

For the Virginius Mine the Revenue Tunnel provided convenient access to the underground workings. The cost of
working the undeveloped ground in the Virginius Mine below
the fourteenth level, or 1,400 feet from the surface, would
have exceeded the value of the ore extracted, even though
each of the five or six levels below that point probably contained silver, with some gold, worth at least $1 million. Taking
ore out via the tunnel eliminated the costs of hoisting and
pumping. Access was convenient and economical, and additional saving could be gained from improved methods of
preparing ore for shipment to smelters.[72]

For a time the tunnel project suffered an uncertain future.
During the first year Reynolds had personally financed the
project, while he searched for money from a variety of sources.
It was, he admitted, a heavy burden. Not until the stockholders of the Caroline Mining Company agreed to underwrite actual costs was completion of the tunnel assured. It was
estimated that the Terrible and Monarch veins would be cut
at a distance of 5,500 feet and the Virginius, at 6,270 feet.
The latter point, Reed concluded, would be reached in 1892.
In fact, it was another year before the tunnel intersected the
Virginius vein, and the distance from the entrance was con-
siderably greater than had been anticipated.[73]

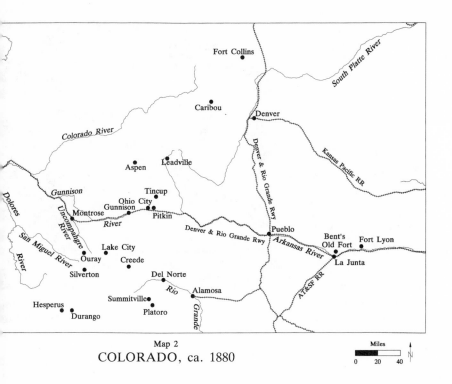

Map 2

COLORADO, ca. 1880

Miles

0   20   40

N

Above: Revenue Mill, Sneffels, Colorado. One of John Ashenfelter's freighting teams, with wagon, is approaching the mill. *(Courtesy, Colorado Historical Society, neg. F36940)*

Below: Virginius Mine, Ouray County, on Mount Sneffels at an altitude of 12,300 feet. Provisions were carried to, and ore was carried from, the mine by John Ashenfelter's mule trains. *(Courtesy, Colorado Historical Society, neg. F36935)*

bove: Freight wagons on Canyon Creek Road, linking Ouray and the Revenue Mill
t Sneffels, Colorado. *(Courtesy, Colorado Historical Society, neg. 36928)*

elow: Commodore Mine, Creede, Mineral County, Colorado. *(Courtesy, Colorado istorical Society, neg. 36920)*

Above: Mines at Summitville, Rio Grande County, Colorado, ca. 1900:

1. Chandler Tunnel 3. French Tunnel 5. Old Annie Cut
2. Ida Tunnel 4. Ida Shaft House 6. Surface extraction of ore

(Courtesy, Colorado Historical Society, neg. 36934)

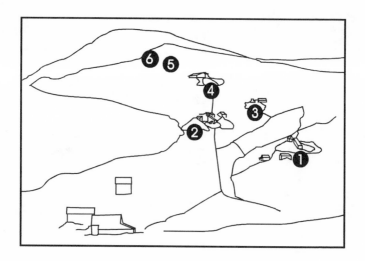

Above: Frank Hough Mine on Engineer Mountain, southwest of Lake City, Hinsdale County, Colorado. *(Courtesy, Colorado Historical Society, neg. 36929)*

Below: Gold Links Mine and Mill, north of Ohio City, Gunnison County, Colorado, ca. 1910. *(Courtesy, Colorado Historical Society, neg. F36941)*

Above: One of A. E. Reynolds's mines near Pitkin, Gunnison County, Colorado. *(Courtesy, Colorado Historical Society, neg. 36919)*

Below: *Left to right,* J. P. M. Humphrey, clerk; Albert Eugene Reynolds; David G. Miller, mining engineer; and Charles F. McKenney, administrative assistant, in Reynolds's office, Equitable Building, Denver, Colorado, ca. 1910. *(Courtesy, Colorado Historical Society, neg. F36930)*

Anna Reynolds Morse Garrey, Carl J. Sigfrid, B. T. Poxson, and George
H. Garrey, ca. 1938. *(Courtesy, Colorado Historical Society, neg. 36939)*

5

An Abundance of Silver

THE Revenue Tunnel was an engineering feat that focused the mining industry's attention on the Sneffels Mining District at Ouray. The project brought fame and fortune to A. E. Reynolds and Hubbell W. Reed, the men who planned the undertaking and persevered against what were at times almost insurmountable obstacles. Reynolds raised the money and acquired the machinery necessary to drive and equip the tunnel, and Reed provided the day-to-day supervision, which ended successfully with the tapping of the Virginius vein deep inside the mountain. Through the tunnel the ore of the Virginius and other mines was transported to a new state-of-the-art concentrating mill, from which concentrates, together with high-grade ore, were shipped to smelters. The returns averaged in excess of $330,000 a year until the end of the century, giving Reynolds the means to acquire mining properties elsewhere in Colorado.

By 1900 Reynolds was a giant among the state's mining men. His reputation had been built in large measure on the output of wealth from mines at Ouray. In addition to the Revenue Tunnel Company, he was the chief executive officer of the Caroline, Glacier, Wheel of Fortune, and Cumberland Mining Companies, which utilized the adit for access to veins of gold and silver inside Mount Sneffels.

In addition to Ouray, Reynolds owned numerous mines throughout western Colorado. He bought mines the way some of his friends bought well-bred horses. He established a persistent pattern, buying properties, making them the central assets of a new corporation, and selling stock to investors in order to recover, at minimum, the original cost, ideally more, and to create a fund with which to develop and operate the property. Reynolds invariably retained control of the company with a majority of stock. At the same time he enlisted the support of wealthy men, particularly easterners, who, because they respected Reynolds's ability to make money from mines, became investors in many of his enterprises.

Reynolds first employed this technique of using other people's money to make a mine with ventures on Mount Sneffels near Ouray and Telluride. He repeated the technique, with varying degrees of success, at Platoro in Conejos County, Summitville in Rio Grande County, Creede in Mineral County, Aspen in Pitkin County, Pitkin and Tin Cup in Gunnison County, Lake City in Hinsdale County (where Reynolds had earlier begun his mining career in Colorado), Rico in Dolores County, and Hesperus in La Plata County. Although most of these properties had potential as large producers of gold or silver ore, the principal moneymakers were the mines at Ouray and Creede. At the latter place the Commodore and nearby mines where highly successful.

Construction of the Revenue Tunnel, an adit that eventually extended more than 7,000 feet into the mountain, began in the fall of 1888. The difficult task of drilling holes in rock for powder charges was initially done by hand. Drills operated by compressed air were introduced in the spring of 1889, and electricity was the main source of power by the time the project ended.[1]

Despite a steady decline in the market value of silver, work on the adit continued at a steady pace in 1892. The tunnel reached the Virginius vein early the following year. Workers cut a thin vein at a distance of 7,335 feet from the entrance on January 9, 1893. Although uncertain, Reynolds concluded this was not the long-sought pay streak but a spur or feeder of the Virginius vein. Two weeks later miners reached the elusive goal. The vein comprised a total of 24 inches of ore separated by approximately 12 inches of barren rock. It was located at a vertical distance of 3,040 feet from the surface.[2]

At that point a connection with the Virginius Mine was excavated to a point approximately 800 feet above the tunnel. As early as October 1892 miners in the upper workings had cut a station at the thirteenth level to set an electric hoister and commenced construction of a winze to link the mine with the tunnel. After the work was under way, it became apparent that the fourteenth level had to be run in order to make the connection. From the tunnel level the incline was at an angle of 50 degrees and measured 5 by 7 feet. It was designed to be enlarged to 7 by 12 feet and divided into three chutes to accommodate ore, waste, and an electric skip. Once the project was completed, the connection provided abundant ventilation for the tunnel and upper workings and allowed ore to be economically removed from the lower levels of the Virginius Mine through the adit.[3]

The ongoing downward movement of silver prices was a matter of grave concern. On the eve of the 1892 presidential election Reynolds had predicted that a victory by Grover Cleveland would be disastrous for silver producers. Cleveland was, according to Reynolds, a gold standard man who, if elected, would break the ranks of the silver men in his own party. That would doom hopes for congressional action to stabilize the price of silver. Without that legislation silver would continue downward, placing in jeopardy the mines on Mount Sneffels.[4]

Cleveland was elected in November 1892, and nine days after the new president's inauguration the low price of silver forced Reed, with Reynolds's approval, to adopt drastic measures to cut operating costs. On March 13 he reduced wages from $3.50 to $3.00 per day for men employed in the Revenue Tunnel, except drillmen and helpers. Similar reductions were imposed at the Virginius Mine on June 10. This prompted a response from a neighboring mine. After dinner miners from the Humboldt descended on the Virginius to protest the reduction, after which men from both mines asked for their time and "went down the hill" to Ouray. Largely because the walkout was spontaneous, lacking any effective organization, most of men drifted back to work the following week. However, paying off employees who left their jobs imposed unneeded strains on the company's already fragile finances. The brief walkout also created a bitterness that heightened tension among management, Reed and his foremen, and the rank and file of the miners.[5]

By July 1 the local economy had collapsed. The Panic of 1893 and the ensuing depression curtailed operations in the Revenue Tunnel and the Virginius Mine. Because they were the largest employers among area mines, this had a devastating effect on Ouray. Merchants were desperate for money, but Reed, unable to obtain returns on ore shipments, could not pay outstanding bills. Furthermore, without funds he could not reduce labor costs because layoffs had to be accompanied by payment of wages; otherwise the men would file liens against the property.

It was up to Reynolds to save the Ouray enterprises. He mollified most of the local merchants by guaranteeing payments. This gained him time to raise money elsewhere. He contributed funds of his own and obtained money from M. D. Thatcher. Reynolds also asked the New York investors to advance money to assist in paying debts, including wages, and to carry forward work on the extension from the tunnel to the Virginius Mine.

With one exception, the New Yorkers refused to put up the needed money. H. S. LeRoy sent $1,000, his share of what Reynolds had requested. The others did not pay a penny until Reynolds went to New York to convince them that it was in their interest to protect their investments at Ouray by putting up additional funds. Eventually he did secure $20,000, and this, with belated payments for ore by smelters, carried the Caroline Mining Company through the crisis.[6]

From 1890 through 1894 the Virginius Mine recorded gross profits in excess of $300,000 a year. Its best year was 1890, when the property earned more than $500,000. By 1894 gross income had dropped to slightly more than $100,000, a reflection of falling prices for silver and dislocation caused by the switch from extracting ore through a vertical shaft to access through the Revenue Tunnel.

The Glacier Mining Company, owned principally by Reynolds and Thatcher, was equally successful. However, there are no statistics for production, shipments, expenses, and profits prior to 1895. The Glacier property, extending beyond the Virginius property for 2,500 feet, had been worked through the Virginius Mine since 1893. The Revenue Tunnel was eventually extended beyond the Virginius claim in order to gain easy access to the Glacier claim and then to the next claim on the line of the Virginius vein, owned by the Hector Mining Company. Reynolds and Thatcher were the leading stockholders in that enterprise.[7]

While crews completed the uprise to the Virginius Mine, finishing touches were added to the tunnel. Down the middle of the adit a 2-foot-gauge double track of 35-pound steel rails was laid to handle traffic in and out of the tunnel. On the right-hand side a ditch 12 inches wide and 18 deep was cut to carry water. The flow was particularly heavy from the upper workings of the Virginius Mine. On the left side a 4-inch pipe conveyed air from the compressor to mechanical drills. During construction a 15-inch pipe carried pure air to the working face of the tunnel.[8]

Cars on the double track carried men and materials into the tunnel and returned filled with ore, which was dumped into bins at the top of the mill. Originally mules furnished the motive power. One mule with a driver hauled from six to eight loaded cars. As many as twelve mules were used daily.[9]

In an effort to reduce transportation costs, Reynolds ordered from the General Electric Company electric locomotives for moving all loads in and out of the tunnel. In October 1896 animals were replaced by electric trams, which operated at speeds of 8 miles an hour. One locomotive pulled trips of from fifteen to twenty-five cars and operated day and night. The switching of cars at either end continued to be handled by men with mules, and animals were used to haul ore from the entries and drifts that ran from the adit to various working properties. The electric motors provided a savings in transportation costs of about $1,000 per month.[10]

In addition to the hauling system, electricity was used to light the tunnel, the mill, and adjacent buildings. Along the approximately 2-mile length of the tunnel, lights were placed at intervals of from 200 to 300 feet. Electricity in the form of direct current was generated by waterpower from three units below the tunnel on Canyon Creek.[11]

Electric lights were also installed in the structures at Sneffels, a company-owned hamlet of homes near the entrance to the tunnel. Formerly called Porter's, it was located at an altitude of 10,300 feet and was 9 miles southwest of Ouray. The community's population fluctuated between 500 and 750 men, women, and children. The administrative personnel and their families resided in fifteen houses, while the men who worked in the tunnel and the mines lived in boardinghouses. The company operated three four-story boardinghouses to accommodate the bachelor workmen, and those whose wives and children resided in Ouray or elsewhere. Each of the buildings accommodated about 100 men, who enjoyed the comforts of central steam heating, electric lights, hot and cold running water, bathhouses, barbershops, a library, and a reading room. Room and board, which cost the company about $0.60 a day for each man, were part of the miners' wages.[12]

In 1898 the school census revealed that Sneffels was the second largest population center in the county. It had its own school, which was attended by from twelve to fifteen children. Businesses in the community included the general merchandise store operated by George Porter, a cobbler's shop, a photographic studio, and a livery stable. Reynolds owned one-third interest in the store for a number of years and finally bought out Porter's remaining interest in 1899. Daily mail service was available at the post office, which was in Porter's store. For residents who wanted a greater variety of shops and entertainment, a stagecoach made daily runs to and from the mining hamlet and Ouray.[13]

Sneffels emerged as a community during construction of the tunnel and continued to grow as production increased from the properties along the tunnel's length. With the completion of the adit, the mining camp at Virginius was abandoned because the mine was worked from below. Men entered and exited the property via the tunnel, and ore was taken by way of the tunnel to the mill for processing.

The cost of the facilities at Sneffels, the tunnel, and the connection to the Virginius Mine was approximately $400,000. This was funded in part from the sale of the Revenue Tunnel Company's capital stock, face value $250,000, all of which was sold at par. Another $150,000 were advanced by the Caroline Mining Company, to be repaid from royalties on Virginius ore that passed through the tunnel.[14]

A large sum of money was also committed to the construction of a state-of-the-art mill at Sneffels to treat all of the ore that came out of the tunnel from claims owned by the Caroline and Glacier Mining Companies. Construction was to have begun as soon as the tunnel intersected the Virginius vein, but the collapse of silver prices following the Panic of 1893 forced a delay. Plans were completed and work started on the foundation in the fall of 1893. In July 1894 work began on a building 96.5 feet high, 175 feet long, and 48 feet wide. The structure was built on the slope of the mountain so that gravity could be used to move ore from the top to the bottom floors. A covered rail track carried cars laden with ore from the tunnel to the upper level of the mill, where there were two storage bins, each with a capacity of 250 tons.[15]

The mill was modern in every respect. It utilized Blake crushers, Cornish rollers, and a battery of twenty 700-pound stamps to crush ore for treatment on jigs and concentrating tables. The crushed ore was sized as coarse, intermediate, and fine grades for treatment in jigs.

The Revenue Mill was a typical concentrating plant of that day, but with two exceptions. At the upper end coarse concentrating took the place of the costly hand sorting that had been the practice in the Virginius Mill. At the lower end the tailings from the jigs were crushed with stamps and treated on tables to save the last of the silver and gold values, which otherwise would have gone to the dump. Although the principal product was silver, each ton of concentrates carried from 0.5 to 1 ounce of gold.[16]

The tunnel and mill reduced the cost of mining and the preparation of ore for the market, assuring profitable working of the Virginius Mine and nearby properties for the foreseeable future. Initially the mill treated about 75 tons of ore each day, reducing 5 tons to 1, producing in all about 15 tons of concentrates. The advanced technology saved a higher percentage of the values than had been possible in the old Virginius Mill. Water needed for concentration was taken from the drainage box in the tunnel. It entered the mill at a temperature of 60 degrees Fahrenheit and did not freeze on the jigs or tables during the coldest weather.[17]

The capacity of the mill was quadrupled within two years. From the start it had processed ore from the Virginius and the Glacier claims and was jointly operated by the Caroline and the Glacier Mining Companies. In 1896 the original mill was expanded, and alongside it under a single roof a new mill was erected. One mill processed ore from the Virginius; the other, newer unit treated ore from the Glacier property. Together they were the called the Revenue Mill, which had a daily capacity of 300 tons of ore. The Virginius Mill measured 175 by 68 feet and the Glacier unit, 175 by 60 feet. They were similarly equipped with modern crushers, rolls, stamps, screens, jigs, and tables.[18]

The larger workforce required for the tunnel and the mill made the Revenue Tunnel Company and related enterprises prime targets of a new wave of militant unionism. The Western Federation of Miners, founded in 1893, targeted precious metal mines in an effort to create one large industrial union in the western states. Strikes occurred in Idaho at Coeur d'Alene and in Colorado at Leadville, Cripple Creek, and elsewhere. Because of the Revenue's proximity to Telluride, a center of WFM agitation, it was inevitable that the unionizing movement would spill across Mount Sneffels to the Revenue properties.[19]

Reynolds was no friend of labor organizations. Along with M. D. Thatcher and H. W. Reed, he was determined to shut down the Revenue Tunnel and related properties rather than submit to a union. Recognition, he believed, would mean surrendering control of the property to the union. Throughout his career as a mine operator Reynolds never wavered from that position.[20]

The first of a long series of confrontations with the Western Federation of Miners occurred in December 1896, when the day and night shifts walked out in protest of allegedly abusive treatment of some men by the shift bosses. Andrew Reynolds, who was the cashier in the Ouray office, conveyed to his older brother reports that the real cause for the strike was an effort by the union to force the large number of Italian immigrants to either join the organization or find employment outside the district. The younger Reynolds reported that a large number of Italians had indeed joined the ranks of the WFM.[21]

In response to the strike Reynolds ordered Reed to curtail operations, keeping only a handful of nonunion men active in the mine and the mill. After about thirty days he sent representatives to recruit men from the lead mines of Missouri and Wisconsin. With imported workers, whom Reynolds refused to call strikebreakers, production was restored to about half of capacity by the end of January 1897, and it was projected that production would be back to normal by the end of February.[22]

A union of mine operators was no more acceptable to Reynolds than was an organization of workers. In March 1902 he turned down an invitation from Charles A. Chase, secretary of the Telluride Mining Association, to participate in a meeting of mine operators at the Brown Palace Hotel in Denver. Reynolds stated emphatically that he would not recognize the right of any organization to dictate to him how to manage his business affairs. Furthermore, if the owners created an organization for their protection, they would be bound at some time to treat with organized labor. Reynolds said he would not place himself in a position where eventually he would have to negotiate with labor unions. Rather, he would insist on the right to conduct his own affairs without interference from any organization.[23]

In spite of an ongoing threat of labor strife, Reynolds's properties in Ouray County remained productive and profitable through the latter years of the 1890s. The Revenue Tunnel and Revenue Mill allowed related enterprises to function as a single firm in fact, if not in name. H. W. Reed coordinated, in addition to the tunnel and mill, activities of the enterprises served by the tunnel and mill—the Caroline Mining Company and Glacier Mining Company—and he was the superintendent of the Hector Mining Company, which owned 2,500 feet on the Virginius vein beyond the Glacier claim.

The Hector Mining Company was organized in 1890 at Reynolds's suggestion with the long-term goal of linking the north and south faces of Mount Sneffels, from the Ouray to the Telluride side, with a tunnel. He broached the topic to John H. Bradley, a longtime friend and member of the New York dry goods firm of Buckley, Wiling and Company. Attracted by Reynolds's assurances of large dividends, Bradley enlisted the support of William F. Havemeyer, a prominent member of the family that dominated the sugar refining industry and an active investor in a wide range of enterprises.[24] Reynolds, Havemeyer, Bradley, and H. W. Reed incorporated the Hector Mining Company in August 1890. That enterprise owned the Cimarron Mine in Marshall Basin, 3 miles from Telluride in San Miguel County. Havemeyer provided $25,000 for the purchase of the mine, with the understanding that he would hold all of the Hector stock and receive all dividends until he had been fully reimbursed. Each man received 10,000 shares, and the balance of 10,000 was sold by Havemeyer to friends in New York City.[25]

The Hector Mining Company produced gold and silver ore, but the output was seldom enough to pay expenses and to retire the debt incurred in opening the mine and related facilities. In order to upgrade the second-class ore, the Cimarron Mill was erected at the entrance to the mine's fourth level. The mill utilized waterpower except during the winter, when more expensive steam power had to be used. To move coal and supplies to the mine and ore to the railhead at Pandora, Reynolds made an agreement with John A. Porter, president of the Smuggler-Union Mining Company, to lease part time that firm's wire (cable) tram. In return Reynolds agreed to buy fuel from Porter's coal mining enterprise near Durango. By eliminating the need for pack burros, the tram saved the Hector Mining Company as much as $500 per month in transportation costs.[26]

As the manager of the San Miguel County property, Reynolds was under constant pressure from Bradley and Havemeyer to increase production in order to pay dividends to stockholders. Bradley, whose health was precarious, needed the income to meet personal expenses. Havemeyer, who was independently wealthy, later admitted that he had assured his friends who bought the Hector stock that the company would pay monthly dividends. When that did not happen, Havemeyer agreed to compensate Reynolds, who paid fictitious dividends to three New York investors.[27]

In order to excavate the tunnel from Marshall Basin to an intersection with the Revenue Tunnel, Reynolds and his associates reorganized the Hector Mining Company in 1896, doubling its capital stock to $100,000. The additional shares were exchanged, in part, for property along the projected line of what was called the Ophir Tunnel. Other securities were sold to create working capital. At the same time the management of the Hector Mining Company organized the Hector Tunnel Company to underwrite the cost of the adit.[28]

The Hector Tunnel Company, in which Reynolds, M. D. Thatcher, and W. F. Havemeyer were the key investors, contracted with Reynolds for the construction of the adit. That contract was canceled within six months, and two years later the Hector Mining Company acquired the Hector Tunnel Company, exchanging 4 shares for 1. By that date Reynolds and Thatcher each controlled 42.5 percent of the company's stock, Le Roy owned 13.3 percent, and Havemeyer owned less than 2 percent. The work of advancing the Ophir Tunnel continued month after month. Occasionally crosscuts were driven into adjacent ground in order to produce ore to keep the Cimarron Mill running at near capacity.[29]

By 1900, as the Ophir Tunnel inched southward, the Revenue Tunnel was in need of reorganization. The ground above the adit had for all practical purposes been mined out. Evidence of this was found in the sharp drop in the Caroline Mining Company's output after 1897. That year the enterprise experienced a near-record production of 5,980 tons of ore, the cash receipts from which amounted to $524,358.84. By 1899 the output of ore had declined to 1,072 tons, and even though the average value increased to $92.05, the cash receipts dropped to $98,721.81. The following year the Virginius Mine yielded only 10 tons, the proceeds from which amounted to $1,005.68.[30]

Fortunately the Glacier Mining Company increased its output as that of the Caroline Mining Company declined. Ore production in 1897 exceeded 6,000 tons, the cash receipts from which amounted to $448,393.71, the highest to date. In 1899 the Glacier claim yielded 9,591 tons of ore, and cash receipts amounted to $863,167.23.[31]

By contrast, the Hector Mining Company, unlike the Caroline and Glacier firms, produced relatively large amounts of gold as well as silver. For that reason it earned relatively large profits on a small annual output of ore. From 1890 to 1898 the Hector Mining Company obtained from Cimarron Mine and adjacent claims 3,358 tons of ore, the cash receipts from which amounted to $638,819.43.[32]

The decline of the Virginius Mine, for whose benefit the Revenue Tunnel had been excavated, forced Reynolds to conclude that in the interest of operating efficiency and economy, the Caroline, Glacier, and Hector properties should be operated as a single mine by one corporation. In a circular letter to stockholders he proposed consolidation of the Revenue Tunnel, Caroline, Glacier, and Hector companies as the Revenue Tunnel Mines Company. M. D. Thatcher, who with Reynolds owned most of the stock in the four enterprises, was at first reluctant, but after adjustments in the accounts of the Caroline and Glacier to equalize each firms' earlier share of the cost of sinking Virginius shaft, he accepted Reynolds's plan.[33]

Incorporated under the laws of the state of Colorado on August 4, 1900, the Revenue Tunnel Mines Company had an authorized capital of $3 million divided into shares with a par value of $1 each. Most of these were exchanged for the stock of the consolidating firms. The Caroline and Glacier companies each received 1 million shares. An additional 700,000 shares were exchanged for the stock of the Hector companies and the Revenue Tunnel. That left in the treasury 300,000 shares, proceeds from the sale of which were to be the source of funds for operations and development.[34]

The only cash to exchange hands in the consolidation was for the purchase of the Revenue Tunnel Company stock held by the Caroline Mining Company. The new corporation acquired 16,810 shares at a cost of $15 each, or a total of $252,150. The stock was canceled, and the Caroline Mining Company waived any claim on the shares of the Revenue Tunnel Mines Company given in exchange for the stock of the Revenue Tunnel Company. As a consequence, the stockholders of the Revenue Tunnel Company divided 122,850 shares.[35]

The Revenue Tunnel Mines Company operated all of Reynolds's properties on the adit except the Cumberland and Wheel of Fortune enterprises. The Cumberland Mining Company had been organized in March 1891 to work the Cumberland, Nashville, and Banner lode mining claims that Reynolds had contracted to purchase from John Rapalje, Frederick Herbst, and Charles Underhill. The tunnel intersected the new company's property, at which point a drift was driven on the vein. Production of silver-galena ore was limited until the completion of the Revenue Mill because the Cumberland properties yielded mostly milling-grade ores.[36]

The Wheel of Fortune Mining Company was formed in 1899 after Reynolds purchased the Wheel of Fortune and three additional claims from W. P. Ryman of Philadelphia. These properties, together with those Reynolds had attempted to put into the abortive Ruby Mountain Mining Company ten years earlier, were sold to the Wheel of Fortune Mining Company in exchange for 100,000 shares of its capital stock, half of which went into the treasury to secure funds for operations and development. These were sold mainly to New York investors, including Herman S. Le Roy, Theodore Rogers, Francis Schell, A. V. H. Stuyvesant, and Charles A. Starbuck.[37]

The property was located near the Revenue Tunnel and extended up the mountain more or less parallel to the direction of the adit. A crosscut from the adit intersected the Wheel of Fortune vein, which was composed of silver in combination with galena and gray copper. Production from the vein was valued at about $30,000, restricted to a remnant of a rich pocket of ore that had been mined by the predecessor Wheel of Fortune Consolidated Mining Company.[38]

The consolidation coincided with a major change in the local management of the Revenue Tunnel. In September 1901 Hubbell W. Reed resigned as superintendent, leaving Ed Krisher, until then the mine foreman, in charge of the property. W. A. Garret continued as foreman at the mill. Reed ostensibly gave up the position he had held for more than twenty years to relocate to Salt Lake City because of his health. In fact, he may have ended his long-term relationship with Reynolds for other reasons.

Reed appeared to have been miffed about something, and the timing of his resignation suggests that it was the consolidation of the properties on the tunnel into a single company. Reynolds and Thatcher, who owned jointly more than 70 percent of the stock in the companies in question, suggested the merger and voted its approval. Reed, a minority stockholder in the Caroline, Glacier, and Revenue companies, was not consulted prior to the decision to merge them, along with the Hector companies, to form the Revenue Tunnel Mines Company.

There is one other plausible explanation for Reed's departure: he may have realized that the properties of the Revenue Tunnel Mines Company were no longer capable of yielding the large profits of previous years. The ground at and above the level of the tunnel was for all practical purposes mined out.[39] Recognizing that the glory days were past, Reed was ready to retire to Salt Lake City to enjoy the substantial wealth he had accumulated from mines at Ouray.

Reynolds's reaction to Reed's resignation was one of disappointment. He had hoped that they could go along together to get the Revenue Tunnel Mines Company's property in shape to sell it. It would be fitting, he remarked to Reed, if they could have finished the task they had started together twenty years earlier.[40]

The property continued to be worked after 1901, mostly by lessees. Over a period of twenty years it yielded 125,000 tons of ore but after Reed's departure did not again pay dividends. Reynolds devoted the next two decades to attempts to sell the property.[41]

By 1901 Reynolds attention was, and had been for some time, directed in large measure to other mining camps throughout Colorado. In addition to Ouray and interests previously acquired in Lake City, he had sizable holdings in the Ute Mining District near Platoro in Conejos County. It seems likely that he was first attracted to the area because at least one of his Aspen friends had investments there. David M. Hyman owned the Gladstone claim, which had a common boundary with one of Reynolds's claims.[42]

Reynolds acquired interests in three enterprises at Platoro. He secured titles to the Parole and Parole No. 2, which became the principal assets of the Parole Mining Company, incorporated in Illinois in November 1889 with an authorized capital of $64,000. Nearby Reynolds developed the Forest King Mining Company and the Senate Gold and Silver Mining Company, formed in 1889 and 1890, respectively. The Platoro properties remained in operation for only a short time because the ore they produced did not pay the expenses of development and operation.[43]

Investors in the Platoro ventures were mostly eastern men of considerable wealth. Exceptions were Mahlon D. Thatcher, the Pueblo banker; Charles P. Palmer, a promoter of Conejos County properties; and Albert Smith, a Denver lawyer. The principal backers of the Forest King and Senate companies were New York City men, including Charles Robinson, a member, with Reynolds and C. D. Arms, of the Aspen Pool; Robert Schell; A. V. H. Stuyvesant; and Theodore Rogers, a banker. H. A. Magee, a Chicago attorney, and Charles F. Morse, an executive of a prominent Chicago manufacturer of mining equipment, bought substantial amounts of the Parole Mining Company's stock.[44]

Reynolds also acquired interest at Summitville, located northwest of Platoro. Charles P. Palmer, who had been an expert witness for the Durant interests during the Aspen apex suit, was instrumental in directing Reynolds's attention to mining properties at Summitville, on the Continental Divide in Rio Grande County. It was there that Thomas Bowen acquired the sizable wealth that underwrote his successful election as U.S. senator from Colorado in 1883. For a time the mines were large producers of gold, but with the exhaustion of the oxidized ores near the surface, production declined and soon ended. The low-grade sulfides that abounded at depth could not be effectively treated with available technology to make them profitable shipping ores.[45]

Reynolds purchased the Golconda Gold Mining Company in June 1891 and then sold three-eights interest to Charles P. Palmer, through whom he had acquired the property. Reynolds anticipated that he could dispose of a substantial block of the enterprise's stock to his friends in the East. This proved impossible because Palmer, as superintendent, could not find high-grade shipping ores. What he found was low-grade ore, and it was, Reynolds conceded, of little use to anybody.[46]

Over a period of three years expenditures at Summitville exceeded income by at least $80,000. This additional burden came at a time when Reynolds was plagued by problems related to the nationwide panic and the ensuing depression. In desperation he leased the mine in 1893. Eventually mounting costs forced him to shut down the property in 1898. Two years later Reynolds made an agreement to combine the Golconda Gold Mining Company and T. N. Barnsdall's Consolidated Gold Mining Company. There was no specific date for this consolidation, except that it was to occur at some time in the future.[47]

Long before Reynolds gave up on Summitville, he was looking for investment opportunities at Creede. That camp came into being when N. C. Creede, for whom it was named, discovered the Holy Moses Mine, followed in short order by the Amethyst claim. Both were sold to David H. Moffat, prominent Denver banker and industrialist. News of these purchases set in motion a rush of fortune seekers to the area.

Investment opportunities at Creede may have been first called to Reynolds's attention by Charles P. Palmer, who had arranged for the acquisitions at Platoro and Summitville. In August 1891 Palmer suggested that since he had heard nothing but good reports from the new mining camp, his friend should acquire Tom Bowen's interest there. Bowen owned the Ridge Mine. Reynolds made no effort to acquire the property, probably to his regret, for it later became a large producer of silver ore.[48]

Within less than two months Reynolds acquired claims at Creede through the efforts of men with whom he had been associated in the Aspen apex suit. Byron E. Shear and I. L. Johnson, partners in an Aspen law firm, joined forces with Colin Timmons, an engineer and mine promoter, to buy up properties at Creede. In need of an experienced entrepreneur to carry out their plan, they turned to Reynolds, who, because of his activities at Aspen and Ouray, could raise, if necessary, large amounts of capital and direct the development of mines.

With Timmons as agent, Shear, Johnson, and Reynolds purchased several claims. The best of these—the Commodore, Sunnyside, New York, and Pittsburg—were on or near the rich Amethyst vein that ran through Bachelor Mountain. From Mary A. and Samuel D. Coffin they purchased the New York claim on October 21, 1891. From John C. Mackenzie and William P. McGillilard they purchased the Commodore claim on December 10, 1891. From the Coffins they bought three-fourths interest in the Pittsburg claim on December 18, 1891. From A. C. Dore they secured the Sunnyside claim on January 22, 1892.[49]

With these purchases they controlled a sizable piece of potentially rich ground on West Willow Creek. The best of the acquisitions in terms of eventual earnings were the Commodore and the New York, which were among the six large producers that straddled the Amethyst vein. From south to north the Bachelor, Commodore, New York, Last Chance, Amethyst, and Happy Thought accounted for 90 percent of the silver, lead, gold, and zinc, aggregate value of $37.5 million, produced by mines at Creede from 1891 to 1911. the earnings of these properties varied from a low of $2 million to a high of $11 million.[50]

The acquisition of the New York involved Reynolds in disputes over ownership of the claim. In 1892 Henry R. and E. O. Wolcott and other owners of the Last Chance, which cut across the New York, insisted on the right to work the area in controversy. When Reynolds and the co-owners of the New York threatened a lawsuit, a compromise was effected. The property claimed by both parties was placed in a new corporation, the New York and Chance Mining Company, whose stock was divided among the owners of the New York and Last Chance claims. Reynolds acquired 27.5 percent of the new enterprise's stock and served as its secretary and treasurer.[51]

He was also general manager of the New York and Chance Mine. With Alexander Thornton as local superintendent, Reynolds drove a a deep tunnel to intersect the Amethyst vein. To facilitate this work, iron pipes carried water from a point above the falls on West Willow Creek to dynamos installed at the mine. Electricity provided lights in and about the mine and power for mechanical drills.[52]

After advancing about 500 feet without striking any mineral, the tunnel intersected a valuable ore body. This came as a surprise to the Wolcott brothers and their associates, who, in order to avoid the cost of litigation with the New York claim, had given up what they thought to be barren ground. In part to control production from the new ground, and also to reduce operating costs because of the declining price of silver, the operations of the Last Chance and the New York and Chance Mines were combined in August 1893. S. Z. Dickson and E. H. Crawford, manager and superintendent, respectively, of the former assumed responsibility for both properties.[53] No longer in charge of the New York and Chance, Reynolds directed his energies to the development of the Commodore and other properties and to litigation that threatened his interest in the New York claim.

The discovery of a large ore body in the New York and Chance Mine prompted Mary A. Coffin, one of the original locators of the New York claim, to sue Reynolds and his friends on grounds that they had purchased the property from her for a nominal sum when they knew in fact that it was worth a very large amount of money. On grounds that the buyers had committed fraud, she asked that the contract for the sale of the property be set aside by the court.[54]

The controversy had its origin in the manner in which the New York claim had been located. Initially George K. Smith and Omer V. Cole, partners who had obtained a grubstake from Samuel D. Coffin, a real estate man in the San Luis Valley, staked out the claim south of N. C. Creede's Amethyst and parallel to the Last Chance claim. Subsequently Cole gave up prospecting and surrendered his share of what he thought was a worthless New York claim to Smith, who then restaked it as a joint venture with Mary A. Coffin, wife of S. D. Coffin, his partner in the search for wealth at Creede.

In October 1891 the owners of the Last Chance had their claim resurveyed to include about 500 feet of what was the New York claim. When Smith and Coffin objected, the owners of the Last Chance insisted they would pursue their right to the property through the courts. In order to defend their interest, Smith and Coffin turned to Colin Timmons, a local mining engineer, offering him half of their New York claim in return for money to develop the property and hire a lawyer to defend their title to it. In October 1891 Timmons arranged for Isaac L. Johnson, an attorney, to acquire one-sixth of the New York claim in return for defending it against encroachment by the owners of the Last Chance.[55]

In April 1893, before the formation of the New York and Chance Mining Company, Reynolds, Johnson, and Byron E. Shear, at the suggestion of Timmons, purchased the remainder of Coffin's interest in the New York claim for $15,000. Reynolds also purchased Timmons's interest, previously acquired from Coffin, for $100,000. In November 1893, after the discovery of rich ore in the New York and Chance Mine, Coffin charged that Timmons, Johnson, Shear, and Reynolds had conspired to cheat her out of a property whose true value they knew but withheld from her at the time of the purchase. Coffin gained a temporary injunction against Reynolds and associates in November 1893, but the court dismissed that action the following January on grounds there had been no intent to defraud.[56]

Undaunted, Coffin pursued her charges through the legal system. The case dragged on until May 1899, when Judge Calvin P. Butler, in U.S. District Court, Denver, ruled that the evidence revealed that the plaintiff had been thoroughly satisfied with the sale at the time it was made and had given no thought to recovery of the property until it proved to be of some value. It was unfortunate, the judge continued, that the plaintiff should have parted with a valuable property for a small consideration, but in the absence of fraud, there was no remedy in the courts. Judgment was for the defendants.[57]

Among the congratulatory messages that followed the close of the Coffin suit was one from C. A. Hallam, who had been David M. Hyman's close associate at Aspen. Writing from Deadwood, South Dakota, where he was secretary and treasurer of the Two Johns Mining and Milling Company (named for John W. Gates and John A. Drake), Hallam remarked, "I hope you have no more big mining suits. Two such as Aspen and Creede ought to suffice for a life time." The second suit, unlike the first, did not end in a compromise, and it left Reynolds and his associates in full control of the properties they had acquired from George K. Smith and the Coffins.[58]

Neither the New York nor the New York and Chance properties were Reynolds's most valuable property at Creede. By the time the Coffin litigation had been resolved, Reynolds's activities in Mineral County centered largely on the Commodore Mining Company, of which he was the major stockholder. Acquired in 1891 by Reynolds, Johnson, Shear, and Timmons, the claim was divided in 1893, giving Reynolds and Shear each 33 percent and Johnson, 15 percent. Timmons's share was sold to Owen E. Le Fevre and Charles F. McKenney, who received 12 and 6.3 percent, respectively. Reynolds later purchased Shear's interest in the property.[59]

Development commenced in 1892 with the sinking of a shaft. At a depth of 97 feet assays of ore varied from 180 ounces to as much as 500 ounces of silver per ton. Further development was delayed, in part because the owners were preoccupied with the New York claim and also because the Commodore Mining Company was not formally organized until 1895. Until then the money for large-scale development, particularly the driving of one or more deep tunnels, was not available.[60]

The mines on Bachelor Mountain originally sank shafts to tap the Amethyst vein but quickly opted for tunnels in order to avoid the high cost of hoisting ore and pumping water from great depths. Eventually all of the mines were worked through adits because they provided drainage without the inconvenience and expense of pumps. Tunnels were also convenient and economical passageways for removing ore.[61]

The first tunnel on the Amethyst vein was started in 1892. The Nelson Tunnel ran from West Willow Creek just south of the Bachelor claim, with the goal of cutting the vein at depths of from 400 to 1,400 feet. It was driven 2,100 feet without encountering significant amounts of ore. A continuation of that project, the Wooster Tunnel, extended it a distance of 8,850 feet to the Amethyst claim. The Amethyst, Last Chance, and New York Mining Companies paid royalties for transportation of ore and drainage of water. The Last Chance was idle for three years before its flooded workings were drained by the tunnel, permitting the resumption of mining operations.[62]

The Commodore was the only large mine that did not participate in the Nelson Tunnel project. When asked by J. T. Wallace to join in the construction of the adit, Reynolds and his associates replied that given the Commodore's location, it should have its own opening and mine its ground through a tunnel it controlled. Taking advantage of its topography, and an agreement with the neighboring Bachelor Mining Company for use of a portion of its ground, the Commodore drove an adit to the vein. Eventually the company completed three adits (numbers three, four, and five), the last of which extended more than 4,000 feet to intersect the vein.[63]

After three years of development work, including equipping the mine for a large output, Reynolds and his associates organized the Commodore Mining Company, which was incorporated under the laws of the state of Colorado in 1895. Twenty percent of the authorized capital of $1 million in shares was set aside to be sold to obtain money for development and operations. Some of this was purchased by Reynolds, thereby strengthening his position as the leading stockholder in the enterprise. Most of the remainder was purchased by William F. Havemeyer and his friends in New York.[64]

The company rapidly became a large shipper of high-grade ore. With Reynolds as president, C. F. McKenney as secretary and treasurer, David G. Miller as manager, and Alex Thornton as superintendent, the mine paid large dividends without interruption for the next ten years. The Commodore proved to be rich in ore beyond the imagination of its owners. In October 1897 Miller informed Reynolds that there was more ore in sight than he had ever seen in his life and all of it good grade. The mine's output, he continued, could be maintained at from 150 to 200 tons a day.[65]

Rich ore was also extracted from the adjoining Sunnyside claim. That property, owned jointly by the Commodore and the Amethyst Mining Company, led to a long-standing controversy over who should mine the property. This pitted Reynolds against David H. Moffat and was complicated by each side's contention that it owned the apex and was therefore entitled to all of the disputed property. After about a year the dispute was resolved with the formation of the Bristol Head Mining Company to mine and control the ground in controversy. Moffat was president; Reynolds, vice president; and James A. McClurg, general manager.[66]

The prosperity of the Commodore Mine was reflected in its record for paying dividends. In 1899 alone the company declared dividends totaling $0.625 a share on a par value of $1. In addition, management had created a reserve fund of $150,000, equal to $0.125 a share, making the earning for the year equal to 75 percent of the par value of the stock. Reynolds ventured the opinion that, given the low price of silver, this was a remarkable achievement, unmatched by any other silver mine in the United States or elsewhere.[67]

By 1900 the Commodore, equipped for large-volume output, accounted for about half of the silver produced at Creede. Electricity generated by waterpower was used to provide power throughout the mine. All underground levels were connected by uprises. Ore was transported to the entrances of the three tunnels and from there conveyed by bucket tramways to ore bins at the railroad. The Denver and Rio Grande Railroad transported the ore to smelters at Pueblo and Denver.[68]

Despite the Commodore's magnificent performance, Reynolds recognized that there was little reason to be optimistic about the property's future. The upper workings above the drainage tunnel were being rapidly exhausted and could be operated at the current rate probably no more than two years. Influenced by the Bachelor Mining Company's success in a shaft below the Nelson Tunnel, Reynolds proposed exploration below number five tunnel. If an ore body were found at greater depth, the Commodore could continue profitable operations for an indefinite period, particularly if it could obtain leases on the lower levels of neighboring claims. He conceded, however, that to perpetuate the enterprise, it was wise to look for properties beyond the Creede Mining District. In fact, he was investigating claims on Red Elephant Mountain in Clear Creek County.[69]

When the output of the Creede mines declined, as had occurred at Ouray, Reynolds was already active in mining districts elsewhere in Colorado. He owned properties in Gunnison County, some at Tin Cup, and, farther south over Cumberland Pass, an immense block of claims in the vicinity of Pitkin and Ohio City. By the turn of the century he was prepared to devote time and money to the development and operation of these assets, which he had largely neglected until then.

6
Searching for New Bonanzas

IN the spring of 1891 A. E. Reynolds acknowledged to a friend that he once again had mining fever. He was contemplating the purchase of the Gold Cup Mine and adjacent properties at Tin Cup, Gunnison County, Colorado. Because of previous bouts with this malady, Reynolds was already the owner of mines at Lake City, Ouray, Platoro, and Summitville, and he retained a small part of what had been large interests at Aspen. Before the close of 1891 he was dickering for properties at Creede, in what became Mineral County. Before the end of the decade he acquired the Emma Mine at Dunton, Dolores County. The Gold Cup Mine was the first of many Gunnison County properties that Reynolds, and associates, acquired over a period of thirty years. Most of these were several miles south of Tin Cup in and around Pitkin and Ohio City, where for a time silver and gold mines were hailed as a bonanza, another Creede according to local boosters. In the end the Gunnison County mines as well as the property near Rico fell short of expectations; nonetheless they were an important part of Reynolds's mining activities for the remainder of his lifetime.

Tin Cup was one of the first mining camps in Gunnison County. After the rush to Leadville in 1879 prospectors traveled over the Collegiate Range to Taylor Park, the location of the headwaters of the Gunnison River, where they worked numerous placers. Inevitably the search for the mother lode, the source of the placer gold, led to a thorough examination of the region. By the early 1880s Tin Cup was a center of mining activity. The chief obstacle to the community's growth was its lack of a rail connection. The high cost of transporting ore by wagon over the Continental Divide to the railroad at St. Elmo, 10 miles to the east via Alpine Pass, was a major cause for the decline of mining activities.[1]

In 1891 Reynolds acquired properties on East Gold Hill south of Tin Cup. In addition to twenty-two newly patented claims, he bought the Gold Cup Mine, owned by the Gold Cup Consolidated Mining Company, a New York enterprise, of which Emile Vatable was the principal stockholder. Isaac L. Johnson, a longtime associate who had a lease on Gold Hill properties, persuaded Reynolds that the Gold Cup was a valuable property. H. W. Reed and Angus Snedaker traveled from Ouray and Aspen, respectively, to make investigations, concluding that the mine could quickly pay back the cost of the entire group of properties, comprising some 300 acres. On their recommendation and with the assurance of financial support from Mahlon D. Thatcher, Reynolds decided to buy.[2]

From Vatable he secured 350,000 shares of the Gold Cup Consolidated Mining Company at a cost of $105,000 and assumed an existing debt of $18,999. This made him the majority stockholder in the enterprise. For the balance of the stock he offered $0.15 a share and acquired all but 50,000 shares. The holdouts, Reynolds believed, thought he would eventually have to pay them twice that amount. On this point they were disappointed since he foreclosed on the company for debts incurred in its operation and in December 1891 organized the Gold Cup Mining Company, a Colorado corporation, whose stock he sold in large amounts to New York City friends, including William F. Havemeyer, and Herman S. Le Roy.[3]

Initially Reynolds was convinced it would be a big mine, but he was wrong. Snedaker, the superintendent, concluded that the property had been systematically gutted by the previous owner. At first Reynolds dissented, attributing the Scotsman's pessimism to the likelihood that natural water channels had cut off the ore at intervals, making the operation of the mine more difficult than anticipated. He was reluctant to believe that he could have been blatantly cheated by Emile Vatable. However, within a month Reynolds admitted that he had been the victim of clever manipulation. Experience revealed that the numerous faces of ore in the incline shaft were nearly worthless facades behind which there was nothing of value. The bulk of the ore had been skillfully extracted from behind and the opening out of which it had been taken carefully concealed.[4]

Convinced that nothing could be gained from seeking a new ore contact at greater depth in the Gold Cup at a time when silver prices were falling, Reynolds and Thatcher decided to close the mine. In late February 1893 Snedaker suspended operations, employees were paid off and discharged, and the property was turned over to a caretaker, George W. Russell, a former Indian Territory wagon master and onetime foreman of the Reynolds ranch in the Texas Panhandle. Any thought of renewing operations vanished because of a panic in the financial market and the collapse of silver prices on June 26. The property remained idle for nearly three years.[5]

It was reopened in 1896, with Isaac L. Johnson as lessee. He secured from Reynolds and Thatcher an option on 60 percent of the Gold Cup stock. Within three months he encountered an ore body that local newspapers called a bonanza, prompting Reynolds to inform Thatcher that they had stopped operations too soon. However, the value of the discovery was greatly exaggerated. It was of modest value, comprising 3 or 4 feet of high-grade ore and a large volume of milling ore.[6] This was one of the rare occasions when the mine made a profit for the lessee.

The Gold Cup remained under lease to Johnson for twenty-five years. Because there were no returns, Reynolds and

Thatcher assisted him from time to time by contributing stock, the proceeds from the sale of which were earmarked for development of the property. In return Johnson maintained the mine and consistently paid local taxes until 1917, when he fell in arrears. The lease was repeatedly revised and extended until neither Johnson nor Reynolds was certain of its provisions.[7] However, by leaving the property in Johnson's care, Reynolds was free to devote his attention to the accumulation of two large blocks of mining claims less than 12 miles south and west of Tin Cup.

These properties were in the vicinity of Pitkin and Ohio City. The former, located in a narrow valley traversed by Quartz Creek and surrounded by mountains, had been the scene of a silver mining boom from 1879 to 1883. A second boom was launched in 1890 but eventually stalled when silver prices declined steadily in 1892 and tumbled downward in 1893 with the start of a depression. At that time Reynolds began buying up properties, convinced that they would be of great value at some time in the future. When some owners resisted, he suspended purchases, biding his time until 1899, when through the efforts of trusted lieutenants he once more picked up numerous properties.

Over a period of about twenty years Reynolds secured control of more than 600 claims, covering nearly 6,000 acres of mineral lands. William J. Fine, an engineer who was also a local banker; William H. Eckbert, a mining engineer; and John F. Pearson, a veteran miner, arranged for the acquisition of the properties. Fine negotiated purchases of private holdings; Eckbert platted the properties, recorded titles in the local courthouse, and filed claims, when appropriate, with the U.S. General Land Office; and Pearson supervised the development and operation of mines. Reynolds secured patents for approximately three-quarters of the acquisitions, many of which were in the vicinity of Ohio City, located south and west of Pitkin, at the confluence of Ohio Creek with Quartz Creek.[8]

Pitkin and Ohio City, only 6 miles apart, were the centers of two distinct mining areas. Immediately north and west of Pitkin in the Quartz Creek Mining District was the Lime Belt, extending from the town up West Mountain into an upland basin known as Chicago Park. To the west of Chicago Park and across a divide was the Gold Belt, located in the Gold Brick Mining District, lying entirely within an area drained by Ohio Creek, later called Gold Creek. The principal mines, located from 4 to 9 miles north of Ohio City, were linked to that community by a good wagon road.[9]

In the early 1890s the Lime Belt had allegedly yielded large quantities of silver from mines at or near the edge of the formation. The Fairview and Silver Islet were each credited with production worth about $1 million. The Cleopatra and the Silver Basin each produced silver worth $500,000, and from the Blaine-Tycoon, Terrible, and Maid of Athens the ore was valued from $100,000 to $250,000. This outpouring of wealth had ended, according to local sources, because of the collapse of silver prices.[10]

In 1892, at a time when shallow mines were reported to be highly successful, exploration with a diamond drill, a relatively new method of prospecting, was said to have revealed within Chicago Park ore bodies at greater depth than previously suspected. The Silver Basin Mining Company hired Ben Sadtler, professor of metallurgy and mineralogy at the Colorado School of Mines, to oversee the drilling of a test hole and the assaying of core samples to determine the location of mineralized zones. Large ore contacts had been found, according to widely circulated copies of Sadtler's report, at from 300 to 750 feet. It was suggested that another rich zone of mineralization was located at an even greater depth, on the contact between underlying granite and the limestone.[11]

Reports of Stadler's diamond drill test suggested that mineralized zones were likely to be found on the contacts between strata of blue lime and dolomite. Although this was not substantiated in all cases, it suggested to Reynolds, because of the similarity of the area's geology to that of Aspen and Leadville, the possibility of large-volume, high-value ore production. This was the primary motivation for his acquisition of properties in both the Gold and Lime Belts. With the financial backing of eastern friends, initially Charles A. Starbuck, president of the New York Air Brake Company, Reynolds acquired a large block of mineral properties and then organized a company to seek silver ore at depths of from 300 to 750 feet.[12]

On January 16, 1901, Reynolds and two officers of the New York Air Brake Company, Starbuck and J. C. Thompson, incorporated the Colorado Smelting and Mining Company of Colorado. Chartered in New Jersey with an authorized capital of $5 million, the enterprise took possession of approximately 3,000 acres of mineral land that Reynolds owned by that date. In Chicago Park some three hundred claims were located in a horseshoe-shaped area 5 miles long and from 1 to 2 miles wide. In spite of the corporation's name, it had no plans for erecting a smelter.[13]

The Colorado Smelting and Mining Company bought from Reynolds his mineral lands in the Quartz Creek and Gold Brick Mining Districts. In exchange he acquired all of the stock issued by the enterprise, comprising three-fifths of the authorized shares. Initially he received 1.5 million shares for properties mainly in Chicago Park. After July 1, 1902, when the war tax on stocks, imposed at the start of the conflict with Spain in 1898, was lifted, he acquired another 1.5 million shares in exchange for additional claims. One-third of the stock, or the proceeds from the sale thereof, he returned to the treasury to be used to underwrite development and operations.[14]

As was his habit, Reynolds invited longtime friend and business associate Mahlon D. Thatcher to make a substantial investment in the new mining enterprise. When the Pueblo banker declined, Reynolds offered Starbuck an interest in the Colorado Smelting and Mining Company, but he was reluctant to invest in the enterprise on a large scale. He limited his investment to 96,000 shares.[15]

In an effort to raise funds to develop the Ohio City property, Reynolds offered stock to other friends in New York. Among others, Phoebe Robinson bought 100,000 and Theodore Rogers of the Metropolitan Bank, 10,000. They, along with Starbuck, paid from $0.15 to $0.20 a share, netting the company approximately $40,000.

Reynolds's Gunnison County associates acquired large minority interests in the enterprise. As the owners of numerous key mining properties north and west of Pitkin, W. J. Fine, W. H. Eckbert, and J. F. Pearson were in positions to assist the Colorado Smelting and Mining Company's exploration of the Lime Belt. In exchange for stock they sold mining claims that were strategically located in the areas where Reynolds planned adits or shafts to explore down to the granite contact.[16]

Under Pearson's direction openings had been started in Chicago Park and at the base of West Mountain four months before the Colorado Smelting and Mining Company was formally incorporated. The Silver Basin Mine shaft, which had been sunk by the Pitkin Mining Company in 1893, was reopened and extended downward in search of contacts between strata of limestone and dolomite. Reynolds bought 80 percent of the Pitkin company's stock from its majority stockholder, Chicago meatpacker Jack Cudahy. It was estimated that the shaft would reach a rich mineral contact at a depth of about 600 feet.[17]

A contract for deepening the Silver Basin shaft was awarded to W. H. Kennedy of Creede in December 1900. He was required to make 50 feet a month, which meant that his target date for completing the project was June of the following year. Kennedy was also awarded the job of running a tunnel under West Mountain.[18]

The adit was designed to intersect a contact at a distance of about 1,500 feet. Originally called the Gray Eagle, the West Mountain Tunnel was advanced at the rate of 150 feet a month toward a contact thought to be a vein of quartz at a distance of 2,100 feet from the portal. It was assumed that at that point mineral ground would extend for a distance of 1 mile on either side of the tunnel and upward a height of 800 feet.[19]

After approximately a year Reynolds canceled Kennedy's contract and hired his own crew to complete the Silver Basin and West Tunnel openings. That decision came after a drunken brawl by the contractor's men in August 1901 and an ongoing problem of absenteeism because of the men's addiction to whiskey. Reynolds could not accept the losses, estimated at from sixty to ninety working days.[20]

Normally tolerant of the consumption of alcohol in modest quantities, Reynolds objected strongly when employees, friends, or siblings allowed drinking to interfere with the performance of their responsibilities to employers, other workers, or family. He informed Pearson that a "new deal" was to be imposed and rigidly enforced. Employees were to be informed that they would not be allowed to retain their jobs if consumption of alcohol prevented them from efficiently carrying out assigned tasks. This edict must have solved the problem of alcoholism, for Reynolds did not again raise the issue with his superintendent. However, neither the Silver Basin shaft nor the West Mountain Tunnel yielded appreciable amounts of silver ore.[21]

With its own crews the Colorado Smelting and Mining Company started work on four more adits in the Lime Belt. From Hall's Gulch, north of Pitkin, Pearson's men drove tunnels in opposite directions. By advancing to the north, he sought to cut the contact in an area called the Mineral Farm. The objective was the ground beneath formerly productive mines that had filled with water. A tunnel would not only drain the properties but would also permit them to be worked economically from below without the expense of pumping water and hoisting ore.[22]

Driving south from Hall's Gulch, Pearson's crew sought to explore below the shallow workings of Silent Friend Group, plus the Robinson and Ferry claims. A decade or more earlier the 250-foot Silent Friend incline had yielded valuable ore, but the mine could not be worked at greater depth because of water. The adit, by draining the claims, afforded Reynolds and his associates an opportunity to tap what they hoped would be rich ore bodies at reasonable costs.[23]

Two more tunnels were driven above Hall's Gulch in search of mineral contacts. From Armstrong Gulch an adit was driven in an easterly direction to undercut the Dominion, Terrible, and adjacent claims. After advancing about 500 feet, work ended without finding the contact.[24]

The Sutton Tunnel, the highest in altitude, was designed to explore at depth claims near the top of Fairview Mountain. These included the Fairview, Cleopatra, Little Tycoon, and Jim Blaine, all of which at one time had been large producers of silver. The adit was advanced a distance of only 350 feet, at which point work stopped without having encountered workable mineralized zones.[25]

The failure to tap deep silver deposits in the Lime Belt was a disappointment to Reynolds. Nonetheless, he rationalized this setback, insisting that the exploratory openings had been undertaken not to reach ore contacts but to meet the U.S. General Land Office's requirements for securing patents on mining claims lying ahead of and above the adits. For all of his effort Reynolds acquired little or no mineral, but he gained numerous patented mining claims.[26] In light of failures to find any commercially valuable ore contacts, he must have suspected that the area was of little, if any, value but refused to say so to associates.

While active in Chicago Park, Reynolds acquired an interest in property within 1 mile of the mining camp of Bowerman, 3 miles southeast of Pitkin. In 1903, when there was a sizable boom in that section of Gunnison County, veteran prospectors J. C. Bowerman and Stephen Dunn brought Reynolds a suitcase full of rich gold ore specimens taken, they said, from the Independence lode mining claim. In order to explore the property, Reynolds organized the Independence Gold Mining Company, of which he was president. Bower-man and Dunn received a majority of the enterprise's stock in return for deeds to eight mining claims and one mill site. William F. Havemeyer, as was his habit at that time, purchased 10,000 shares because of his faith in Reynolds's judgment.

Armed with a lease and purchase option from the Independence Gold Mining Company, Reynolds invested $27,000 without finding marketable ore. He shut down operations after less than three months, convinced that the samples Bowerman and Dunn claimed to have taken from the site must have come from an isolated pocket of mineral. Later that year Bowerman agreed to pay $60,000 for Reynolds's interest in the Independence property but failed to complete the schedule of payments.[27]

While acquiring and developing properties near Pitkin and Ohio City, Reynolds actively pursued similar goals in Dolores County, 100 miles south and west of Gunnison County. Near the town of Dunton, on the West Dolores River 16 miles from Rico, the county seat, Reynolds purchased a major interest in the Emma Mine in 1899. This was not the result of another attack of mining fever but an attempt to aid his brother-in-law, Richard Keller, who had secured an option on the property in 1897. Keller immediately sold his option to F. B. Tobey, who, with the support of New York investors, organized the Pactolus Gold Mining and Milling Company to operate the property. In 1898 Tobey defaulted on the contract in a manner that caused the owners to rescind their agreement with Keller. Angered by the obvious injustice of that action, Reynolds came to Keller's rescue.[28]

The principal owners of the Emma Mine, originally only the Emma claim on which there was a small concentration mill, was A. F. Adams, and a number of Rico people, who were represented by Horatio Dunton, a local lawyer. Reynolds convinced the owners that Keller was in no way responsible for the misdeeds of Tobey and his associates, with the result

that the original purchase option was reinstated. When Tobey failed a second time to make the required payment of
$25,000, Reynolds, on the basis of a careful inspection of the
underground workings by his friend Charles F. Palmer, decided to buy the property. The mine and mill became the
principal assets of the Emma Gold Mining Company, organized April 5, 1899, as a Colorado corporation with an authorized capital of 100,000 shares, each with a par value of $1.[29]

Following a well-established plan for launching new enterprises, Reynolds placed 20,000 shares in the company's treasury, the proceeds from which were to be used to pay for
development of the mine. He immediately commenced negotiations with H. W. Fowler, a Chicago manufacturer of railroad car wheels, for one-half of the capital stock. When the
sale did not materialize, Reynolds sold a substantial block of
his holdings to New York friends.[30]

With funds from the sale of treasury stock, Keller, as local
manager, commenced operation of the mine and mill. Tunnels were driven into the side of the mountain to reduce or
eliminate reliance on shafts for hoisting ore and pumping
water from the lower depths, which also significantly reduced
the cost of extracting ore and transporting it to the mill.[31]

In addition to expanding underground workings, the Emma
Gold Mining Company acquired adjacent mining claims, coal
lands, and timberlands and erected a new mill in which it
installed stamps 300 pounds heavier than those in the original mill to pulverize ore prior to treating it on Wilfley concentrating tables. Reynolds hoped to increase the percentage of
gold and silver in the concentrates. On average one hundred
men were employed, divided about evenly between the mine
and mill. In 1903 and 1904 from 40 to 50 tons of concentrates
were shipped daily. According to the mining industry press,
production was large and the company appeared to be prosperous.[32]

In fact, the mine and mill operated only sporadically over a
period of several years. The company gained large returns on

crude ore and concentrates, but expenses by far exceeded income. In the first three years of operation ore returns amounted to a total of $120,000, while the cost of operating the mine and mill was $200,000. It was utter folly, Reynolds stated to Keller, to keep the property open when the income did not meet the payroll and other charges. As late as 1908, the year before Reynolds turned the mine and mill over to lessees, the Emma Gold Mining Company earned slightly more than $54,000, but operating expenses exceeded $84,000.[33]

The enterprise suffered from a technical problem that it tried without success to solve: values equal to the amount of gold and silver saved in the mill were lost in the treatment process. The inability to recover more than 50 percent of the gold and silver in the ore meant that the company consistently operated at a loss. In his search for a remedy Reynolds built and equipped a new mill with larger stamps and experimented with a number of processes designed to improve the efficiency of ore concentration. The result was higher costs without commensurate improvements in the output of the mill.[34]

Frustrated by the Emma Mine's failure to earn profits for investors, Reynolds put the property on the market. A succession of prospective buyers examined it, but no one was willing to buy, in part because the $350,000 price tag was out of proportion, given the difficulty of retrieving values from the ore, to the potential for earnings. Belatedly Reynolds lowered the price to $250,000, and then to $200,000, without attracting potential buyers. After repeated failures to dispose of the mine and mill, the Emma Gold Mining Company leased its property to Frank Stampfel, a longtime employee, in 1909. This permitted Reynolds to devote his attention to his other assets, particularly the claims lying north of Ohio City in Gunnison County's Gold Belt.[35]

There Reynolds hoped to develop a prosperous mine as well as to enlarge his holdings of potentially valuable properties. In 1904 he shifted the main thrust of the Colorado Smelting and Mining Company's activities from the Quartz Creek Mining

District westward to the adjoining Gold Brick District. In doing so, he was influenced by persistent failures to find ore contacts at depth and by the fact that low prices for silver did not offer much hope for profitable mining operations. At a time when silver was selling for $0.55 an ounce, gold brought a handsome return of $20 per ounce.

The area north of Ohio City was already the location of a successful mining venture. Adjacent to the Colorado Smelting and Mining Company's large block of mining claims, the Raymond Consolidated Mining Company commenced excavation of a tunnel in February 1904. It was designed to drain the Midnight, Monte Carlo, and Raymond Mines, formerly large producers of ore that had been abandoned because water inhibited operations below a depth of 250 feet. In a distance of 2,107 feet the Raymond Tunnel cut fourteen veins, six of which revealed gold as well as silver in sufficient quantities to justify extraction and treatment. A 100-ton mill was erected at the entrance to the adit.[36]

Owners of adjacent properties mobilized capital to drive parallel adits, hoping to cut similar veins. Within a distance of less than 5 miles along Ohio Creek, four tunnels were driven during the years from 1904 to 1907. The first, in the order of appearance, was the Carter, located south of the Raymond. To the north of the Raymond were the Gold Links; the Belzora-Bassick, with two openings; and the Sandy Hook. Three of the four, including the Gold Links, erected amalgamation and concentrating mills in conjunction with mining operations.[37]

The Gold Links Tunnel was located 5 miles north of Ohio City and 4 miles over the hill from Pitkin. Originally Reynolds, Eckbert, and Pearson, owners of the Gold Links group, planned to organize a new company to drive a tunnel through the property and beyond into claims they hoped to acquire at some future date. Subsequently Reynolds changed his mind and convinced his associates that they should sell their claims to a company that would commit substantial resources to driving the adit in order to tap mineral resources that were inaccessible from the surface.[38]

In June 1904 they sold their properties to the Colorado Smelting and Mining Company. In exchange for more than a dozen strategically located mining claims, Reynolds, Fine, Eckbert, and Pearson received 1 million shares of stock. The company commenced a tunnel to pass through the Gold Links and other claims en route to the Sacramento Mine, a large producer of gold and silver ore in the early 1890s.[39] It was located to the east and more than 500 feet above the tunnel level. When construction stalled at a point 1,700 feet from the portal for lack of funds, Reynolds had to find another way to assure the completion of the project.

Within a year a new enterprise was created to construct the Gold Links Tunnel. On June 5, 1905, Reynolds, Charles F. McKenney, and William J. Fine incorporated the Gold Links Mining Company. A Colorado charter authorized 1 million shares of stock, each with a par value of $1. On June 16, 1905, four of the five directors—Fine, Reynolds, McKenney, and Humphrey—voted to accept Reynolds's offer to exchange the Gold Band group and the End Line, thirteen claims in all, for all of the company's capital stock. Reynolds agreed to return to the treasury 10 percent of the shares, proceeds from the sale of which were to underwrite development and operations.[40]

Also on June 16 the directors of the Colorado Smelting and Mining Company and the Gold Links Mining Company, who were the same people, conveyed each to the other enterprise one-half interest in claims lying adjacent to, in front of, and above the portal to the Gold Links Tunnel. This cleared the way for joint ownership and use of the tunnel. The Colorado Smelting and Mining Company owned and worked the ground to the left (north) of the adit, while the Gold Links Mining Company owned and worked the ground to the right (south) of the tunnel.[41]

Furthermore, the Colorado Smelting and Mining Company transferred to the Gold Links Mining Company all claims lying to the right (south) of the tunnel. In return for this action Reynolds agreed to drive the adit to a point 3,000 feet from the entrance. This was to be completed no later than July 17, 1910.[42]

With 90 percent of the new company's shares in his possession, Reynolds moved quickly to market what he did not need to maintain personal control of the corporation. He retained 443,099 shares and sold the remainder. He conveyed just under 100,000 shares to small investors and another 400,000 to Pittsburgh oil magnate Theodore N. Barnsdall.[43]

Barnsdall acquired 35 percent of the Colorado Smelting and Mining Company's outstanding shares. His actual cost was $0.15 a share, or a total of $208,650, in the form of cash and promissory notes scheduled to mature over a period of several years. Reynolds, who was normally guarded in his predictions about the outcome of high-risk mining ventures, suggested that this investment by the oilman would earn him $1 million.[44]

By selling Barnsdall's notes to banks in Denver and Pueblo, Reynolds, acting for the two companies, acquired the money to complete the Gold Links Tunnel and to contract for the erection of a 100-ton amalgamation and concentration mill near the portal. He made James E. Lyon, a trusted employee then at the May Day Mine at Hesperus, supervisor of construction and sent him to Ouray to confer with W. A. Garrett, for the Revenue Mill was to be the model for the new facility at Ohio City. The stamps, most of the machinery, and the lumber came from the San Luis Land and Mining Company's Independence Mill at Crestone. Reynolds purchased the plant and relocated most of it to the site north of Ohio City at a savings, according to his estimate, of from $40,000 to $50,000 over the cost of new equipment.[45]

The erection of the mill raised questions about the proper disposal of tailings. The Raymond Mill had dumped its waste into Ohio Creek, a common practice at the time. Responding to the threat this posed to aquatic life, the Colorado Fish and

Game Commission ordered construction of a dam and settling ponds to prevent tailings from entering the watercourse.
Rather than comply with the order, the Raymond Tunnel
owners suspended operations for several months.

Reynolds was unsympathetic with the commission's efforts
to prevent pollution of the stream. He argued rather bellig-
erently that if the people of Gunnison County thought that
catching fish was more important than developing mines and
mills, he would halt construction of the Gold Links Mill.
Operators, he insisted, were victims of the commission's "hum-
bug." He suspended construction for a time but continued
work in the tunnel. However, three years later the Colorado
Smelting and Mining Company, owner of the mill, constructed, in response to a threatened suit by the state, a dam
and settling basins to impound mill tailings in order to
prevent further pollution of the local creek and, farther
downstream, the Gunnison River.[46]

Putting the Ohio Creek property in operating condition
required, exclusive of additional mining claims, an expenditure of $500,000. The mill, with water- and steam power,
amalgamation plates, concentrating tables, and accessories,
cost $75,000. Within a year $25,000 were spent in erecting
and equipping an additional building. Carrying the main
tunnel to a distance of 3,000 feet, and beyond, together with
cross-drifts, required an expenditure of $150,000. The in-
stallation of a flume to carry water from Ohio Creek to
turbines at a power station near the tunnel and mill required
an investment of another $6,000 in 1909. Electricity for
lighting and the powering of machinery for the greater part
of each year yielded a saving in the consumption of coal
amounting to from $40 to $200 per day, depending upon the
season of the year.[47]

The mill commenced operation in December 1907. After
less than two weeks Reynolds ordered it shut down because
the income derived from mining and processing ore failed to
pay operating expenses. The heavy burden of debt, and a

tight money market in the aftermath of the Panic of 1907, meant that he could not risk operating the property at a loss. Although one hundred stamps had been available from Crestone, only thirty had been installed, and seldom were more than twenty in operation at one time. The rate of ore extraction frequently did not match the capacity of the mill.[48]

The Gold Links Mine and Mill were not the big profit maker that Reynolds and Barnsdall had anticipated. In 1908, the first full year of operation, the property lost more than $23,000. A profit of more than $15,000 in 1909 was followed by a record net income of over $67,000 in 1910. Earnings fell sharply in 1911 and 1912, however, followed by a substantial loss of more than $11,000 in 1912.[49] At this point Reynolds and Barnsdall, who had been meeting the company's bills, decided to cut their losses by reorganizing operations at Ohio City.

In 1912 Reynolds, as president and major stockholder, allowed the Colorado Smelting and Mining Company's New Jersey charter to lapse. Also, to protect stockholders' interest in that enterprise, he obtained from the district court a judgment to satisfy a debt of $55.663.41, money advanced in previous years by some of the stockholders as voluntary assessments on their shares. This he held in trust while forming a new corporation. First the Colorado Smelting and Mining Company (New Jersey) absorbed the Gold Links Mining Company, giving 2 shares for 1. Then the New Jersey company surrendered its stock and assets to the Colorado Smelting and Mining Company, chartered in Colorado on June 6, 1912. The new corporation was to take over all of the properties in the vicinity of Ohio City and Pitkin.[50]

The reorganization was never completed, and no property was deeded to the new corporation. Reynolds's plan to remake the enterprise was blocked when his onetime trusted associates, John F. Pearson, William J. Fine, and William H. Eckbert, conspired to seize key mining claims on which taxes were in arrears. Pearson had been authorized by Reynolds to

negotiate with the county commissioners to obtain concessions on taxes due for past years. Instead, with the coopera-
tion of local authorities, the three men took advantage of
Reynolds's absence from the state to gain reassessments on
valuable claims along Ohio Creek. By lowering the value of
each claim to less than $100, Pearson and his associates could
secure tax deeds without sending formal notifications of that
action to the Colorado Smelting and Mining Company, the
Gold Links Mining Company, or Reynolds as president of
both corporations.[51]

The conspirators, according to Reynolds, were motivated
by nothing more than greed. In fact, they may have been
acting to protect their investments in the two companies. They
were among creditors who had lost their claims against the
Colorado Smelting and Mining Company when Reynolds and
Barnsdall gained almost complete control of the enterprise
through a court-ordered sale of the property. By acquiring
tax titles from Gunnison County, they were in a position to
demand payment of their claims, or other compensation, as a
condition for removing a major obstacle to Reynolds's plans
for consolidation and reorganization.[52]

After unsuccessfully challenging the tax titles in district
court, Reynolds entered into time-consuming negotiations
with the holders of the tax deeds. Fairness, he insisted, should
be the basis for cash purchases. From the Gunnison Bank and
Trust and several individuals he reclaimed ninety properties,
paying a bonus of 25 percent above the original cost of the
certificates. He was unwilling, however, to pay Eckbert and
Pearson what he labeled as exorbitant prices for their tax
titles. They asked, among other things, that he repurchase
400,000 shares of the Colorado Smelting and Mining Company's nearly worthless stock at a cost of $44,000 and pay a
bonus of 10 percent to redeem the titles. He did eventually
acquire the tax titles, but it is not clear what concessions he
had to make to Pearson and his associates in order to complete the transaction.[53]

The redemption of tax titles cost Reynolds and Barnsdall, who for all practical purposes were the owners of the Colorado Smelting and Mining Company, more than $30,000. Barnsdall contributed nearly $17,000, and Reynolds managed to provide $13,632 by some means or another. He was not altogether certain how he did so at a time when his financial affairs were in a shambles. This raised the amount of money the companies owed him, he informed Barnsdall, to $232,225. That debt accounted largely for his inability to meet the current needs of his other mining enterprises.[54]

The consolidation and reorganization were to have been the initial step in a plan to raise money to revitalize operations through the Gold Links Tunnel. The property was idle at the time. Work had been suspended in November 1912 because the company could not extract ore on a scale that permitted the operation of the mill at a rate that would generate income to pay all the expenses of extracting and processing ore.[55]

With a new company Reynolds had hoped to put the property in a condition to earn profits for the investors. By raising through the sale of stock sufficient money to mine from 100 to 150 tons of ore a day, he planned to run the mill at from two-thirds to full capacity. He estimated that if enough ore were mined daily to utilize all thirty stamps, the net profits to the companies would be on the order of from $20,000 to $25,000 a month. With an additional 4,000 feet of ground ahead, and the likelihood of striking four or more veins, the property would be, he believed, an attractive investment and would establish a record of consistent dividends. These plans were abandoned when he had to devote available time and money to redeeming portions of the holdings sold by Gunnison County officials for nonpayment of taxes.

In 1913, as soon as most of the tax deeds had been purchased, Reynolds, with Barnsdall's support, asked the Colorado secretary of state to revoke the Colorado Smelting and Mining Company's corporate charter. Three years later Reynolds petitioned the district court in Gunnison County for a judgment declaring that the firm was insolvent and authorizing its sale to satisfy creditors for unpaid debts. The assets of the firm were sold under judgment by the sheriff of Gunnison County in June 1917.[56]

That action gave Reynolds the satisfaction of thwarting the designs of his former associates. J. F. Pearson initiated the litigation, seeking payment of a claim for services plus interest amounting to $3700. As trustee for the stockholders of the Colorado Smelting and Mining Company, Reynolds filed a counterclaim for $43,000, representing payment of voluntary assessments on stock in previous years. He then brought suit in his own name in the amount of $239,000 for advances and payments of the company's bills, asking that all claims be prorated by the court. When the claims were combined, Pearson collected only $50, and the value of his stock, along with that of Fine and Eckbert, was reduced by 12 percent. In this way, Reynolds informed Barnsdall, he had squared accounts with the people who had used tax titles to jump claims.[57]

By purchasing the Colorado Smelting and Mining Company's assets, bidding the amount owed him as an individual and as trustee, Reynolds anticipated that he and Barnsdall could put the property in a condition to resume mining and milling operations. All that remained to be settled were fees arising from the litigation and the purchase of two dozen tax deeds for key properties in the Lime Belt. Reynolds's hopes were dashed when Barnsdall died in 1917. Robert Law Jr., Barnsdall's son-in-law and one of the executors of his estate, refused to put anymore money into Colorado mining schemes.

In an effort to pay expenses, Reynolds leased the mine and mill at Ohio City. Local residents Al Plewis, his son M. O. Plewis, and a Mr. Morris and his son extracted from the Gold Links Tunnel ore that was treated in the mill, operated by James E. Lyon at the portal. The returns to the company were negligible, but the lessees paid the taxes and performed the annual assessment work, as required by federal mining law, on unpatented claims.[58]

Interest in mining revived after the outbreak of World War
I in Europe. The conflict created an expanded market for a
variety of minerals, causing prospectors to examine once
again mining claims in and around Pitkin, Ohio City, and Tin
Cup. The manufacture of large quantities of weapons and
munitions stimulated a demand for the additives used to
make alloy steel, particularly tungsten and molybdenum.
Because both metals were found in the area, it appeared that
another mining boom was about to occur in southeastern
Gunnison County.[59]

For a brief time Isaac L. Johnson, the longtime lessee of the
Gold Cup Mine, experienced the new prosperity. While continuing to work properties on East Gold Hill south of Tin
Cup, he took advantage of the high price paid for molybdenum to organize the Bon Ton Leasing Company, which
purchased the Bon Ton group of mines located north of
Pitkin. The firm erected a mill on Quartz Creek to utilize the
oil flotation method to extract molybdenum and other metals.
The nearby Molybdenite Mine was also a producer of the
metal. However, the small volume of output did not warrant a
large expenditure for special processing equipment, and
production of the rare metal ended.[60]

For a brief time Tin Cup was the scene of a tungsten boom.
A discovery south of the mining town raised the possibility
that the Gold Cup Mine could yield tungsten as well as gold
and silver ore. As in the case of molybdenum, tungsten
production was short-lived. I. L. Johnson did not mine tungsten or, for that matter, much, if any, gold or silver ore. In fact,
during the war years Johnson made little progress on a tunnel
from Willow Creek to drain the lower depths of the Gold Cup
property.[61]

By creating renewed demand for silver, the war revived
interest in Gunnison County mines. From 1915 to 1919 the
price of silver approximately doubled to about $1.20 an
ounce, the highest it had been since long before the slump
brought on by the Panic of 1893 and the repeal of the

Sherman Silver Purchase Act. In 1920 the price fell to $0.85 an ounce, then climbed above $1 when Congress, by the terms of the Pittman Act, guaranteed a minimum price of $1 to domestic producers in order to replace some 290 million ounces melted down and sold to the United Kingdom during the conflict.[62]

Reacting to the revival of silver prices, Reynolds sought to sell the huge blocks of claims he controlled at Pitkin and Ohio City. The managers of the Chino Copper Company, with extensive properties in New Mexico, showed some interest in the Gold Links Tunnel. It is not known what value Reynolds placed on the property, but since the Raymond Tunnel was on the market for $600,000, his price was probably equal to that amount and perhaps even higher because the Gold Links had a better record of production. However, nothing came of this inquiry.[63]

The high price placed on the property probably did discourage prospective buyers. James E. Dick, agent for the Akron Mines Company at White Pine, southeast of Pitkin, thought that Reynolds was asking too much for the Gold Links Tunnel and mill. Dick examined the mine's surface areas and arranged with the caretaker to open the tunnel to permit inspection of the vein 2,150 feet from the portal. After making several visits to the property, Dick discontinued his investigation. He suggested it was worth no more than $250,000, one-half to one-third of the value that Reynolds placed upon it.[64]

Reynolds understood that the value of the properties on the Gold Links Tunnel could be properly tested only through systematic exploration, and that would require the application of a very large amount of capital, probably $150,000 or more. He had tried without success to raise the requisite capital in the past, and there was no reason to think that he could do so in the future. Nonetheless, he held firmly to the conviction that the properties at Ohio City, if not Chicago Park, would pay large returns if ample capital could be devoted to development and operations.

Recognizing that working the Gunnison County properties was out of the question, he tried to sell assets elsewhere. With the industry in decline and most of his mines idle and incapable of generating income, Reynolds offered to sell mines at Ouray, Creede, Summitville, and Platoro. The expense of upkeep on those properties was draining what little money he derived from leases. Other properties at Lake City as well as elsewhere in western Colorado added to his financial burden, for taxes had to be paid on patented claims even when they were inactive, and only costly annual assessments prevented unpatented claims from reverting to the public domain.

Above: Thoroughbred Hereford yearling heifers on the Reynolds Ranch, Channing, Texas, ca. 1900. *(Courtesy, Colorado Historical Society, neg. F36926)*

Below: Cutting alfalfa on the Reynolds farms, La Junta, Colorado, 1910. *(Courtesy, Colorado Historical Society, neg. 36932)*

Cutting wheat on the Reynolds farms near La Junta, Colorado, 1910. *(Courtesy, Colorado Historical Society, neg. F36931)*

7
Decline of the Mining Industry

By 1900 or shortly thereafter the mining of precious metals in Colorado had entered a period of decline that continued, with only brief interruptions, throughout the twentieth century. The prosperity that A. E. Reynolds had taken for granted in the 1890s vanished for a number of reasons. High-grade deposits of gold and silver ores were largely worked out, and many mines that had reputations as large producers of dividends for investors ceased production or were turned over to lessees in the hope that royalties would pay the cost of upkeep, including taxes. Silver mines suffered an additional burden as persistently low prices worked against the prospect of profitable operations on low-grade ores. Mineowners faced rising costs for milling, in part because of the need for investment in increasingly sophisticated and costly equipment to save mineral values. Sources of capital dried up as people with money turned to manufacturing and commercial enterprises that promised larger, more consistent returns on investments.

As Colorado's foremost mining entrepreneur, Reynolds experienced declining activity and income in the twentieth century. The Virginius Mine, access to which was through the Revenue Tunnel, was largely mined out above the tunnel level and paid its last dividends in 1901. The Commodore Mine at Creede, another large producer of silver, paid its last double-digit dividends in 1901, and subsequent returns to investors, twelve in the next fourteen years, averaged only 2.5 percent annually. Other properties at Summitville, Platoro, Lake City, Aspen, and Boulder County as well as in other states failed to live up to Reynolds's persistently optimistic expectations. Adverse conditions did not deter Reynolds from continuing his quest for the elusive bonanza. There was, he insisted, another Virginius or Commodore somewhere in western Colorado waiting to be discovered. This conviction was reinforced when Reynolds experienced two brief successes: a gold mine near Hesperus, west of Durango, and a silver-copper producer on Engineer Mountain between Lake City and Ouray. These were profitable, but they were not equal to the big mines of earlier years and were exceptions at a time when most of Reynolds's properties were shut down or in the hands of lessees. He remained convinced throughout his final years that if he could raise the capital for systematic, large-scale exploration and development, most, possibly all, of his mines would be capable of yielding handsome profits to investors.

After Hubbell Reed relocated to Salt Lake City in 1901, Reynolds decided to dispense with a superintendent and assumed personal direction of mining on the claims astride the Revenue Tunnel. Ed Krisher and H. Y. Russell, foreman and engineer, respectively, carried out Reynolds's instructions, but they were hampered by lack of funds because most of the available money had been devoted to the building of a coal-fired, steam-generating electrical plant in Ouray and a transmission line to the tunnel at Sneffels.

Prior to resigning, Reed had directed the sinking of a shaft from the tunnel level to a depth of 700 feet. Since the area above the tunnel had for the most part been worked out, nearly all profit-making ore having been removed, the company's future depended on following the vein downward. Hoisting ore and pumping water required power in excess of the combined output of the hydroelectric plants on Canyon Creek. For that reason a power plant was erected in Ouray.[1]

By the time the generating station was completed, Reynolds had temporarily abandoned plans to work below the tunnel. Instead, he drove the Revenue adit south along the Montana vein, while from the Telluride side the Ophir Tunnel he advanced to the north, also along the Montana vein, the objective being a passageway from one side of Mount Sneffels to the other. The adits penetrated low-grade ore that supplied the mills at each portal. A rise from the Revenue and a winze from the Ophir, the combined effort traversing 670 feet, were completed in 1902.[2]

Although work on the tunnels was funded largely out of operations, additions to the Revenue Mill and the electric plant created a heavy burden of debt that the company had little prospect of paying at the current level of operations. In an effort to keep the firm solvent, Reynolds asked stock-holders to make a voluntary contribution of $0.06 a share. The failure of that effort convinced Reynolds that he should seek a sale of the property. In September 1902 he gave a three-month lease and an option to the Guggenheim Exploration Company, asking $2 million for the Revenue Tunnel Mines Company. After a careful investigation of property above and below the tunnel, Daniel Guggenheim declined to complete the purchase.[3]

The future of the Revenue Tunnel Mines Company remained uncertain until August 1904, when miners struck a rich ore body 500 feet below the tunnel. In two years the returns on the ore amounted to more than $836,000, from which profits of more than $206,000 enabled Reynolds to pay creditors, including a large debt with the Thatchers' banks in Ouray and Pueblo. Good times vanished before the close of the year 1906, as the ore body weakened and finally disappeared. When production failed to pay expenses, Reynolds halted operations.[4]

In early 1907 Reynolds, with Thatcher's approval, leased the property to employees. Krisher agreed to take the lease only if he could divide the ground into blocks, which were subleased to the men who had been working in the mine. This proved to be rewarding to all parties, particularly the company, for it earned nearly $15,000 in royalties over a period of less than a year and a half. Reynolds ended that arrangement in 1908 when the incline between the Ophir and Revenue Tunnels threatened to collapse because the lessees had failed to maintain it in proper condition.[5]

Determined to generate income from the property to pay mounting debts, Reynolds hired Edwin H. Platt, a mining engineer, to serve as superintendent of the Revenue Tunnel Mines Company. Platt conducted operations on a large scale until his hard-driving management techniques alienated employees, causing the majority, mainly Italian and Slavic immigrants, to demand their pay and to go down the hill. Platt was ecstatic, for he disliked what he called "dagoes" and Austrians. After replacing the immigrants with native-born Americans, he noted in a letter to Reynolds that it was gratifying to hear conversations in English. It was, however, a pyrrhic victory, for he acknowledged that the new employees would not stay for any length of time. Furthermore, they were far less efficient than the workers who had walked off their jobs.[6]

The walkout exacerbated already critical financial problems. In order to forestall legal action by creditors, Reynolds arranged to acquire, at a cost of $300,000, Mahlon Thatcher's stock, after which the Revenue Tunnel Mines Company, a Colorado corporation, was sold through an exchange of stock to a new corporation, the Revenue Tunnel Mines Company of Wyoming. The successor enterprise, formed in 1911, with Reynolds controlling more than 90 percent of the capital stock, acquired all of the assets of the older firm and emerged from the transaction free of most of the debts that had plagued operations at Ouray for several years.[7]

After the reorganization Reynolds was even more determined to sell the property on Mount Sneffels. He granted to W. E. Wheeler, a Telluride banker, a two-year option to offer the enterprise to the London Exploration Company, the operator of the Tom Boy Gold Mining Company at Telluride, for $750,000. When nothing came of that effort, Reynolds offered the property to William J. Cox, manager of the neighboring Camp Bird Mine. Once again a sale failed to materialize, leading Reynolds to conclude that the price placed on the property was unrealistic; that is, it far exceeded any estimate of value that could be derived from an examination of the property.[8]

Nonetheless, Reynolds's objectives in placing the property on the market were partially fulfilled. In 1911 the Tom Boy Company, through its parent organization in London, bought ten claims on the Telluride side of Mount Sneffels, those served by the Ophir Tunnel, paying $445,000. This enabled Reynolds to redeem the notes he had given to Thatcher for Revenue stock and to pay off most of the corporation's outstanding debts. Momentarily the company enjoyed financial solvency, a condition that could not last unless new ore bodies were discovered. For this reason Reynolds renewed his effort to sell the remainder of the property.[9]

Finally in May 1913 J. P. Sidwell, a Chicago businessman and president of the Atlas Mining and Milling Company, owner of the Atlas Mine and mill at Sneffels, made a firm offer to buy the Revenue Tunnel and related properties. The contract, initiated by Sidwell personally rather than as an officer of Atlas, called for the payment of $190,000 over a period of nearly two years. Sidwell made only one payment before his sudden death, and the company's directors were unwilling to honor the purchase agreement with Reynolds.[10]

Within a year after the Atlas contract failed, E. H. Platt, acting as agent for Reynolds, negotiated a sale of the property to British investors organized as the St. John Mines (Colorado). The contract, dated May 19, 1914, stipulated that the purchaser would pay $197,222.23 over a period of twenty-seven months for the Revenue Tunnel Mines Company, the Cumberland Mining Company, the Wheel of Fortune Mining Company, and related properties. Fifty percent of the money was to go to the Revenue Tunnel Mines Company, 30 percent to the Cumberland Mining Company, and 20 percent to the Wheel of Fortune Mining Company. As a large stockholder in each of the corporations, Reynolds anticipated substantial gains from the transaction.[11]

From Reynolds's view the sale was a way of getting out from under an enormous personal debt that had accumulated in recent years. Besides numerous small obligations, he owed three banks more than $286,000, secured by mining and other corporate securities. The Thatcher brothers' First National Bank of Pueblo carried $139,062.67 of that amount, followed by the First National Bank of Denver with $112,936,96, and the Denver National Bank with $34,473.82. An agreement with the banks dated April 26, 1915, pledged Reynolds's proceeds from the sale to the reduction of debts.[12]

That document indicated that Reynolds's personal interest in the properties would yield for him more than half of the proceeds from the sale. He owned 98 percent of the Revenue Tunnel Mines Company, for which St. John Mines had agreed to pay slightly more than $45,000. He also owned 85 percent of the Wheel of Fortune Mining Company and 20 percent of the Loyal Mining Company, each of which was to receive $40,000. He was to receive 39 percent of the $60,000 for the Cumberland Mining Company. In all Reynolds was to secure $116,000 from the sale, enough to pay off more than one-third of his bank debt in Colorado.

However, long-term financial relief remained as elusive as ever, for once again a sale of the Revenue Tunnel Mines Company was not completed. In part this was because Reynolds was unable to clear up the titles to all of the properties owned by the three companies. More important, the failure was largely attributable to World War I. When the government of Great Britain banned the export of funds, St. John Mines could not complete the purchase agreement. That firm made only two small two payments totaling $15,000. On December 21, 1916, the date when a payment of $50,000 was

due, the company defaulted. Reynolds offered the English
investors more time to complete the transaction, but they
decided to let the contract lapse.[13]

The decision to give up the property may have reflected, in
part, the diminished value of the Revenue Tunnel Mines
Company's property because of the loss of the mill to fire in
January 1915. At the time Superintendent Platt was convinced
the company would seize upon the loss to break the contract.
Instead, the company negotiated a modification of the purchase agreement, by the terms of which the loss of the mill,
valued at $20,000, was to be shared equally by the buyer and
seller. Reynolds's share was to be deducted from the final
payment for the property.[14] However, without amalgamation
plates and concentration machinery there was no way to
process the large volume of low-grade ore produced from
properties on the tunnel. It was only a question of time until
St. John Mines forfeited the contract.

The manner of termination was, in Reynolds's view, highly
questionable, although within the terms of the contract. On
December 20, one day before the default, officials of St. John
Mines demanded of Reynolds the sum of $3,000, which he
had agreed to provide for improvements on the properties.
Without waiting for a response, the British officials appropri-
ated that amount from money Reynolds had made available to
E. H. Platt at Ouray for payments to local creditors. In
addition, the company retained approximately $12,000 from
the sale of materials salvaged from the fire-gutted mill. That
money, Reynolds contended, belonged to him. He retaliated
for these high-handed tactics by placing a hold order on
payments from smelters on ore. This enabled him to allocate
the money to the payment of bills that had been incurred in
producing the ore.[15]

Unable to sell the Revenue Tunnel, Reynolds turned his
attention to other properties. The Commodore Mine at Creede,
long a moneymaker for investors, suffered a sharp decline by
1905, yielding only small annual dividends for the next ten

years and, after 1915, none at all. The decline of operations at Creede was similar in many respects to what had happened to the Revenue Tunnel at Ouray.[16]

Convinced that the ground at and above the Commodore Tunnel was nearly mined out, Reynolds authorized the sinking of a shaft below the tunnel. A 450-foot incline was completed in April 1902, at which time the Commodore Mining Company sought leases from owners of adjoining properties. There was no response, leading Reynolds to conclude that neighbors were counting on the Commodore to pay all the expenses of pumping water from their properties in the course of draining its own. Unwilling to assume that burden, Reynolds redirected the Commodore's mining operations to higher ground and explored possibilities for acquiring properties outside of the district.[17]

In July 1902 Reynolds warned stockholders that if operations were limited to the tunnel level and above, the Commodore Mine would be exhausted in approximately two years. In order to perpetuate the company, he suggested, it was necessary to acquire additional properties. To that end he proposed that the enterprise increase its capitalization, using the newly authorized stock to buy mines at Creede or elsewhere.[18]

What he had in mind was a group of gold claims on Red Elephant Mountain in the Downieville Mining District, Clear Creek County, about 40 miles west of Denver. The Commodore Mining Company purchased more than two dozen claims from Frederick S. Stephen and Philip R. Stanhope, organized as the S. and S. Mining Company, giving 300,000 shares of Commodore stock for the properties in 1902. Stephen was the nephew of William Mackenzie, who headed the Alliance Trust Company in Dundee, Scotland. The Lawson Tunnel, named for a nearby community, was driven into the mountain a distance of more than 3,000 feet through hard granite. Three veins were cut, only one of which contained values large enough to pay for mining, and that proved impractical because of an excessive flow of water.[19]

The Lawson Tunnel was a failure. An expenditure of $175,000 over a period of two and a half years proved, Reynolds informed Stephen, that the ground was utterly worthless. Even when it was apparent that the search for gold would not succeed, Reynolds continued the effort an additional six months to complete a raise into the old workings of the White Mine. He wanted to test the accuracy of stories then circulating at Lawson that a large amount of valuable ore had been left in sight. At an additional expenditure of about $10,000, he proved that the rumors were groundless.[20]

The Lawson venture was the first of two properties outside of Creede in which Reynolds hoped to perpetuate the Commodore's operations. In December 1908 he arranged with J. B. and Frank L. Ross for a lease and purchase option on three-quarters of the Congress Gold and Copper Company's property at Silverton, San Juan County. He notified the Commodore stockholders that he had taken an option on the property, advancing $10,000, and that if an inspection indicated that the agreement should be canceled, he would personally refund the money to the treasury. After examinations by David G. Miller and H. Y. Russell, Reynolds terminated the agreement. Then the Commodore's future was tied to working the ground beneath the tunnel level, forcing Reynolds to revive the effort to consolidate the properties on the Amethyst vein.[21]

Plans for consolidation had been proposed by owners of adjoining properties, but these were not acceptable to Reynolds because he insisted that the Commodore Mining Company had to retain control of its own ground, through which access was possible at reasonable cost to the unworked ground below the tunnel level. While biding his time, Reynolds leased the upper workings in order to secure money to pay for the upkeep of the property and to pay small dividends annually to investors. In 1910 he ended the leases, and the company resumed working the mine. In 1915 Simon Guggenheim expressed an interest in the properties at Creede, suggesting that Reynolds again take up the question of consolidation with the owners of the other properties.[22]

This was finally accomplished in 1917 when, largely through the efforts of Denver attorney Gerald Hughes, the American Smelting and Refining Company arranged for a thorough test of the lower ground at Creede. Consolidation was accomplished by creating the Creede Exploration Company, one-fourth of which was owned by the Commodore Mining Company. The area was drained by pumping water from the Amethyst shaft. Within two years the effort failed. No ore of commercial value was discovered, and the company was liquidated. At that point lessees working the upper levels seemed sure to exhaust the mine within three years.[23] This left Reynolds no alternative but to pursue mining interests elsewhere.

Summitville and Platoro were potentially valuable properties, but both fell short of Reynolds's expectations. At Summitville he owned the Golconda Mining Company, whose claims encompassed nearly one-half of the mining district. Some of these had produced rich ore in the 1880s. Most of the remaining claims, including the famous Little Annie, were the property of the Consolidated Mining Company, usually called Consol, owned by Theodore N. Barnsdall. Reynolds and Barnsdall agreed to combine their properties but lacked the money to carry out the scheme, which called for extensive development, operations, and treatment of low-grade ores.[24]

It was the lack of high-grade ores and the need to concentrate most of what was available before shipment that doomed Reynolds's plans for Summitville. The remoteness of the site, approximately 30 miles southwest of Del Norte in Rio Grande County; heavy snowfall that isolated the community more than half of each year; and the high cost of transportation discouraged efforts to develop the properties. Equally disturbing, the fine gold embedded in quartz, carried in the predominant copper ore, could not be concentrated efficiently with available technology. Only a fraction of the gold could be saved, not enough to pay for the cost of mining, milling, and transportation to smelters at Durango or Pueblo.[25]

In an effort to find an effective method for processing the abundance of low-grade ores, Reynolds turned for help to anyone who professed to have the necessary technology. The American Concentrator Company, Joplin, Missouri, tested 4 tons of Summitville ore in January 1902 without coming up with an effective method of treatment. When John Philip Schuch, operator of an ore sampler at Cripple Creek and vice president and general manager of the Hartford Gold Extraction Company, claimed to have the right method for saving all the gold in ore from the Golconda, Reynolds eagerly allowed him to conduct tests at Summitville. Schuch claimed that his experiments with cyanide to leach gold from the ore were successful, but a fight with associates within the Hartford company for control of the enterprise prevented him from erecting and operating a mill at the mine. Reynolds canceled the experiments and leased the property in the hope that royalties would cover most, if not all, of the expenses of the property's upkeep.[26]

Efforts to make a mine at Platoro were equally unsuccessful. The mining claims in Conejos County had been idle for at least a decade when, in 1904, Reynolds was asked if he wanted to sell the two groups of claims that made up the Forest King and Parole Mines. Although nothing came of that inquiry, it did prompt Reynolds to ask David M. Hyman about putting his Mammoth Mine into an option agreement. Four years later, when looking for a property that could be developed and marketed to eastern investors, Reynolds asked friends who owned stock in the Forest King and the Parole Mining Companies to join him in securing a lease and option on the Mammoth and to underwrite construction of a mill if the ore in sight justified that investment. David G. Miller, Reynolds's trusted engineer, completed a careful inspection of the Mammoth vein that traversed all three properties. Assays of samples revealed that the values were not there.[27] Disappointed, Reynolds looked elsewhere for a productive mine.

He found what he wanted near Hesperus, La Plata County. In May 1903 three prospectors located the May Day, Gold Rule, Cimarron, and Kenton claims on the La Plata River about 12 miles west of Durango. They worked the May Day vein at the surface in a crude and indifferent manner until October of the same year and sold their interest to Charles E. McConnell, a Durango banker who was A. E. Reynolds's brother-in-law, and to David G. Miller, who was superintendent of the Commodore Mine at Creede. The purchasers attempted unsuccessfully to raise money to pay for the property and its development before asking Reynolds for financial assistance.[28]

He organized the May Day Gold Mining Company in December 1903. A Colorado corporation, it had an authorized capital of $3 million in shares of $1 par value, two-thirds of which were acquired by Reynolds and T. N. Barnsdall. The Pennsylvania oilman advanced the money to complete the purchase. Reynolds insisted on returning to the company's treasury 20 percent of the issued stock, the sale of which provided funds for development and operation.[29]

The May Day was developed according to Reynolds's high standards for economical operation. Under Miller's immediate supervision an incline shaft was sunk on the vein to a depth of 170 feet. On encountering water, Miller, with Reynolds approval, installed a power plant to operate mechanical drills in driving two crosscut tunnels, one for a distance of 800 feet, the other for 2,100 feet. The upper adit cut the vein at a distance of 750 feet, 180 feet below the bottom of the shaft. The second, 400 feet below the first, intersected the vein at a distance of 1,782 feet. From both portals wire tramways carried ore to storage bins at a railway switch.[30]

The mine, on the west side of the La Plata River, did not have immediate access to rail transportation. In order to secure room for operating facilities, the company purchased on the opposite bank the Golden Rule Placer claim and a portion of the Towne homestead. Erected on that land were a rail terminal for a switch that ran to the Denver and Rio Grande Southern Railway, an ore dump, storage bins, and a boardinghouse for seventy-five to one hundred men.[31]

The May Day was a moneymaker. It paid its way from the start. The shaft was sunk through shipping-grade ore, the proceeds of which contributed to repaying Barnsdall for the cost of the property and for improvements. The May Day was, according to Reynolds, "one of the best little things" he had ever taken hold of. Ore, mined in large quantities at small cost, was worth from $30 to more than $100 a ton. The cost of mining, freight, and treatment at the smelter, only 16 miles away, did not exceed $15 a ton. It cost only about $0.06 to produce $1 of gold.[32]

In all the company paid sixteen consecutive monthly dividends of $10,000 and four extra dividends of the same amount. Barnsdall was fully reimbursed for money advanced to buy the property, and he earned in addition $0.2875 on each of 260,000 shares that had originally cost him $0.125 and $0.875 on an additional 130,000 shares that had cost him nothing. The big production from the mine ended by the close of 1907, but some activity continued for the next several years.[33]

After that year mining was confined largely to adjacent properties. In 1906 Reynolds, in behalf of the May Day company, had purchased by an exchange of stock controlling interest in the Chief Mining Company when it appeared that the May Day vein extended beyond the limits of the original claims. This proved to be incorrect, and much to Reynolds's annoyance, some two hundred stockholders in the Chief Mining Company, after enjoying the rewards of the May Day's initial output, showed no interest in making voluntary assessments to revive the mine after it had fallen on hard times.

Determined to breath new life into the enterprise, Reynolds bought adjacent claims, including the Pay Day and the Midnight groups. In January 1911 he joined his brother Charles and David G. Miller as incorporators of the Pay Day

Mining Company, which worked through the May Day Mine to extract ore from the rich Idaho vein. This activity prompted legal action by the Pueblo people who owned the Valley View Consolidated Mining Company. A suit in federal district court dragged on for two years before Reynolds's claims in behalf of the Pay Day Mining Company were upheld. In 1915 Reynolds sold all of the claims originally acquired from the Chief Mining Company to the Valley View Consolidated Mining Company and used the funds to underwrite development of the remaining property. The Idaho vein was lost because of a geological fault, and efforts to find it were unsuccessful. The May Day property was shut down in November 1915 and remained idle for several years.[34]

In 1907, at a time when the May Day vein appeared to be approaching exhaustion, Reynolds decided to reopen the Frank Hough Mine in Hinsdale County. Located at 12,200 feet above sea level on the north side of Engineer Mountain, the mine had not been worked since the early 1880s, when it was owned jointly by Reynolds, Henry C. Thatcher, John H. Maugham, and John S. Hough. Production ended in 1884. That year John A. and Mahlon D. Thatcher acquired the interests of their deceased brother, and those of John Maugham, in settlements of Maugham's debts owed the Pueblo bank. The property was inactive until Reynolds decided to reopen it in 1907.

After securing a lease and purchase option from the Thatchers, Reynolds organized the Frank Hough Mining Company to work four claims through the refurbished shaft of the old mine. Money for this purpose was secured as a loan from the May Day Gold Mining Company to the Frank Hough Mining Company, plus the sale of stock to eastern investors. Reynolds's goal was to evaluate the vein at the 400-foot level by means of a drift, with a winze to a depth of another 100 feet to determine if the quality and quantity of the ore body justified a tunnel from the Ouray side of Engineer Mountain to intersect the vein.[35]

For three years Reynolds remained hopeful that the Frank Hough would develop into the big mine he needed to take the place of the Virginius-Revenue and the Commodore. During that time the mine earned $153,000 from ore returns, and the prospect of even larger production encouraged Reynolds to commence work on the tunnel. His hopes for the Frank Hough were dashed when the surface structures were destroyed by fire in January 1911 and the shaft collapsed. Unfortunately, development on the vein had not advanced to the point where Reynolds and his associates could say with any degree of certainty that the quality and quantity of the ore body justified an expenditure of at least $40,000 to complete the Frank Hough Tunnel. For that reason the mine was abandoned.[36]

After the loss of the Frank Hough Mine, Reynolds reexamined some of his older properties. In Hinsdale County and elsewhere he owned numerous mines that had not been worked for many years. Some of these, he believed, had potential as producers of gold or silver ore if he could mobilize the capital to develop and operate them on a large scale.

The Ocean Wave Mine near Lake City was, in Reynolds's view, a worthy investment. It had been opened in 1876 by Kansas City, Missouri, investors, including Howard M. Holden, a prominent banker. It shut down in 1880 and remained idle for many years. The mine had been productive, but the company suffered from bad management. It made the mistake of erecting a smelter to treat the mine's output, unaware that the locality did not produce the mix of ores needed to assure the furnace's success.[37]

Convinced that the Ocean Wave ore body continued downward, Reynolds proposed to cut it with a tunnel driven to a point 500 feet below the bottom of the shaft. In 1899, with financial backing from eastern friends, he bought the property from Holden and organized the Ocean Wave Mining and Reduction Company. As president and major stockholder Reynolds hired J. J. Abbott, a local engineer, to drive the tunnel a distance of 1,500 feet, where it was expected the ore body would be intersected. After advancing only 1,200 feet, work was suspended in 1901 because the company had exhausted its funds. The property remained idle for more than a decade.[38]

In 1914 Reynolds reached an agreement with his cousin Frank Van Horn, who had been foreman of the Commodore Mine, to continue work on the Ocean Wave Tunnel. Van Horn was to expend $25,000, for which he was to be compensated from returns on ore and $25,000 in company shares. Ore extracted in driving the tunnel amounted to only $759, and Van Horn spent $34,000 in two years without reaching the vein. Two years later, still short of the ore body, Reynolds finally shut down the Ocean Wave Tunnel, and it remained idle during the remainder of his lifetime.[39]

When the Ocean Wave Mine proved unproductive, Reynolds turned his attention to other enterprises in the Lake City area. These included the Argenta, Golden Fleece Extension, Lake View, and Palmetto Mining Companies, in all of which he owned large interests. These properties had been inactive for years, and their value was largely unknown.

The Argenta Mining Company, originally incorporated by Reynolds and M. D. Thatcher in December 1890, owned mining claims that gave it control of valuable waterpower sites on the Lake Fork of the Gunnison River. This enterprise was the successor to an English firm, the Argenta Falls Silver Mining Company, whose assets the Coloradans purchased at public sale. In this way they gained control of potentially valuable mining claims, including the Belle of the West, Minerva, and Western Belle. The Minerva encompassed Argenta Falls, a potentially valuable source of waterpower between Lake San Cristobal and Lake City.[40]

Reynolds, in behalf of the Argenta Mining Company, secured permits to develop the waterpower of the lake and the falls. It was reported in 1900 that he had acquired all properties around the lake with the intention of raising the water level at least 11 feet. The objective was to increase the flow of water for generating electricity to Lake Fork, Capitol City, Lake City, and several mines on Henson Creek.[41]

According to the same report, Reynolds planned to use the power to operate an electric tramway from Lake City, the terminus of the Denver and Rio Grande Railroad, up Henson Creek to mines on Engineer Mountain. By reducing the cost of transporting ore from Capitol City to Lake City, a distance of 10 miles, from $10 per ton by teams and wagons to $2 a ton by rail, Reynolds's scheme was certain to encourage the reopening of several mines. These included the Lelle, Vermont, Czar, Moro, Independence, Yellow Medicine, and Frank Hough.

If the report was correct, for some unknown reason Reynolds did not complete plans for the waterpower or tramway projects. However, in 1904 he encouraged the Argenta Mining Company to join with two nearby enterprises in which he was a large stockholder, the Golden Fleece Extension Mining Company and the Lake View Gold Mining and Milling Company, to consolidate all or part of their mineral holdings with the Golden Fleece Consolidated Mining Company, of which Thomas B. Stearns was president. A prominent Denver engineer, Stearns controlled the Hinsdale Mining and Development Company, operator of a hydroelectric plant at Crooke's Falls, below Argenta Falls on the Lake Fork of the Gunnison River.[42]

The consolidating enterprises received for distribution to stockholders one-fiftieth of the Golden Fleece Consolidated Mining Company's 1 million shares. Reynolds and Thatcher each acquired slightly more than 9,000 shares, while J. J. Abbott claimed more than 2,000. These would have been valuable holdings if Stearns had found a market for the waterpower potential of Argenta and Crooke's Falls. Because of the region's sparse population and the decline of mining activities after the turn of the century, Stearns's project was limited to a small plant at Crooke's Falls, from which the town of Lake City derived it electricity.[43]

Nearly twenty years later Stearns, with the approval of a majority of stockholders, transferred the waterpower rights of the Golden Fleece Consolidated Mining Company to the Golden Fleece Mining and Milling Company. Incorporated in Colorado in August 1919, the new firm had as its president J. L. Hulen, a western mining entrepreneur who had allegedly made a fortune from marketing potash. He planned to construct an enlarged hydroelectric plant and use the power to work mining claims. The surplus electricity was to be sold to consumers, public and private, throughout the region. This venture was no more successful than its predecessor, with the result that Reynolds's dream of harnessing the enormous power potential of Lake San Cristobal and the falls on the Lake Fork of the Gunnison was never realized.[44]

Disappointments became the rule, not the exception. Reynolds's other mines in Hinsdale County were unproductive, as were those near Aspen in Pitkin County. Except for some stock in the Smuggler Mining Company, he had disposed of his interests in David M. Hyman's properties by the 1890s. He remained, however, the principal stockholder in two groups of mines at Highlands, above Aspen. The Tarifa and the Etcetera groups, adjacent mining claims, had been located by brothers John W. and McKay Robinson, local miners who had worked some of David M. Hyman's mines at Aspen. Reynolds, with J. W. Robinson and associates, incorporated the Tarifa Mining Company in 1892 and the Etcetera Mining Company in 1893. The principal investors, except for Reynolds, were eastern participants in the Aspen Pool, which had funded the apex suit that had pitted Hyman and Reynolds against Jerome B. Wheeler and others.[45]

The two companies owned ground that contained low-grade silver ore in combination with lead. Extraction was to be through the Tarifa Tunnel, but at a distance of about 1,800 feet a heavy flow of water wrecked the mine. The loss halted operations, and the Tarifa property was abandoned. Discouraged, the investors gave up on the Etcetera. Reynolds lost the nearly $15,000 that he had advanced the two companies. The Hurricane Mining and Milling Company took a lease and option on the Etcetera in 1918 but made no payments in the next three years.[46]

The only other Colorado properties were in San Juan and Boulder Counties. In the vicinity of Silverton Reynolds owned one-fifth of the Eastern Star Group, comprising four lode mining claims, and one-eighth of the American lode mining claim. These properties had no record of production. Reynolds stopped paying taxes after a number of years. In 1912 the owners of the adjoining Polar Star claim brought the Eastern Star group through a tax deed. Reynolds's investment plus interest, amounting to almost $10,000, remained on his books at the time of his death in 1921.[47]

Equally unproductive were properties in Boulder County. In 1898 Reynolds bought the Eagle Bird claim at Caribou, once a large silver-producing camp. In the next four years he acquired adjacent properties, including a fraction of the American Flag claim and two-thirds of the Josie Mansfield placer. The total cost of all the claims was about $40,000.[48]

In 1915 Reynolds gave a lease and option on the Boulder County properties. Henry R. Lowe offered $47,500 for the claims, through which he proposed to drive a long tunnel to reach the Caribou vein. Lowe also secured an option on adjoining property owned by T. W. Barnsdall but failed to carry out the ambitious scheme. Reynolds's Caribou property remained inactive during the remainder of his lifetime.[49]

The several mining claims that Reynolds owned or controlled in other western states held little promise of development because of the depressed mining industry. Two properties were in Arizona Territory. The Black Prince group at Chloride, near Kingman, was, in Reynolds's view, a potentially valuable property. So convinced was he of the outcome that he organized the Black Prince Mining Company in 1899, even before Colin Timmons had completed the sinking of a shaft to a depth of 250 feet. Reynolds, along with his eastern friends who had invested in the enterprise, was disappointed when Timmons failed to find gold ore in quantities that justified further development.[50]

A similar outcome occurred with the Big Four group near Prescott, Arizona Territory. The four claims had been acquired by Frederick S. Stephen and Philip R. Stanhope in the name of the S. and S. Mining Company in 1901. Subsequently the partnership proved unworkable, and they transferred two-thirds of the property to Reynolds in September 1902. Reynolds held onto this interest and continued to pay taxes on the claims until 1916, even though he derived no income from them.[51]

A venture in New Mexico Territory was equally unsuccessful. Reynolds, along with Charles F. McKenney, J. A. Thatcher, and Charles J. Hughes Jr., invested $1,500 in the Iron Mask claim, Moreno Mining District, Colfax County, in 1898. They did so to assist Newton J. Thatcher, who had been instrumental in developing David M. Hyman's mines at Aspen during the celebrated apex suit of the 1880s. There is no evidence that Reynolds and his associates received any return on their investment or that they retained any long-term interest in the property.[52]

A similar outcome occurred with a copper property in Utah. In the spring of 1899 Byron L. Shear and Isaac L. Johnson, with whom Reynolds had been associated in numerous ventures, asked him to advance $3,000 to initiate development of unpatented claims in Bingham Canyon. Unknown to Reynolds, his associates had secured an option on the Rob Roy group, on which they spent a large amount of money for development. In an effort to ascertain the worth of the property, Reynolds sent Hubbell W. Reed to make an investigation and to assess needs for additional work. He recommended further development of the Rob Roy Tunnel.[53]

In November 1899 Reynolds, reacting to rising costs that appeared to be out of control, sent David G. Miller to Utah to pay all outstanding obligations and to close the mine. The cost of this ill-fated venture to Reynolds was never fully calculated. However, he invested in development substantially more than the amount original advanced to Shear and Johnson, and the Utah property earned no income.[54]

Reynolds added a second copper property, located near Ely, Nevada, to his mining empire in 1907–1908. He became the principal owner of eight mining claims located 2.5 miles west of Ely, Nevada, when he rescued his wife's brother-in-law Charles E. McConnell from the embarrassment of a bank failure and the threat of criminal action by disgruntled depositors. As part of the settlement with creditors Reynolds completed payments on McConnell's purchase option and became the majority stockholder in the Ely-Revenue Copper Company, incorporated in Colorado in 1907.[55]

Efforts to sell the property were unsuccessful. Numerous leases and purchase options were given, but none was completed. The debt-ridden enterprise added to Reynolds's burdens at a time when his own finances were in a shambles. His only long-term investment in mining property outside of the United States was nonproductive of needed revenues. In 1889 Reynolds, with Charles D. Arms, a Youngstown, Ohio, businessman; Myron H. Beach; and Harris A. Wheeler, organized the Colorado Exploration and Mining Company, which acquired mining claims in Thunder Bay District, Ontario Province, Canada. Beach, a Chicago attorney, handled the mine's affairs. Wheeler, who had served in the army in Indian Territory, was president and superintendent of the Michigan Military Academy, Orchard Lake, Michigan. Wheeler was the largest stockholder, owning 42 percent of the stock. Reynolds held 30 percent, probably in an effort to assist Wheeler in making a success of the venture.[56]

In this he was disappointed. The company owned 688 acres of land that contained silver and iron ore deposits. Located on the north shore of Lake Superior approximately 200 miles northeast of Duluth, Minnesota, the property was largely wilderness. Before the enterprise could develop the mineral potential of the land, the Panic of 1893 caused the collapse of the price of silver. Thereafter efforts to promote a sale of low-grade iron ore deposits were consistently unsuccessful. Reynolds and Wilford Arms, the son and heir of Charles Arms, divided the cost of paying unpaid taxes in 1912 and agreed to share that expense in the future. However, Reynolds lacked the funds to meet that commitment, and the taxes were nearly ten years in arrears at the time of his death in 1921.[57]

Unable to derive income from potentially profitable but largely idle mining properties, Reynolds turned to real estate promotion. When that venture only added to his debts, Reynolds, dogged by persistent adversity, turned again to mining. He was convinced that there was yet another bonanza of gold and silver awaiting discovery in western Colorado, and he was determined to find it.

8
End of a Career

As Colorado mining activity declined in the first decade of the twentieth century, A. E. Reynolds turned his attention more and more to the development of land he owned in the Arkansas River valley, most of it across the river from and east of the community of La Junta. That property, comprising approximately 3,000 acres, was initially devoted to feeding and preparing for sale thoroughbred Hereford calves shipped from Reynolds's ranch in the Texas Panhandle. Following the sale of the ranch and the construction of the Fort Lyon Canal, which provided irrigation water for all but a small fraction of the property, Reynolds decided to subdivide and offer farms for sale. He sold some to farmers and speculators on long-term contracts, but some of the new owners defaulted on their mortgages when revenues from crops did not equal the annual payments. Reynolds repossessed the farms and eventually sold most of them to German immigrants who had come to the area to work in sugar beet fields.

As a post trader at Fort Lyon, at Las Animas, Colorado Territory, Reynolds gained his first impression of the agricultural potential of the Arkansas River valley. The fertile soil of the river bottom, with accessible water for irrigation, had great potential for growing crops. After leaving the area to establish stores in Indian Territory, he seized upon the opportunity to acquire tracts of land near the military post where he had been a resident-merchant from 1867 to 1869. He probably bought tracts of 640 acres with the intent of marketing them at a profit. It is unlikely that at that time he thought about the possibility of utilizing the land for farming or ranching.

In 1870, after the Cheyennes and Arapahoes had relocated to Indian Territory, the mixed-bloods who lived with the tribes were awarded land in the Arkansas valley by the U.S. government. By the terms of the Treaty of Fort Wise, October 14, 1865, each mixed-blood was entitled to claim one section, or 640 acres. The government issued patents for numerous Indian claims along the north side of the Arkansas River, covering, according to Reynolds, a large percentage of the land from La Junta to the Colorado-Kansas line.

Some of the claims were in the vicinity of a canal that had been excavated by the Bureau of Indian Affairs in 1864 to encourage the tribes to take up agriculture. The canal fell into disuse following the relocation of the Cheyennes and Arapahoes to Indian Territory. However, some of the choicest Indian claims were in the vicinity of the canal, which later qualified them for first rights to water from the Arkansas River.[1]

Among the thirty-one people who received patents for Indian claims were the mixed-blood children of William Bent, the proprietor of Bent's Fort on the Santa Fe Trail. As one of the commissioners who negotiated with the Arapahoes and Cheyennes, Bent was largely responsible for the Indian claims provision of the Treaty of Fort Wise. Of the Bent children, George, Charles, and Julia were well known to A. E. Reynolds. The two men and Ed Guerrier, Julia's husband, were clerks and interpreters in Lee and Reynolds's store at the Indian Agency, initially located at Camp Supply and later at Darlington. Through the Bents and Guerrier owners of Indian claims who wanted to sell their patents contacted Reynolds, who made numerous purchases. Some he acquired for friends and acquaintances; two he retained for himself.

In this way Reynolds became the owner of two sections of land near La Junta. Indian Claim B had been issued to Jenny Lind Crocker. Reynolds always referred to her as the widow

Crocker. Indian Claim 12 had been awarded to Armama (or Aramama) Smith, daughter of John Smith; an interpreter at Camp Supply; and his Cheyenne wife.[2]

The title to one of the properties remained in doubt for several years. Mary Bridget Campling, a resident of La Junta who claimed to be John Smith's niece, challenged Reynolds's right to Indian Claim 12. She produced a warranty deed, allegedly from John Smith's son, William Gilpin Smith, and charged that Reynolds's deed from Armama Smith was dated after the woman had died. Reynolds was convinced that William Gilpin Smith was a fraud, and although he knew that Armama Smith had legally conveyed the property and that she was still alive, he could not convince the court of the correctness of his position. Consequently the Colorado District Court for Otero County, following a hearing on the dispute in May 1893, ruled six months later that the property belonged to Campling.

That judgment was appealed. At a new trial in 1897 Reynolds offered the testimony of Ed Gurrier and Joe Weiglein, both of whom had worked in the agency store in 1870. They had taken Armama Smith to Dodge City and witnessed the conveyance of Indian Claim 12 to Reynolds by warranty deed in the presence of a justice of the peace. Furthermore, Armama submitted affidavits that she was alive and well in Oklahoma. In November the court reversed itself, ruling that Reynolds was the rightful owner of the disputed land.[3]

Indians claims were of little value until the 1880s, when irrigation systems were built in the Arkansas valley. According to the warranty deeds, Reynolds paid $1,500 for each of two sections, or $1.17 per acre, in 1870. This was a good price for unimproved land at the time. In May 1884 he offered to sell the two sections at $7 an acre, but there were no buyers at that price. Five years later he valued the land and water rights at from $20 to $25 per acre.[4]

By that date irrigation schemes were in fact under way near La Junta. In 1883 Otis L. Haskell, a Denver real estate pro-

moter, had incorporated the Arkansas River Land Town and
Canal Company with the goal of providing water for 300,000
acres. This plan was too ambitious for the time. Haskell
reorganized the corporation in 1886 and sold it the following
year. The new owners adopted the name La Junta and Lamar
Canal Company. When farmers failed to obtain the water for
which they had paid subscriptions, they organized a mutual
stockholding enterprise, the Fort Lyon Canal Company, in
July 1898. Litigation with the previous owners and the holder
of a mortgage on the canal was not resolved until 1903, at
which time the Fort Lyon Canal Company was declared the
owner of the canal and adjudicated water rights.[5]

The formation of the Fort Lyon Canal Company caused
Reynolds to reconsider the utilization of his land at La Junta.
Until 1899 he had used the property primarily for pasture
and for producing hay for feeding thoroughbred Hereford
calves and mixed-breed steers shipped from his ranch near
Tascosa, Texas. That year he instructed James H. Crosley,
who was the local manager, to convert some of the land to the
production of crops, which could be irrigated with water
from the Fort Lyon Canal. As he gradually phased out cattle
operations, Reynolds devoted most of the property to the
production of oats, wheat, and sugar beets.[6]

Unable to give personal attention to crop raising at La
Junta, Reynolds hired Crosley to farm the land. After leasing
additional land in 1900, Reynolds invited George W. Williams, the younger of two brothers who had been feeding
thoroughbred calves from the Texas ranch during the winter
months at Burdick, Kansas, to be his second farmer. Williams
moved to La Junta, starting a business relationship with
Reynolds that was to last more than twenty years.

The terms governing Williams's management of the leased
farm were spelled out in detail by his employer. Williams was
to be paid $40 a month and have the use of a house rent free,
but he was to provide his own board. Insofar as he was able, he
was to take charge of the farm, doing all of the plowing,

planting, tending to crops, and harvesting. Reynolds insisted that he was not hiring a "boss farmer to take charge and hire others." Furthermore, Williams was not to accumulate any private property, particularly livestock, that might mix with Reynolds's purebred calves.[7]

Before the close of 1900 Reynolds further expanded the size of his holdings at La Junta by purchasing what had been Indian Claim 13. That tract had been awarded originally to Julia Bent, who sold it to pioneer cattleman John W. Prowers. Prowers's heirs sold the land to Thomas H. Marshall, who, in turn, conveyed 1,221 acres to Reynolds in January 1901. Marshall sold the balance of the section to farmers who owned adjoining lands.[8]

The La Junta Farm, as Reynolds called the property, comprised 2,780 acres. Three hundred forty-five acres were bottomland south of the river and 8 miles east of La Junta. The remainder was north of the Arkansas (opposite La Junta) and from 3 to 5 miles east of the community. Some 2,150 acres were traversed by ditches that carried irrigation water from the Fort Lyon Canal. The tillable land was planted in alfalfa, wheat, oats, peas, and beans. After the construction of factories at Swink and Rock Ford, much of the land was devoted to the production of sugar beets. In addition, Reynolds owned, under Crosley's supervision, a herd of graded Hereford bull calves and another of high-grade calf steers at La Junta. Most of these animals had been transferred from the Panhandle ranch shortly after it was sold to the Prairie Cattle Company in 1902.[9]

The cattle remained at La Junta only a few years. Most were sold to breeders, and the remainder were transferred to the EJM Ranch near Delta. Edward J. Mathews had worked for Reynolds at the Panhandle ranch before locating at Montrose, Colorado, where he established a wholesale and retail grocery business. In addition, he was president of the Paonia Packing Company, canners of fruits and vegetables, and the E. J. M. Cattle Company. In 1916 Mathews sold the ranch and livestock and paid off the notes he had given Reynolds for cattle.[10]

The end of ranching operations at La Junta was prompted by Reynolds's decision to utilize more of the land for the production of crops. As a cost-saving measure Reynolds dismissed James H. Crosley as farm manager in 1904, at which time George W. Williams assumed direction of all farming operations. Under his management land formerly devoted to pasture and the production of hay was plowed under and planted in crops. By 1907, 400 acres were devoted to wheat, more than 200 acres to sugar beets, 40 acres to peas for hog food, and 100 acres to oats. In addition, there were seven orchards. The following year Williams tended more than two hundred hogs and about three hundred head of cattle. The latter were scheduled for relocation to western Colorado.[11]

In farming, as in mining, Reynolds insisted on applying advances in technology in an effort to increase the efficiency of operations. In order to prepare the land for tillable crops, Reynolds acquired a steam traction engine from the Lowell Steam Plow Company of Kansas City, Missouri. The 25-horsepower, double-cylinder engine, with a 32-inch drive wheel and a ten-bottom gang plow, water wagons, and other accessories, cost about $2,000. After one year, during which the engine performed satisfactorily, Reynolds traded it in for a 35-horsepower, double-cylinder engine to draw the ten-bottom plow. This proved to be adequate when the ground was moist, but when the soil was dry, the plow overloaded the engine. Reynolds's "engineer" solved that problem by substituting three gangs of 28-inch discs, which turned the soil to a depth of 7 inches, 5 more than the gang plow.[12]

Expanded crop production failed to yield a profit. Disappointed, Reynolds decided to sell the farm in 1906. This decision reflected, at least in part, a need for money to underwrite mining operations in Gunnison County and elsewhere. In fact, after failing to persuade New York financier Bernard M. Baruch to underwrite gold mining at Ohio City,

Reynolds borrowed from him $65,000 on a short-term note, using the La Junta farm as collateral. This money was used to drive the Gold Links Tunnel. However, when the mine failed to yield anticipated large profits, Reynolds, faced with Baruch's demand for repayment, had to find a new source of money.[13]

Through the efforts of Henry Wilcox and Son, Reynolds borrowed from Cornell University the money with which to repay Baruch. The loan, in the amount of $65,000, was for a period of eight years at 6 percent interest per annum. The note in that amount was secured by a mortgage on Reynolds's unsold La Junta farms and stock in the Fort Lyon Canal Company.[14] The contract was designed to encourage sales at La Junta. For all land sold in the future, Cornell University agreed to carry for purchasers mortgages at the rate of $50 an acre. Reynolds had to accept a second mortgage on the remainder of the purchase price if it exceeded $50 an acre.

Since it was unlikely one person could purchase all of the available land, Reynolds decided to subdivide it into smaller tracts of from 80 to 150 acres each. These he offered for sale with rights to water from the Fort Lyon Canal. Initially he named his brother Charles as the agent to handle all transactions. After Charles declined to relocate from Denver, Andrew J. Reynolds Jr., the oldest of A. J.'s three boys, for whom A. E. Reynolds had paid the cost of a law degree at Harvard, accepted the position and opened an office in La Junta.[15]

Sales promotions were undertaken throughout the Middle West in an effort to attract prospective buyers of farmland to La Junta. Traveling agents visited communities in Kansas, Nebraska, Missouri, Illinois, and Wisconsin to talk to people about buying irrigated farmland in the Arkansas River valley. Interested parties came as excursion groups by train to look at Reynolds's farms and at nearby land offered by various promoters of irrigation projects.[16]

The most successful of the traveling agents was S. A. Porter, who spent most of his time canvassing the southeastern counties of Nebraska. A high percentage of the excursions to

La Junta, and a large proportion of the buyers of Reynolds's farms, were from Lancaster, Cass, and Otoe Counties.[17] They resided in or near the towns of Bennett, Palmyra, Syracuse, Hickman, and Eagle.

Between 1910 and 1914 Reynolds's agents sold eleven of the twenty-one farms. Seven of the buyers were farmers, who lived on and worked the land. E. N. Eveatt, S. P. Stryker, J. G. Patterson, J. A. G. Strickland (two farms), George W. Williams, and J. J. Zook produced mainly grains, alfalfa, and sugar beets. After paying down one-fourth of the purchase price in cash, the farmers had to depend for the most part on income from crops to pay annual taxes, water assessments, and installments on principal, plus interest to Reynolds. Lack of water from the Fort Lyon Canal because of a three-year drought, recurring hail, and poor management doomed some of these efforts to failure.[18]

Four of the buyers—Dr. D. G. Gibbons, J. R. Megahan, J. D. Poe, and Dr. W. F. Trobitt—were speculators. They were business- and professional men who gambled that the farms would appreciate in value and could be sold at a profit at some future date. In the meantime they placed the operation of their farms in the hands of tenants on the assumption that the proceeds from crops would meet all of the annual expenses. In this they were disappointed. Drought, deficient irrigating water, recurring hail, and a lack of competent farmer-renters combined to deny them the income they had counted on, with the result that they, like the farmer-owners, fell in arrears on their payments.

In spite of a highly organized campaign, Reynolds sold only a little more than half of his farms. He attributed this lack of success, at least in part, to the fact that the farm units were unusually large and, by standards of that day, also very expensive. None contained fewer than 80 acres, and the largest was 150 acres. The minimum price for the land was $125 per acre, and some sold for $135, even $150 per acre. At that time most of the people who came to Colorado in search of irrigated farms were from the Middle West, and they wanted about 40 acres, for which they hoped to pay no more than $40 an acre. Numerous irrigation land companies, many in the Arkansas valley, that offered property of that size and price had agents on the trains from the East to steer prospective buyers to their projects. Some buyers bought dryland farms. Nonirrigated farms on the eastern Plains could be purchased from railroads at a fraction of the cost of irrigated land.[19]

Not only did Reynolds fail to dispose of all of his land at La Junta, but limited sales also failed to earn for him any profits. Almost all of the purchasers fell in arrears on their payments, forcing Reynolds to renegotiate their contracts. When defaults occurred, he often bought back portions of farms and in some instances took back all of the properties.

Because of buybacks and repossessions, fifteen of twenty-one farms were unsold in January 1915. In an effort to dispose of remaining properties, Reynolds entered into negotiations with the Catholic Colonization Society of Chicago. That organization, working with Bela A. Unger, a Hungarian immigrant salesman of boundless energy, proposed to place Belgian farmers on the ground. Although the colonization scheme failed, Reynolds authorized a joint effort by his nephew and Unger to place European farmers experienced in growing sugar beets on the La Junta property.[20]

The three men hoped to recruit Germans, recent immigrants from Russia, who lived in Chicago, Kansas, and elsewhere in the Middle West. In the course of their sales promotion they discovered at Rocky Fort, only 15 miles from La Junta, a group of so-called Germans from Russia who as renters of farms were experienced in the production of sugar beets on irrigated land. They were, according to Reynolds, men who knew how to work the land and make it pay.[21]

These people were the descendants of Germans artisans and farmers who had relocated to Russia at the invitation of Catherine the Great and her grandson in the eighteenth and nineteenth centuries to settle on the southern lands recently won from Turkey. The immigrants, people of many religious persuasions, were encouraged to develop Russia's agriculture, commerce, and industry. In return for establishing farms and villages in the middle Volga River valley and in the area north of the Black Sea, they were permitted to perpetuate their native culture, including their own language, schools, and religion, and were exempt from military service.[22]

Their descendants sought refuge elsewhere when, commencing in the 1870s, Czar Alexander II introduced a program of Russification that took away the right to perpetuate German culture. Because of this, and also because of the growing scarcity of land for agriculture, families sought new homes elsewhere, particularly in the United States, Canada, and Argentina. The first Germans who migrated to America in the 1870s were the vanguard of a wave of refugees, many of whom came to Colorado at the turn of the century. Opportunities for employment in the sugar beet fields of the Arkansas River valley attracted them to Rocky Ford, Crowley County, and to other parts of the state. Initially they rented land, but their long-term goal was to purchase their own farms and to create their own communities.

Eighteen or nineteen of the German families at Rocky Ford relocated in the fall of 1915 to farms that A. E. Reynolds had created by further subdividing unsold land. The units varied in size from 40 to 60 acres and sold for an average price of $125 per acre for irrigated land. They had little or no money to make a downpayment, in lieu of which Reynolds required that they erect houses for their families on their farms. They should have had income aggregating at least $15,000, perhaps as much as $20,000, from the sale of crops they had grown in Crowley County. Unfortunately, according to Reynolds, "they were cleaned out by hail," with the result that he had to advance from $500 to $1,000 to each family in order to move from Rocky Ford.[23]

The newcomers created a close-knit community dedicated to perpetuating their traditional culture. To this end they organized their own evangelical Lutheran church and a school in which some, if not all, instruction was in German. The original purchasers were John Blum, Peter Busch, George Dorsch, Henry Engelman, Philip Engelman, Jacob Erlich, Fred Freidenberger, Henry Hergengrader, Alex Herrman, Peter Kindsvater, George Lorenz, Jacob Maier, David Mayer, Henry Schimpf, Henry Schwein, Jacob Schwein, Henry Schweitzer, Henry Will, and Mikael Will.[24] At the request of the new farmers Reynolds advanced the money for the enlargement of the local school; the new addition provided rooms for German-language classes. He also donated land for St. Paul's Evangelical Lutheran Church and for a cemetery. The burial ground, he insisted, had to be accessible to people of all faiths.[25]

In an effort to derive immediate profit from land sales, Reynolds seized upon a suggestion by A. J. Reynolds, his nephew and agent, that the farmers seek loans from the federal government to pay for their land. A. J., with A. E.'s approval, organized the Bent's Fort Farm Loan Association, which applied to the new Farm Loan Bank in Wichita for loans on the farms purchased by the Germans from Russia. The bank approved twenty-four loans aggregating $85,900 for farms comprising 1,614.64 acres of land. The differences between the loans and the value of the contracts for the farms, plus unpaid advances for housing and cultivation of crops, were carried by Reynolds in the form of second mortgages. As of June 15, 1918, the second mortgages amounted to $110,758.77, the experiences of the previous three years suggesting that future returns would come in slowly, if at all.[26]

Reynolds's inability to secure full value from the sale of the La Junta farms contributed to the near collapse of his personal finances. He had counted on sales of his immense mining assets, but, with the exception of the Telluride properties, he had failed to earn any appreciable income from that source. Furthermore, at the very time that he was called upon to put

up more than $75,000 to save one of his wife's brothers-in-law
from the embarrassment of a bank failure, investment funds
that he had counted on for the development of mining
properties failed to materialize, and disappointing speculations in corporate securities absorbed what income he derived from other sources.

The Panic of 1907 was a key turning point in Reynolds's
personal fortunes. The disorder in the financial market,
although relatively brief, ended for Reynolds more than three
decades of prosperity and marked the start of what proved to
be a long and difficult effort to stave off financial collapse.
This turn of events was complicated by the failure of the two
public banks in Durango. When the Smelter City State Bank
closed its doors on December 7, 1907, irate depositors brought
criminal charges against President Charles E. McConnell for
allegedly accepting money on deposit after he knew that the
bank was insolvent.[27]

Reynolds acted quickly to save McConnell from the embarrassment of a public trial and imprisonment. To depositors
and others creditors Reynolds gave assurances that he would
work with them to minimize the impact of the bank's failure.
This may have made a settlement of the bank's affairs more
difficult, for it contributed to the view among some Durango
residents that Reynolds, a rich man, could raise any amount
of money in McConnell's behalf and would do so "for the sake
of family pride."[28]

Negotiations with a depositors' committee dragged on for
about a year. In November 1908 Reynolds and Richard Keller,
another of his wife's brothers-in-law, were presented with
three propositions, the first of which called for the issuance of
three-year, 5 percent notes to all depositors. The second
stipulated that depositors were to be paid one-half in cash
and one-half in the stock of the Ely-Revenue Copper Company, a Nevada mining enterprise that McConnell had acquired
with bank assets. The third required that deposits of $50 or
less be paid in cash and that all other depositors be paid 25

percent in cash, 37.5 percent in Ely-Revenue stock, and the balance in three-year, 5 percent notes. Only the last of the proposals was acceptable to Reynolds. This, with some modification, was eventually accepted by the bank's receiver and approved by the District Court for La Plata County.[29]

Reynolds and Keller agreed to underwrite the cost of settling the Smelter City State Bank's affairs. By the terms of an agreement dated November 28, 1908, Keller assumed 25 percent of the cost and Reynolds, the remainder. The total cost was more than $72,000. Of that amount Keller paid less than $12,000, leaving Reynolds to assume 85 percent of the cost. Nearly five years later Reynolds and Keller modified their original agreement, recognizing that in the division of assets remaining after the bank settlement, Reynolds was to have 85 percent and Keller, 15 percent. At issue was the stock of the Ely-Revenue Copper Company and scattered parcels of land.[30] The real estate, mostly in the vicinity of Farmington, New Mexico, was of little value at the time and contributed nothing to solving Reynolds's ongoing financial problems.

The Panic of 1907, which brought about the failure of McConnell's Durango bank, complicated Reynolds's business affairs in other ways. It delivered a severe blow to oilman Theodore N. Barnsdall's personal fortune and ended plans he had developed with Reynolds to pay for the large-scale operation of the Gold Links Tunnel at Ohio City and the combined Golconda-Consol properties at Summitville. By earlier supplying the $86,000 with which Reynolds purchased the May Day Mine, Barnsdall had earned dividends double the amount of his investment. This feat he hoped to repeat in Gunnison and Rio Grande Counties, but he was forced by creditors to devote available funds to the payment of debts.[31]

Reynolds was troubled by large personal debts of his own, the result, at least in large part, of speculation in corporate securities. Over a period of more than thirty years he had bought and sold large quantities of the common stocks of the New York Air Brake Company and the American Smelting and Refining Company. He had also gambled with Mexican Central Railway bonds and speculated in silver futures.[32]

The New York Air Brake stock proved to be highly volatile, subject to extreme short-term fluctuations, suggesting that it was manipulated by speculators. Initially Reynolds acquired stock in the enterprise because of a long-standing friendship with Charles A. Starbuck, president of the company. In time Reynolds concluded that with access to information from a top executive, he could anticipate fluctuations and make them work to his advantage. He may have profited in the short term from buying and selling New York Air Brake shares.

Between 1891 and 1912 Reynolds bought and sold more than 3,000 shares of New York Air Brake common stock. It is not clear that information from Starbuck enabled Reynolds to make money from speculation in the stock, but there were occasions when he bought cheap and sold later when the stock had advanced substantially in price. Some of this stock Reynolds purchased as a member of speculative pools, including 350 shares with his friend David M. Hyman and another 2,000 with Hyman and others.[33] It is certain, however, that whatever profits he may have gained from playing the market prior to 1907 were more than offset by losses after that date.

In the aftermath of the Panic of 1907 the price of New York Air Brake stock fell dramatically over a period of several months. In early May 1907 common was selling at $128 per share. After the summer's financial disturbance the price dropped to $93 in mid-October and to $50 before the end of the year. The stock remained unstable because the company did not pay dividends from October 1907 until July 1910.[34] Reynolds, who paid an average of $126.20 for his holdings, suffered substantial losses from which he never fully recovered.

The irony of Reynolds's speculation in New York Air Brake stock is that he assumed that profits from this activity would liquidate most, if not all, of his outstanding mining debts, which were very large by the first decade of the twentieth century. In fact, losses in the stock market compounded his financial problems. He owed Hyman alone more than $100,000. The first New York Air Brake stock pool, which Hyman sold out at ninety, resulted in a direct loss to Reynolds of more than $41,000, plus the numerous advances he had made over the years in margins to protect his interest in a falling market.[35]

Subsequently Reynolds purchased an additional 1,000 shares of New York Air Brake stock, which he turned over to Hyman as collateral for unpaid debts. When the company rebounded after the start of World War I in Europe, Hyman decided to sell the stock at $99 in early May 1915. Reynolds pleaded with him to wait, insisting that there was ample evidence that the price would advance beyond $100, probably as high as $125 or $150 within a few months. Reynolds was concerned, however, that the stock, whatever it price, pay his debt to Hyman, who would then return 75,000 shares of Commodore Mining Company stock, which he held as collateral.[36]

Hyman refused to delay the sale. The proceeds from that transaction wiped out Reynolds's debt and also gave him $3,175. Since he had advanced $20,000 in margins to protect the stock in previous years, his actual loss on the sale was in excess of $16,000. By September New York Air Brake stock was selling at $152.50, enough to have netted Reynolds a tidy profit of nearly $40,000 if the sale had been delayed.[37]

New York Air Brake advanced sharply in 1915 and continued to rise thereafter as the company's earning were augmented by the production of cartridge cases, fuses, and shells for Great Britain. This allowed the company to increase annual dividends from 6 percent in 1915 to 11.5 in 1916 and to 20 percent the following two years. Reynolds used the proceeds from dividends as well as the sale of some stock to pay a portion of what had become a staggering burden of debt. Collectively he owed the First National Bank of Pueblo, the

First National Bank of Denver, and the Denver National Bank more than $286,000 on loans that had been secured mainly with New York Air Brake stock. With the sale of the Revenue Tunnel Mines Company and related properties to the St. John Mines in 1915, Reynolds had pledged his share of the proceeds, more than $115,000, to the reduction of his bank debt. That transaction was aborted in 1916 because of conditions brought on by the world war, forcing him to hope for an advance in New York Air Brake stock to pay the banks.[38]

During the war years Reynolds eliminated a large share of his bank debt. In part he accomplished this because of the upward movement of New York Air Brake stock. He also gained a temporary windfall when the farms at La Junta were refinanced through the Federal Farm Loan Bank. However, this did not end his involvement with New York Air Brake securities. He continued to buy common shares, and, as events turned out, he held them until their depreciation in value threatened to rule out any possibility of recovering a major share of his original investment.

Speculation in this stock was a difficult habit for Reynolds to abandon. From 1916 to 1920 he maintained a separate account of 1,000 shares with his New York broker, A. A. Hausman and Company. The stock remained relatively stable in 1916, but in the following year reverted to its usual pattern of erratic behavior. By November 1917 Hausman was threatening to close the account, forcing Reynolds to commit an additional $26,000 in margin. After the Armistice the stock began a downward spiral as the company reported its first deficit in nearly ten years. This prompted Hausman to suggest that Reynolds dispose of his shares, advice that was ignored. In November 1920 the broker, in order to protect the account, sold 500 shares at an average of $80.50. Reluctantly Reynolds concluded that there was little prospect of advances and authorized the sale of the remaining 500 shares at $81. It was time, he concluded, to take his losses, amounting to nearly $20 a share, and to get out of the market. Within a month the stock dropped to $66, which would have resulted in an additional net loss of more than $30 a share.[39]

In thirty years of speculation Reynolds, convinced that by holding onto New York Air Brake stock he would eventually make a big profit, actually lost a large amount of money. Guided by "insider" advice from Charles Starbuck and other officials, Reynolds stubbornly refused to sell when the price went up, always anticipating further advances. Some of his closest friends, even his stockbroker, complained that he consistently refused to take advantages of price rises to liquidate his holdings. Conversely he doggedly held onto shares during long slides, anticipating that a reversal would eventually carry the stock to new heights.[40]

It is not possible to determine accurately the outcome of Reynolds's speculation in New York Air Brake securities. It is apparent, however, that his losses, particularly after 1907, were consistent and, except for a brief period during World War I, very large. As a conservative estimate they probably added up to more than $50,000 and may have been on the order of $100,000. Most of this loss occurred at a time when Reynolds could not afford reverses of such magnitude.

In an effort to improve deteriorating personal finances, he redirected his efforts to mining, convinced that among his many properties in western Colorado there was a bonanza of mineral wealth waiting to be discovered. The two most promising mines, he believed, were the Golconda at Summitville, Rio Grande County, and the Emma at Dunton, Dolores County. The latter was the better option because it had well-equipped underground workings and a mill and required the least amount of capital to make it a productive enterprise.[41]

Over a period of about twenty years Reynolds had invested a large amount of money at Dunton. Although potentially a rich mine, yielding an iron sulfide ore that ran about one-third gold and two-thirds silver, it had seldom met operating expenses because the equipment in the concentration mill had saved no more than half of the mineral values in the low-grade ore, which made up the bulk of the mine's output. In 1909 Reynolds leased the mine to a longtime employee, Frank Stampfel, who over a period of three years shipped a large volume of high-grade ore that netted him $75,000 in profits, plus $30,000 in royalties for Reynolds. By establishing a record for profitable production, Stampfel's success convinced Reynolds that it was time to sell the Emma Mine.[42]

From 1913 to 1919 a number of buyers looked at the Emma Mine, but much to Reynolds's disappointment, he could not complete a sale of the property. His best chance for success was with the Tonopah-Belmont Development Company, one of the nation's largest mining enterprises. That firm sent its consulting engineer, George H. Garrey, to examine the property in 1915. On the basis of his report Clyde A. Heller, Tonopah-Belmont's chief executive officer, signed a lease and bond in April 1916. After three years Heller gave up the lease without exercising the option to purchase. Desperate to earn royalties sufficient to pay expenses, Reynolds gave Frank Stampfel and Robert L. Pellet a six-year lease on the mine's upper workings in October 1919. Less than a year later they sold the lease to the Dolores Silver Mines.[43]

Reynolds turned his attention to the mine's lower workings, which, he was convinced, contained rich ore that would enable him to rebuild his personal fortune. Hope for a bonanza rested upon an assumption that the Emma Mine was similar to the May Day Mine at Hesperus, 50 miles to the south. In the latter property concentrations of gold and silver ore had been found in a "blanket" on the upper surface of an underground deposit of lime shale. Therefore, it seemed likely that enriched mineral could be mined in the same manner in the Emma Mine.[44]

According to Reynolds, what he called his "blanket theory" was substantiated by the absence of mineral in 1,700 feet of the Emma vein along a crosscut from the bottom of a shaft at a depth of 165 feet. The mineral was, Reynolds suspected, blocked from reaching the vein by a layer of lime shale, from

10 to 12 feet in thickness, at a depth of approximately 100 feet. Therefore, the gold and silver ore should have collected along the top of, or perhaps within the upper portion of, the lime shale.

The blanket theory was controversial. Frank Stampfel, a longtime foreman in the Emma Mine, declined Reynolds's request that he supervise the excavation of a crosscut along the top of the lime shale. He warned that the cost of reaching the shale from the shaft would be at least $10,000 more than Reynolds had estimated and that any mineral found there would probably be low grade. Determined to proceed with the project, Reynolds turned to James Clamp, a veteran miner who had been employed at the Virginius and then the Revenue Tunnel for thirty years. He reluctantly accepted the assignment of testing the theory but became convinced, on finding evidence of the mineralized vein 65 feet below the lime shale, that Reynolds was wrong. Even son-in-law Bradish Morse thought that Reynolds, in his effort to solve personal financial problems, had concocted a theory that supported his needs in defiance of objective evidence.[45]

In order to obtain funds with which to test his theory, Reynolds planned to organize the Lime Shale Mining Company in early 1920. Through the sale of stock, half of which was to be assigned to the Emma Gold Mining Company's exploration of the ground below the level of the West Dolores River, ample funds were to be available to underwrite wages and supplies for Clamp's crew of miners. Reynolds sought financial support from, among others, Gerald Hughes, a prominent Denver lawyer, banker, and mining promoter; Pueblo banker Mahlon D. Thatcher, the son of M. D. Thatcher, who had died in 1916; and W. K. Dudley, cashier of the Pueblo Savings and Trust Bank. Dudley withdrew his offer of support, while Hughes and Thatcher insisted on more information before they put up money for the venture. Because of Reynolds's declining health, the incorporation papers were never filed with the Colorado secretary of state.[46]

Despite strained finances, Reynolds decided to personally underwrite the work in the Emma Mine. Without funds or the prospect of any in the immediate future, Reynolds insisted that Clamp pump water out of the shaft and commence a drift along the top of the lime shale. By March 1921 lack of money had forced Clamp to write Reynolds that it was impossible to continue operations on credit. Neither the miners nor local merchants could be held off. Without cash, Clamp predicted, "all the hard work we have done [will] go for nothing."[47]

While Reynolds was pinning his hopes for the future on the Emma Mine, his immediate concern was to turn a profit from the farms in the Arkansas valley. In 1920 he organized, with George Williams, the Bent's Fort Land and Cattle Company to acquire all land that had not been sold, plus two farms that had been taken back from German purchasers. The new enterprise owned 525 acres of land, 416.2 shares of the Fort Lyon Canal Company, livestock (horses, cattle, and hogs), and farm machinery (implements and tools). Williams, who held about one-third of the company's stock, farmed the land and looked after the livestock.

The Bent's Fort Land and Cattle Company offered Reynolds a brief respite from mounting financial burdens. His two-thirds interest in the enterprise served as collateral for loans with which he advanced funds to the German farmers who had purchased land from him. He was en route to La Junta on January 30, 1921, to extend loans at the local bank when he experienced severe indigestion. The train was a few miles south of Denver when the illness occurred. Reynolds continued on to Pueblo, where, after checking into a hotel, he called a doctor. He remained in bed until Wednesday, when, with great difficulty, he returned to his home in Denver, where he again took to his bed. The following morning, although extremely weak, he set out with his daughter and grandchildren by train for Tennessee.[48]

Later Reynolds admitted that he should not have made the journey. It would have been wiser, he confided to an old friend, to have gone to the hospital. In St. Louis the party had to wait three and a half hours for the connection to Nashville. Determined to find a place to rest before he fell into a heap upon the floor, Reynolds prevailed upon the manager of the Fred Harvey restaurant to open the lounge, where he "laid down, enjoyed a cup of extra heavy bouillon," and did not move until wheeled in a chair to the train.[49]

The long journey ended in Old Hickory, a former rural hamlet that had been transformed into an industrial town as the result of economic mobilization during World War I. What had been farmland in the Cumberland River valley, 12 miles northeast of Nashville, became the site of an immense plant erected by the DuPont Powder Company, at the expense of the federal government, to manufacture smokeless gunpowder. In January 1918 construction began on a plant designed to produce 1 million pounds of powder per day. Operation commenced in July and ended immediately following the Armistice in November, at which time some construction was still in progress.[50]

In 1919 the federal government offered to sell Old Hickory as a surplus property. The Nashville Industrial Corporation (NIC), in which Bradish and George Morse, the partners in the Morse Brothers Machinery and Supply Company, a Denver firm, owned one-half interest, was the successful bidder for the facility. Reynolds bought a small interest in the NIC syndicate, which included a number of prominent Tennessee capitalists. Bradish Morse, as general manager, was in charge of selling the buildings, houses, equipment, and machinery.[51]

In order to devote most of his time to the project, Morse established a home in Old Hickory, where Anna and the children joined him for the major part of each year. They invariably returned to Colorado for the summer months.[52] It was at his daughter's home in Tennessee that Reynolds succumbed to the effects of a lingering illness and old age on March 21, 1921, a little more than a month after his eighty-first birthday.

He died without knowing that his last hope for a mining bonanza had eluded him. The Emma Mine closed the day of Reynolds's death, and the blanket theory remained untested. The mine at Dunton joined a long list of Reynolds's properties that were idle for want of working capital.

Five months before his death Reynolds had hastily compiled for his son-in-law what was, admittedly, an incomplete inventory of mining properties. Bradish Morse hoped to sell some of those assets in order to alleviate the old man's financial embarrassment. Reynolds identified twelve groups of claims, on which he placed an aggregate cash value of nearly $2 million. However, in the absence of a market for silver producers, it was impossible to convert the assets to cash.[53]

The empire that Reynolds had assembled over a period of more than forty years passed to his daughter, his only heir. The mines, largely in western Colorado, were burdened with debts, mostly taxes that in many instances were several years past due. During the 1920s Brad Morse, in addition to his management of the Nashville Industrial Corporation, struggled to put his wife's inheritance in sound financial shape.

9
The Legacy

ANNA Reynolds Morse, Albert E. Reynolds's only child, inherited some equities in farms at La Junta and a large amount of mineral property, mostly in western Colorado, comprising undeveloped mining claims and numerous idle mines. The farms, even though they allowed Reynolds to escape from the frustrations of an increasingly stagnant mining industry, added to his mounting debts. Several of the mines had been large producers of silver or gold in past years but were of questionable value in 1921. Reynolds had insisted that the mineral properties were potentially valuable but that he did not have the capital to develop and operate them. Was this correct, or was his legacy to his daughter nothing more than an accumulation of worthless farm mortgages, mines, and mining claims?

Agriculture as well as mining experienced a grinding depression in the 1920s. Reynolds's estate had to continue a long-established policy of annually advancing money to the German farmers to work the land; even then proceeds from crops frequently did not match expenses and allow for the reduction of debts. Several of the men who had purchased farms from Reynolds failed when farm prices dropped sharply commencing in 1920.

The agricultural depression forced the Reynolds estate to repossess many farms. These were sold to new owners or rented, in some instances to the same people who had defaulted on purchase contracts. George W. Williams continued to work the lands of the Bent's Fort Land and Cattle Company and served as overseer of the rented farms.[1]

A portion of one farm was set apart as a monument to the region's history. Since what remained of the ruins of Bent's Fort was on Indian Claim 13, Anna Reynolds Morse gave the site, as her father had intended, to the Daughters of the American Revolution (DAR). That organization had enlisted Reynolds's assistance in placing a granite stone with a brass plate to mark the site of the old fort in 1912. The DAR gave the land to the state of Colorado in 1954, and it became a national park in 1963. Bent's Fort was faithfully reconstructed, and the marker that Reynolds had erected in behalf of the DAR was placed at the entrance to the park.[2]

The mining assets of the estate, for which Morse was administrator, comprised several thousand patented and unpatented mining claims, in all something over 30,000 acres of land. The principal properties were the Revenue Tunnel located at Sneffels, Ouray County; the Commodore at Creede, Mineral County; the Golconda at Summitville, Rio Grande County; and the Gold Links, Gold Cup, and other properties at Pitkin, Ohio City, and Tin Cup, Gunnison County. Additional mines included the May Day near Hesperus, La Plata County; the Emma at Dunton, Dolores County; the Frank Hough, Ocean Wave, and Palmetto near Lake City, Hinsdale County; and the Parole and Forest King at Platoro, Conejos County. Other mining claims were located in Boulder, Pitkin, and San Juan Counties.[3]

There were no cash assets in the estate, which was heavily burdened with debts. Reynolds's business obligations, mostly unpaid loans from Denver and Pueblo banks, amounted to about $150,000. In addition, taxes had not been paid on the mining properties, in some instances for ten or more years. Amounting to as much as $40,000 on the Revenue Tunnel properties and $29,000 on the Gunnison County claims, these obligations threatened the integrity of Reynolds's legacy because county governments in need of money were eager to sell tax certificates to properties on which payments were in arrears. Furthermore, current tax bills for all properties added up to about $50,000 a year.[4]

Bradish P. Morse, who was the manager of his wife's inheritance, was confident that the estate could achieve solvency, but, he cautioned, it would take time, perhaps several years, "to put it on its feet." The immediate challenge was to put some money in the treasury to pay the taxes. To do this, Morse proposed to sell some of the properties to obtain cash, while concentrating efforts on development and operation of the more promising mines.[5]

He was determined to protect his father-in-law's reputation as a mining entrepreneur. First, Morse hoped to prove that the mining properties were of great value and, in doing so, to acquire money with which to pay Reynolds's debts, dollar for dollar. This was a moral obligation that he could not shirk. Bradish Morse's brothers, who had little interest in mining per se, urged him to let the creditors have the properties. This he refused to do.[6]

Some success marked Morse's initial efforts. Before the close of 1921 he had negotiated contracts for the sale of four major properties and leases for several others. He disposed of the May Day on a two-year lease and purchase option at a price of $125,000, with $10,000 in cash. The Commodore lease and bond were for $75,000, with $5,000 in cash. A fraction of a claim at Ouray netted $900. The Ely-Revenue Copper Company's lands at Ely, Nevada, sold for $70,000, payable in early 1922. Purchasers of the Revenue Tunnel properties were obligated to pay $50,000. Leases were signed for the Ocean Wave and Palmetto, and negotiations were in progress for a lease on the Gold Links Tunnel at Ohio City.[7]

None of the sales contracts was completed. In each instance the prospective buyers refused to take up the purchase option after having worked the properties, usually at a loss, for some time. Unable to sell mines, Morse had no alternative but to turn them over to lessees in an effort to generate money with which to pay ongoing expenses.

At the time that Brad Morse sought to bring order out of his wife's chaotic inheritance, he was deeply involved in salvaging the industrial sites in Old Hickory, Tennessee, purchased by the NIC. That corporation was to dismantle and sell the huge smokeless powder manufacturing plant. Bradish became general manager in charge of operations, a task that required that he reside in Tennessee.[8]

Throughout the 1920s Morse made the recycling of machinery and equipment a highly successful business. After disposing of Old Hickory at a large profit, NIC bought additional industrial facilities that had marketable assets. Projects included a chemical company at Kingsford, Tennessee; an oil refinery and a distillery in Kentucky; an iron furnace complex in Georgia; and an ore reduction plant and coking plant in Virginia.

Unable to give full attention to the reorganization of A. E. Reynolds's estate, Bradish Morse turned for assistance to two of his father-in-law's longtime friends and business associates. Gerald Hughes, a prominent Denver resident, and Carl J. Sigfrid, who lived in Ouray, were lawyers with years of experience in handling estates and mining properties. The oldest of three sons of Charles J. Hughes Jr., Gerald Hughes inherited his father's lucrative Denver law practice in 1911 and quickly established himself as an astute lawyer, businessman, and politician. The firm of Hughes and Dorsey, a partnership of Hughes and Clayton C. Dorsey, guided the Reynolds estate through probate court in the years from 1921 to 1925. Berrien Hughes, a member of the firm, handled routine matters, but it was his older brother Gerald who laid out the basic strategy that allowed the estate, besieged by creditors, to come up with a plan to pay its debts, while at the same time gaining court approval of Anna's administration of her inheritance.[9]

An equally savvy lawyer and politician, Carl J. Sigfrid looked after the estate's western slope mining properties.

Born in Chicago and raised in Kansas, Sigfrid graduated from the University of Michigan with a degree in law. He practiced law in Topeka, Kansas, for two years before relocating to Ouray, where he formed a law partnership with Lyman I. Henry. Sigfrid served as city and county attorney. A specialist in mining law, he cultivated a legion of friends in county court houses throughout the region. Therefore, he was the ideal person to solve many of the knotty problems that threatened to deprive Anna Reynolds Morse of her inheritance.[10]

Sigfrid may have been the only person who knew which of Reynolds's mining properties were of sufficient value, given the estate's lack of funds, to merit the expense of holding for future development. Patented claims were subject to property taxes imposed annually by the counties in which they were located. Unpatented claims were also costly. Federal law required annual assessments, or improvements. This work was essential if the estate hoped to retain control of such claims. If ignored, they would revert to the public domain. Sigfrid knew the locations of claims and called upon friends who were also experienced miners to perform the work on time and in a satisfactory manner. Assessments were quickly brought up to date.

A equally pressing problem was property taxes that had not been paid in several years. County governments desperate for money in the wake of a declining mining industry were eager to sell the properties to anyone who had the funds to pay even a proportion of the past-due charges. The records of sales, called tax certificates, could be translated into deeds, thereby allowing properties to pass into the hands of others at nominal costs. This muddied the question of ownership and threatened to deprive the estate of its assets, ruling out any chance of future income from operations or sales.[11]

Long before Reynolds's death his properties had been targets of individuals and corporations that sought to acquire potentially valuable mining claims at little cost. These so-called tax sharks preyed on properties on which taxes were long overdue.[12] Their motives were mixed. Some were looking for silver and gold properties at bargain prices. Other wanted claims for the mining or milling buildings and equipment on them that could be salvaged for resale.

All of these may have been objectives of the Western Oil, Coal and Investment Company, which, Morse suspected, was owned or controlled by Greeley people. That corporation purchased tax certificates for the properties on the Revenue Tunnel at Ouray, the Emma Mine at Dunton, the May Day near Hesperus, and the Gold Links Tunnel at Ohio City. One observer of this activity suggested that it may have been a conspiracy to bust the "grand old mining man of Colorado."[13] It seems likely that the Greeley firm stood to profit from the resale of the claims and perhaps, if there was no other recourse, from the recycling of improvements.

Sigfrid took on the task of saving the properties for the estate. He successfully negotiated with county commissioners and treasurers for reductions of unpaid tax bills, usually at the rate of 50 percent of the amounts due. He redeemed the threatened properties on the Revenue Tunnel at a cost of $14,000. Since the estate had no money with which to meet this obligation, Bradish Morse had to advance the money from his personal resources.[14] However, in seeking to redeem the Emma Gold Mining Company's claims, Sigfrid encountered resistance, for Western Oil, Coal and Investment had petitioned the Dolores County District Court for tax deeds.

In this instance Sigfrid's keen eye for legal detail saved the day for the estate. He insisted that the tax certificates were invalid because the Dolores County treasurer had issued them prior to the close of the grace period, as required by law, during which an owner had the right to halt all proceedings by paying the past-due taxes. The district court upheld Sigfrid's argument, and the estate redeemed its property at a cost of $8,000, plus legal fees.[15]

Sigfrid was equally successful in Gunnison County. He blocked the Western Oil, Coal and Investment Company's attempt to grab potentially valuable properties at Pitkin and Ohio City. In addition, he stopped R. M. McCracken, a local entrepreneur, from converting tax certificates he had purchased for seven Silver Cord claims into deeds. McCracken sought not precious metals but valuable timber in the form of the trees that covered the surfaces of the claims. The Ouray lawyer settled all of the unpaid tax matters at a reduction of 50 percent, paying nearly $15,000 to clear the titles to the mining claims.[16]

Tax certificates, while troublesome for the Reynolds estate, could be highly profitable for people, or corporations, who had the money to buy up potentially valuable properties on which taxes were overdue. As Sigfrid explained to Brad Morse, the purchaser negotiated a price with the county treasurer, or the commissioners, but the certificate carried on its face the sum of all past due taxes, penalties, and interest. If the property was redeemed, the original owner paid the amount on the certificate, and that was for the benefit of the holder of the document. Therefore, the Western Oil, Coal and Investment Company, by paying $3,600 for certificates on the Emma Mine properties, was entitled to $6,025.85, the sum of the amounts on the certificates, unless, of course, the district court determined that there were grounds for altering that amount. In this instance Sigfrid, by insisting that the certificates had been improperly issued in the first place, obtained a reduction of over $800 on the final cost of redemption.[17]

The redemptions, although costly, were necessary if the Reynolds estate hoped to either work or sell its properties. In an effort to obtain money for the estate, Morse planned to organize companies to develop mines at Ouray, at Dunton, and in Gunnison County. He was convinced that there was no market for idle mines and that the only chance of selling them at a fair price was to offer them as working, productive enterprises.[18]

In pursuit of this goal Morse, with Sigfrid's support, proposed first to reactivate the Revenue Tunnel Mines Company. By offering the enterprise's treasury stock to wealthy friends in Nashville, Morse hoped to raise funds to drive the Terrible drift, which had not been worked for more than twenty years, 4,000 feet to the Blue Grass claim, where he expected to find an extension of the Virginius vein that had made the Revenue Tunnel one of the region's largest producers of silver.[19]

In fact, Morse used personal funds to push the Terrible drift toward the Blue Grass ground. As anticipated, the prospect of large returns from a working mine generated the interest of buyers. In April 1923 Judge F. E. Riddle, a Tulsa, Oklahoma, lawyer and mining promoter, signed a five-year lease and purchase option at a price of $1.25 million, with an initial payment of $25,000 due in three months.[20]

Despite Morse's confidence in Riddle, the sale was not completed. The Oklahoma promoter planned to secure the funds needed to fulfill the contract from Tulsa oilmen, who backed out of the arrangement when the price of crude broke sharply that spring. Reluctantly Morse continued personally to fund work on the Terrible drift, hoping to attract another buyer. When none appeared by July, at which time his commitment exceeded $20,000, he decided to end the effort to reach the Virginius vein.[21]

This left five lessees, without purchase options, working at different places in the mine. James Clamp, the longtime foreman when A. E. Reynolds had operated the mine, held three of the leases as an individual or in partnership with other men. Combined royalties in 1922 barely exceeded $1,000, not enough to meet the expenses of taxes and upkeep on the property.[22]

Equally high hopes for the Emma Mine ended in disappointment. At Dunton Morse proposed to test Reynolds's theory that gold and silver had been deposited on or in the strata of lime shale located at a depth of about 100 feet below the level of the number five tunnel, driven from the banks of the West Dolores River. This was the so-called blanket theory that Morse had cast doubt upon when Reynolds employed James Clamp to pump water out the shaft as the first step toward driving a drift across the top of the shale. With the hope of financial support from Gerald Hughes and Mahlon D. Thatcher, Morse proposed to activate Reynolds's projected Lime Shale Mining Company to work the lower levels of the Emma Mine.[23]

However, neither Morse nor Hughes was willing to go ahead with the project unless they could control all of the Emma Mine, and this was impossible because Reynolds had leased the upper level in 1919. Frank Stampfel and Robert Pellet worked the mine for a time, then sold their lease to the Dolores Silver Mines, controlled by William Gillette, a Greeley businessman. Gillette, in turn, sold the lease to Hugh M. Little, a Denver mining entrepreneur who, by opening what appeared to be highly mineralized ground above number five level and adding oil flotation to the cyanide mill, anticipated large profits from the operation of the mine.[24]

This hope was dashed when the ore from the new ground could not be milled at a profit. Unable to generate revenues sufficient to pay expenses, Little gave up the lease and turned the Emma property back to the Reynolds estate in February 1923. This opened the way for Morse to test Reynolds's blanket theory, but by that date he had exhausted his available personal funds in the effort to reach the untapped portions of the Virginius vein at Ouray.[25]

In any event Morse's attention had shifted to the mines in Gunnison County, the properties that Reynolds had considered his most promising assets. Morse decided to complete the development that his father-in-law had started. To this end Morse organized among wealthy Nashville friends two syndicates to underwrite the cost of exploring mining claims west of Pitkin and north of Ohio City. Morse was partially successful in the first instance, but he was unable to fund operations on Gold Creek (formerly Ohio Creek), where the Gold Links Tunnel was located.

A number of Nashville residents subscribed to a partnership with the objective of exploring Chicago Park, the site of
once-productive silver mines. Reynolds had purchased most
of the claims in the area on the assumption that mineralized
veins mined near the surface could be tapped at greater
depth. Using records of a diamond drill test by Ben Sadtler in
1892, Morse convinced himself and his friends that valuable
silver deposits underlaid most, if not all, of the area. According to Morse, Sadtler's test hole had revealed three potentially
productive strata below a depth of approximately 300 feet:
one comprising 5 feet of mineral averaging 21 ounces of silver
per ton; below that another zone 10 feet in depth, with an
average of 15 ounces per ton; and the last, more than 500 feet
below the surface, an 8-foot-thick high-grade deposit carrying an average of 120 ounces of silver per ton.[26]

In order to limit the liability of the investors, the partnership was reorganized as the Tennessee-Colorado Development Company, incorporated in Colorado in April 1922. The
task of sinking what was called the Tennessee shaft commenced in November 1922, with James F. Robinson, a veteran
local miner, in charge.[27] Within a year it was obvious to Morse
that the project was in trouble.

He had estimated that the cost of reaching the first silver-
bearing stratum, at a depth of 326 feet, would not exceed 25
percent of subscriptions. However, he had based that calcula-
tion on the assumption that the Nashville people would
contribute not less than $100,000. In fact, they raised only
three-quarters of that amount. When expenses exceeded
$15,000, the subscribers refused to pay additional assess-
ments. After some equivocation they agreed to increase their
subscriptions to a total of $100,000 but authorized only
$25,000 for the first segment of the shaft.[28]

Sinking a shaft parallel to and within 20 feet of Sadtler's
1892 drill hole proved to be more difficult than anticipated. A
combination of labor problems and water shortages raised the
cost. Within a year the shaft was down about 175 feet, and

expenses to that time amounted to almost $20,000. With only $5,000 to pay for an additional 150 feet, Morse conceded that it looked as though he would have to put up personal funds to complete the project.[29]

He quickly changed his mind. In February 1924 Morse ordered an end to all work on the shaft. He wanted to straighten out the company's affairs before committing additional funds to the project. By that date Robinson's crew had reached a depth of 297 feet at a cost of almost $28,000. It was time, Morse concluded, for a showdown with the Nashville investors. He was confident that when presented with complete information about the work at Pitkin, they would provide the money to continue work on the shaft.[30]

As Morse predicted, the investors did not shut down the work at Pitkin. On March 11, 1924, they authorized a special assessment of 15 percent on their subscriptions to pay the cost of sinking the Tennessee shaft to the first ore contact. Even with the assurance of money to pay expenses, Robinson made headway very slowly. It was not until the end of the June that Morse, confident that the contact was at hand, informed the Nashville businessmen that it was time to send someone to measure the depth of the shaft and to verify the cutting of the first contact that Sadtler had identified at a depth of about 326 feet.[31]

F. A. Goodale, a mining engineer, reached Pitkin in late July at a time when, according to Sadtler's report, the bottom of the shaft should have been in low-grade silver ore. However, there was no mineral. In an effort to test Sadtler's accuracy, Robinson's crew ran a drift from the shaft to the original drill hole. Confident that the ore body was at hand, Goodale gathered samples, which he planned to have assayed in Leadville.[32]

They revealed little of value. Of twelve assays the highest values were 0.3 ounces of gold and 0.8 ounces of silver per ton. The geology of the shaft had conformed to Sadtler's drill hole foot by foot until the first ore contact should have been encountered, but it was not in the shaft or in the drill hole. Puzzled and disappointed, Morse instructed Robinson to halt operations until the Nashville investors decided what they wanted to do. He was convinced that they would back out of their commitment to the project.[33]

The stockholders were unwilling to abandon the Tennessee-Colorado Development Company before determining if the other strata, identified in Sadtler's report, contained silver. At Robinson's suggestion, seconded by Morse, fourteen investors authorized a 5 percent assessment, or $4,150, to contract for a diamond drill to explore to a depth of 200 feet below the shaft. That task was completed in late November without mineral values of any consequence being found. The best sample revealed only 0.04 ounces of gold and 0.6 ounces of silver.[34]

The diamond drill test was the Tennessee company's final activity in Gunnison County. Its failure to find the silver contacts doomed Brad Morse's hopes for raising funds in Nashville to work the Gold Links Tunnel and the Revenue property. What Morse called the Pitkin "fluke" terminated his efforts to operate what had been A. E. Reynolds's properties. Thereafter, Morse focused attention on leasing and selling the estate's assets.[35]

The fiasco at Pitkin raised interesting questions about Sadtler's diamond drill hole of 1892. Crushed over the outcome of the Tennessee shaft, Robinson concluded that Sadtler was either crooked or the victim of a fraud. Morse concurred, but he was inclined to believe that either the 1892 hole had been salted or samples manipulated, and he blamed the driller, a man named Fulton. No one offered an explanation of why Fulton would have altered the record.[36]

The Pitkin project ended at a time when, according to Morse, the mining industry in Colorado was dead. It was impossible to make a mine if, at best, gold returned $10 and silver $0.35 an ounce. Morse's hopes for raising funds in Tennessee for the Gold Links and the Revenue Tunnel had to be shelved. Mining was at a standstill not only in Gunnison but also in Ouray County. At the latter place, according to Sigfrid, not one property was being worked on Mount Sneffels or on Red Mountain, and only about two dozen men were employed in a mining industry whose workforce had once numbered in the thousands.[37]

A stagnated industry worked against Morse's hopes for using proceeds from the sale of mines to pay off the creditors of the Reynolds estate. Only two mines of A. E. Reynolds's once vast empire offered any hope of income. The May Day, under lease and bond to the Cumberland Mines Company, had paid $50,000 toward the purchase price of $125,000, but there were indications that production had fallen off sharply in the previous year. It seemed unlikely that the contract would be completed when the final payment, twice delayed, was due in 1925. Indeed, in December of that year C. O. Keiser, in behalf of the Cumberland firm, formally surrendered the lease and option without making additional payments.[38]

The Commodore presented a brighter outlook, at least for the moment. When Gerald Hughes gave up his lease in early 1923, his mine foreman, Clarence O. Withrow, took over the mine. He had the good fortune to find a large vein of high-grade ore. In fact, this pay streak had been developed by the adjoining Bachelor Mining Company, and it was, according to Morse, the assumption that the vein crossed the boundary between the two claims that motivated Gerald Hughes to take a lease on the property.[39]

Unfortunately for Hughes the vein was not mineralized at the point where he attempted to work it. However, by pursuing the streak, Withrow, as the successor lessee, struck high-grade ore. Between January 1, 1925 and November 1, 1926, Withrow's leasing company shipped more than 44,000 tons of ore with an aggregate gross value of more than $500,000. The Reynolds estate, and its successor, the Reynolds-Morse Corporation, earned royalties of more than $94,000 from Withrow's bonanza.[40]

When the lease expired, it was rewritten as the Withrow-Commodore Lease, with Sigfrid and Morse as minority stockholders. The new enterprise experience a dramatic decline in production. The Reynolds-Morse Company earned only $6,000 in royalties from the Commodore property in 1927–1928. During this time Sigfrid and Morse sold their interests in the leasing company to Withrow, who added Paul H. Graham as vice president and William S. Sloan as secretary of the corporation. Both men were experienced in mining at Creede.[41]

Withrow's operations revealed that the Bachelor Mining Company, owner of a neighboring claim, had extracted high-grade ore from the Commodore Mining Company's property. Morse asked for compensation and suggested a negotiated settlement. Officers of the Bachelor denied any wrongdoing, insisting that all of the ore in question had been taken from within its boundaries. Convinced that the Bachelor people had taken ore illegally, Morse instructed Sigfrid to bring suit in the district court at Creede.[42]

Despite that fact that the evidence clearly supported the Commodore Mining Company's charges, the case dragged on for more than three years, during which time its outcome remained in doubt. The delay was caused, in part, by the evasive tactics of the Bachelor Mine's Denver attorney, Henry C. Vidal, and also by the fact that the presiding judge, Jesse C. Wiley of Del Norte, was in no hurry to reach a decision. Both Morse and Sigfrid were convinced that Wiley would never give a decision if he could find an excuse for not doing so.[43]

Wiley procrastinated until September 1929. His decision was a victory for the Commodore Mining Company, which was given a judgment against the Bachelor Mining Company in excess of $100,000. When the officers of that enterprise did not pay, Sigfrid, at Morse's suggestion, asked the court for a judgment against the company. At a subsequent court-ordered sheriff's sale of the property on March 10, 1930, Sigfrid bought all of the assets, making the Commodore the sole owner of the Bachelor property.[44]

The Commodore-Bachelor suit should have raised questions of conflict of interest on the part of the presiding judge. Throughout the period of litigation Judge Wiley held what proved to be a highly lucrative lease on the Golconda Gold Mining Company's properties at Summitville. Although both Morse and Sigfrid were uneasy about the lease, Wiley seemed confident that his actions were above suspicion, and Henry Vidal either did not know of the lease or chose to overlook it.

By asking for a lease on the Consolidated Gold Mining Company's adjacent tract, Wiley gave Morse an opportunity to arrange for the completion of the long-delayed merger of the Reynolds and Barnsdall interests. The Summitville Mines Corporation was organized in 1926, with the Reynolds-Morse and Barnsdall Corporations, as successors to the Reynolds and Barnsdall estates, respectively, each owning one-half of the enterprise.[45]

The mining of the property was undertaken by a partnership of Wiley and Jack Pickens, who had been a miner at Summitville from time to time over a number of years. According to Ben Poxson, an Alamosa schoolteacher who became a highly successful politician and mining entrepreneur, Pickens had identified a rich surface deposit of gold ore on or near the Little Annie claim but could not obtain a lease that would allow him to mine it. Therefore, he prevailed upon Wiley to secure the lease, which presumably he could do because of the pending Commodore-Bachelor suit. The partners hauled a large quantity of extremely high-grade ore from Summitville to Del Norte and sent it by train under armed guard to Omaha to be smelted.[46]

From 1926 through 1928 Wiley and Pickens shipped from Summitville ore worth more than $469,000. Some of it was worth from $30 to $40 a pound. The Summitville Mines Corporation received royalties in the amount of $104,743. After the deduction of expenses the Reynolds-Morse Corporation was entitled to one-half of $61,373.[47]

After the high-grade deposit was exhausted, Wiley and Pickens had on their hands an abundance of ore containing less than 4 ounces of gold per ton, too low to pay the cost of wagon freight from Summitville to Del Norte. In order to eliminate transportation costs, Wiley and Pickens decided to organize a company to buy the property and to erect and operate a cyanide mill on the site. While making preparations for the new enterprise, Wiley asked for a ten-year extension of his lease. Before his plan could be implemented, he died of cancer in September 1930, and Pickens was unwilling to continue the partnership with Mrs. Wiley.[48]

This left the Summitville property temporarily in limbo, at least until Wiley's lease expired in June 1931. Meanwhile Morse, in order to determine the worth of the property, asked geologist George H. Garrey to make a thorough exploration of the area and to report on its potential for development. After a brief investigation Garrey concluded that Summitville had much merit. He suggested that a company with a capital of not less than $300,000 to erect and operate a good mill could expect large returns on its investment.[49]

Garrey was to spend the last thirty year of his life closely associated with mining properties in Colorado. Born in Reedville, Wisconsin, in 1875, Garrey grew up in Aurora, Illinois, where his father, a physician, had a private medical practice. George graduated from the University of Chicago in 1898. As an undergraduate he played on the football team three years in a row. He taught two years at Aurora West High School before returning to the university to earn a Master of Arts in geology. As a graduate student he was an assistant to football coach Alonzo Stagg. In 1902 Garrey enrolled at the Michigan College of Mines, Houghton, and graduated two years later with a degree, Engineer of Mines.[50]

For two years Garrey worked for the U.S. Geological Survey, then joined the American Smelting and Refining Company and related Guggenheim enterprises. Under the supervision of chief geologist J. E. Spurr, Garrey served as southern manager in charge of offices in El Paso and Mexico City. In 1908 he joined Spurr and Cox, consulting engineers, and when W. Rowland Cox resigned in 1911, Garrey formed a partnership with J. E. Cox for several months before returning to the Guggenheim firms as chief geologist. He remained in that position until 1914, when he opened an office as a consulting geologist and engineer in Philadelphia.

Two years later Garrey assumed charge of the Tonopah-Belmont Development Company's exploration department. That corporation owned or operated mines throughout the western United States and in British Columbia. In that capacity Garrey conducted the investigation that preceded the firm's lease, with purchase option, of A. E. Reynolds's Emma Mine at Dunton, Colorado, in 1916. Garrey remained with Tonopah-Belmont until 1923, when he again opened an office as an independent consultant.

The Reynolds-Morse Corporation hired George Garrey to make an investigation of mining claims at Creede in 1927. As an expert geologist Garrey prepared the technical evidence used by the Commodore Mining Company in its suit against the Bachelor Mining Company for alleged trespass. The success of that litigation led Morse to turn to Garrey again to make explorations of Summitville, Chicago Park in Gunnison County, and the Revenue properties at Ouray.[51]

In the course of completing that assignment, Garrey, with Ben T. Poxson, acquired leases on Reynolds-Morse Corporation's properties. They were the principal stockholders in Fairview-Cleopatra Mines, lessee of claims in Chicago Park, near Pitkin in Gunnison County. Subsequently they secured leases on properties at Summitville and Creede.[52]

Poxson, a successful politician and businessman, was born in Michigan and educated there before relocating to Alamosa, Colorado, where he was appointed principal of the high school in 1915. Eventually he left education for a career in politics, holding a number of appointed offices. In 1926 Poxson joined Herman Emperius, vice president of an Alamosa bank, in securing a lease from the Reynolds-Morse Corporation on the Ocean Wave property at Lake City. Two years later after that venture proved unproductive, they packed up their equipment and headed back to Alamosa, stopping overnight in Creede. There they met William C. Sloan, who had a lease on the Commodore Mining Company's Pittsburg claim. He offered them a sublease, and they accepted, marking the start of a long and profitable association for Poxson with the Creede Mining District.[53]

While Emperius started operations on the Pittsburg claim, Poxson joined George Garrey in the Chicago Park venture. Operating as the Fairview-Cleopatra Mines, they worked ground that Garrey had recently surveyed for the Reynolds-Morse Corporation. There was in sight ample shipping-grade ore to assure the success of the enterprise until the price of silver fell dramatically in the closing years of the 1920s.[54]

The price of silver had been declining for more than half a century. It recovered briefly during World War I and remained relatively high for about four years after the Armistice. From an average price of $0.82 an ounce in 1922 silver declined gradually to $0.53 an ounce in 1929.[55]

With the onset of the Great Depression the market continued to weaken until it dropped to $0.30 an ounce in July 1933. At that point the Commodore Mine at Creede suspended operations until such time as the price of silver permitted it to operate at a profit. Within weeks virtually all silver mines in the American West had halted operations.[56]

Bradish Morse did not live to see this temporary setback for his plans to put the mines of the Reynolds estate in working order. After suffering from a series of ailments for several years, he died of a heart attack in his home, 1555 Sherman Street, Denver, on December 27, 1931.[57] In approximately ten years he showed skeptics that A. E. Reynolds's legacy to his daughter was far from exhausted of silver and gold. The Commodore and Summitville had produced during Morse's brief management of the Reynolds's properties combined gross values of approximately $1.5 million. And despite the decline of mining activity in the early years of the Great Depression, there was ample evidence to suggest that those mines, if not others, could yield large profits in the future. After the death of her husband Anna Reynolds Morse assumed the management of the Reynolds-Morse Corporation. Sigfrid served as her legal adviser, as he had served her husband. Garrey provided technical information about mining properties and their potential for development. Within half a dozen years lessees were working most of the Reynolds properties. The properties at Creede and Summitville had recorded large returns, and there was reason to hope for similar outcomes at the May Day, Revenue Tunnel, and Gold Cup. That achievement prompted the *Mining Year Book,* a publication of the Colorado Mining Association, to recognize Anna Reynolds Morse as an outstanding mineowner in 1937.[58]

The Reynolds-Morse Corporation's mining operations recovered quickly from the Depression-induced slump after President Franklin D. Roosevelt took office in March 1933. His administration quickly implemented programs to reverse four years of severe deflation. In May Roosevelt signed into the law the Agricultural Adjustment Act, to which Senator Elmer Thomas of Oklahoma had successfully attached an amendment giving the Treasury power to purchase and coin silver at a fixed ratio with gold. In December the U.S. Mint was authorized to purchase up to 24.4 million ounces of newly mined silver at $0.6450 an ounce. In the same month President Roosevelt announced that the federal government planned to raise the price of gold by steps to $35 an ounce. The Silver Purchase Act of June 1934 raised the price of the white metal. By executive decree the price of newly mined silver for 1935 was set at $0.7757 an ounce.[59]

The higher prices brought a revival of operations at properties owned by the Reynolds-Morse Corporation. At Creede Ben Poxson's Emperius Mining Company worked the Pittsburg and adjacent claims, while the Commodore-Bachelor

Mines, controlled by the A. O. Smith Corporation of Milwaukee, Wisconsin, acquired rights to two mines after Clarence Withrow's lease expired on the Commodore. After having produced no silver in 1933, the district mines recorded an output of 479,898 ounces in 1934. The opening of a custom mill in 1937, the first since 1915, assured the ongoing output of low-grade ores.[60]

The revival at Summitville, as at Creede, was initiated by Ben Poxson and George Garrey. In July 1933 they organized the Summitville Gold Mines to lease the ground formerly worked by Wiley and Pickens. In order to attract additional capital for the erection of a flotation-cyanidation mill, they created the Summitville Consolidated Mines in April 1934. Poxson and Garrey surrendered all leases and equipment to the new firm in return for one-fifth of its capital stock. That enterprise was controlled by F. R. Smith, president of A. O. Smith Corporation, a Milwaukee manufacturer of automobile frames and other steel products.[61]

The A. O. Smith Corporation expanded operations to Creede commencing in 1937. It created the Commodore-Bachelor Mines, owner of a lease on the Commodore and Bachelor Mines. Edward Thornton served as superintendent of activities at Creede as well as Summitville. The ore was of low grade, and returns did not meet expectations. By 1940 the Commodore Leasing Company, controlled by Poxson and Garrey, had leased the two mines. Within little more than a year the Commodore was exhausted.[62]

Operations in Rio Grande County were far more profitable for the A. O. Smith Corporation, as the Summitville Consolidated Mines was Colorado's leading producer of gold. From 1934 through 1942 the district produced gold, silver, copper, and lead worth almost $4 million. Ninety-five percent of this was gold. To support that output, the company built a town, complete with schools, a hospital, boardinghouses, and dwellings for seven hundred workers and their families. The exhaustion of high-grade deposits, cou-

pled with America's entry into World War II, caused the
A. O. Smith Corporation to give up its lease in July 1942.[63]

At that point the Gold Links Mining Company, controlled by Poxson and Garrey, acquired a lease on the
Summitville property. Formed originally to lease the Gold
Links Tunnel at Ohio City, Gunnison County, the enterprise
worked the Summitville properties for nearly four years.
The mill was converted to a flotation system, dispensing
with cyanidation, to treat ores whose gold content was only
from $3 to $5 per ton.[64]

The Gold Links Mining Company, unlike other producers of gold, continued in operation during World War II
because it also produced copper, which was needed for the
armament industry. The declining grade of ore and dwin-
dling profits brought an end to operations at Summitville
in 1946. By then Garrey, having married Anna Reynolds
Morse in 1938, was devoting much of his time to the management of the Reynolds-Morse Corporation, and Poxson
had centralized his mining activities at Creede.[65]

Poxson's Emperius Mining Company acquired the central portion of the Creede Mining District. Starting with
one-third interest in the Last Chance, the balance of which
was owned by Ralph Granger, Poxson acquired in time the
Amethyst, Bachelor, Commodore, and all other claims on
the Amethyst vein up to the Happy Thought property. He
gained control of the Reynolds-Morse Corporation's holdings in a trade, by the terms of which he surrendered his
one-fourth interest in Summitville for Commodore properties at Creede. The Reynolds-Morse Corporation and Poxson had jointly purchased the Barnsdall Corporation's interests in the 1950s, and it was this one-quarter interest that
Poxson exchanged for controlling interest in the Commodore Mining Company.[66]

Operations at Creede were highly successful. Over a
period of thirty-two years the Emperius Mining Company
produced silver worth slightly more than $30 million. The

average price of silver during that time was $0.71 an ounce.[67]

After Poxson and Garrey gave up their lease on Summitville, the property was worked sporadically for a number of years. The Newmont Mining Company and the General Minerals Company explored the area in the 1950s and 1960s but did not undertake systematic development. A consortium comprising Cleveland Cliffs, Union Pacific Resources Corporation, and W. S. Moore Company investigated the possibility of mining copper deposits. That enterprise completed extensive work underground, built a mill, and completed other surface improvements.[68]

In 1965 the prospect of selling the Summitville site to the General Minerals Company prompted the end of the Reynolds-Morse Corporation. In order to eliminate the potential for double taxation on income from a sale, all assets, following dissolution of the investment company, were distributed to Anna Reynolds Morse Garrey and her children.[69] By that date the Reynolds's legacy had undergone dramatic changes.

Most of what remained of the mineral holdings appeared to have little value. The Emma Mine at Dunton had been sold to a Canadian mining company. The properties at Creede had been exchanged for a one-quarter interest in Summitville. Chicago Park, which had little, if any, potential for mining, had been sold by the county because of unpaid taxes. The May Day and Gold Links were idle. The Revenue Tunnel properties at Ouray had been frequently leased with purchase options but remained unsold and inactive.

A family limited partnership, the Reynolds Mining Company, was formed in 1965 to bring under one management all of the properties derived through the Reynolds estate. The new company disposed of the farms at La Junta, taking in trade a Denver warehouse, which was eventually sold. The mining properties, with the single exception of Summitville, remained inactive.

After General Minerals Company refused to exercise its purchase option, American Smelting and Refining Company and, later, the Anaconda Minerals Corporation secured leases. Anaconda, a subsidiary of Atlantic-Richfield Oil Company, completed diamond drill and other tests, which revealed a vast amount of low-grade gold ore in combination with other metals. The results of this drilling campaign attracted the attention of Galactic Resources, of Vancouver, British Columbia. By 1984 the Canadian firm had purchased Anaconda's data with the objective of opening an open-pit mine and a heap-leaching facility to extract gold from a large volume of low-grade ore.[70]

Heap leaching with cyanide is a variation of a long-standing method of extracting gold and other minerals from ore. A. E. Reynolds had experimented at Summitville with cyanide as a reducing agent shortly after the turn of the century but could not contemplate production on a scale to make this process feasible, given the remoteness of the site. He used cyanide with oil flotation in the Emma Mill, and a similar combination was used by Ben Poxson, George H. Garrey, and the A. O. Smith Corporation at Summitville in the 1930s and 1940s. The modern version of cyanidation differed from the old method mainly in terms of the economies derived from scale. Surface mining was combined with huge leaching pits lined with materials to prevent solutions and metals from soaking into the ground. The pit was to be filled with crushed ore, over which cyanide solution was sprayed. The cyanide dissolved the gold, from which it was precipitated and recovered in marketable form. First employed by mining giant Newmont Mining Company at its Carlin Mine, near Ely, Nevada, in the 1960s, this method of gold recovery was widely adopted throughout the West, eventually at Summitville in the 1980s.[71]

This was not, however, the first heap-leaching project in Colorado. As early as 1984 that technique for recovering gold had been applied to mine and mill dumps in the Cripple

Creek–Victor area of Teller County. The Golden Cycle Corporation, of Colorado Springs, in partnership with Texas Gulf Minerals and Metals, a subsidiary of a French enterprise, jointly owned the Cripple Creek and Victory Mining Company. It recovered gold from the Carleton Mill and Portland properties, as much as 28,000 ounces in 1987.[72] In doing so, it proved that the new method of cyanidation could be conducted safely and profitably. That was not to be the case at Summitville.

Summitville Consolidated Mining Company, a subsidiary of Galactic Resources, entered into a contract with Bechtel Engineering Corporation to develop a mine and leaching plant capable of producing 120,000 ounces of gold and 50,000 ounces of silver per year. It was anticipated that the facility would produce gold at a cost of less than $200 per ounce, or less than two-thirds of the market price of gold at that time. With proven ore reserves of 18 million tons, the operation was designed to continue for a minimum of five years.[73]

Leaching operations commenced on June 5, 1986, making the Summitville plant Colorado's leading producer of gold. By 1988 it ranked not only first in Colorado but also sixteenth in the nation. Because of the altitude and the severity of weather during the winter months, the mine operated from about mid-May to the close of October each year. Leaching continued twelve months of the year. Millions of tons of ore had to be treated with cyanide in order to obtain a large yield of gold. In 1988, for example, the company excavated 2.6 million tons of ore, the average assay for which was 0.04 ounces of gold and from 0.16 to 0.19 ounces of silver per ton.[74]

By March 31, 1992, when cyanide was sprayed on the massive pile of crushed ore for the last time, the project had produced 280,000 ounces of gold worth about $90 million. In spite of this, the company claimed that it had lost $70 million. This was attributed to at least three factors. The faulty design of the leach pad became apparent when a leak developed in June 1989, forcing the premature shutdown of mining operations for the season. Thereafter, production remained low, in part because of problems with the pad and also because of low recovery rates from ore. In addition, the cost of conforming to state and national environmental regulations was, from the company's view, an excessive burden.[75]

In December 1992 the company terminated all operations with a bankruptcy declaration that it had no funds to continue operations. This posed a possible threat that a large volume of cyanide-laced water containing high concentrations of copper could be released to pollute the Alamosa River. In an effort to ward off potential disaster, the state of Colorado requested the intervention of the Environmental Protection Agency, which took over management of the site. The cost of managing the plant and safeguarding its operation was initially estimated at $800,000. This was revised upward to $1.1 million because of high labor costs at the site. The total bill for cleaning up the site has been placed at $60 million.[76] If Galactic Resources or its operating subsidiary, Summitville Consolidated Mining Company, both in bankruptcy by the close of 1992, do not pay the cost of reclaiming the property, the burden by law will probably fall on prior lessees, those who were involved in any way with the Galactic operation, and the landowners.

The owners were the grandchildren and great-grandchildren of A. E. Reynolds. At the time that Galactic Resources sought a lease, the family members who controlled the Reynolds Mining Company dissolved that limited partnership and replaced it with three corporations, each of which was under the direction of a branch of Anna Reynolds Morse Garrey's family. The South Mountain Mining Company was controlled by the children of Eudorah Reynolds Moore; the Aztec Resources Company, by the son of A. Reynolds Morse; and the Gray Eagle Mining Company, by the children of Anna Morse Tippit. Each owned one-third interest in the mining properties, and it was with the three corporations that Galactic Resources negotiated a lease on Summitville.[77]

Eight years later the Canadian firm's bankruptcy and that of its subsidiary meant that they could not pay for cleaning up the Summitville damage. The EPA, forced to assume management of the property and unable to assess the costs on the lessee, asked the former lessees, property owners, and others to fund the reclamation of the site. The wording of the pertinent law appeared to be clearly on the side of the EPA. This raised the possibility that Reynolds's grandchildren and great-grandchildren would be asked to share in reclamation costs, which could lead to their insolvency.[78]

If this occurs, the saga of A. E. Reynolds will have come full circle. As a young man he set out from New York for the trans-Mississippi West in search of business opportunities and the chance to accumulate wealth and community recognition. An aggressive entrepreneur, he acquired fortune, if not fame, and left to his daughter a large legacy, mostly in the form of mining properties of potentially great value. Ironically, long after Reynolds's death a portion of those assets, mining claims at Summitville, threaten to reduce the second and third generations of his progeny to the humble circumstances with which he began his western adventure nearly 130 years earlier.

Notes

1 Western Entrepreneur

1. The birth dates of the children of Henry A. and Caroline Van Horn Reynolds are in the Reynolds Family Genealogy, prepared by Louisa Arps, ca. 1975. All correspondence and documents cited hereafter, unless otherwise indicated, are in the A. E. Reynolds Collection, No. 1220, the Colorado Historical Society, Denver.

2. Biographical sketches, for which Reynolds supplied the data, are in Frank Hall, *History of the State of Colorado*, 4 vols. (Chicago: Blakely Printing 1895), 4:459–60; and Wilbur Fisk Stone, *History of Colorado*, 4 vols. (Chicago: S. J. Clarke Publishing, 1918–1919), 3:544, 546.

3. Hall, *History of the State of Colorado*, 4:549.

4. Obituary of A. J. Reynolds, unidentified newspaper clipping, September 9, 1910.

5. B. P. Morse to Anna Reynolds Morse, September 19, 1921.

6. The biographical sketches in Hall and Stone were written by A. E. Reynolds, as was the custom of that day, but they differ in one important aspect. Hall says that Reynolds came from New York to Junction City, Kansas, and from there traveled to Missouri to open a store. Stone says that Reynolds came to Leavenworth. Reynolds would not have made this mistake; therefore it must have been committed by Hall, who thought that Junction should be Junction City and corrected what he assumed to be an error in Reynolds's sketch. See Hall, *History of the State of Colorado*, 4:549; Stone, *History of Colorado*, 3:544, 546; and "Junction, Leavenworth City," in Mary E. Montgomery, *Lessor Known or Extinct Towns of Kansas* (Topeka: Kansas Historical Society, n.d), vol. 9 (entries are alphabetically arranged without pagination).

7. The origin and evolution of military sutlers and post traders are discussed at length in David Michael Delo, *Peddler and Post Traders: The Army Sutler on the Frontier* (Salt Lake City: University of Utah Press, 1992), esp. chaps. 10–14.

8. Hall, *History of the State of Colorado*, 4:549; LeRoy Hafen, ed., *Colorado and Its People*, 4 vols. (New York: Lewis Publishing, 1948), 4:705–706.

9. The only biography of W. M. D. Lee is Donald F. Schofield, *Indians, Cattle, Ships, and Oil: The Story of W. M. D. Lee* (Austin: University of Texas Press, 1985). The activities of the firm of Lee & Reynolds are treated in chaps. 1–4.

10. A. E. Reynolds to W. C. Sheldon, April 15, 1886, and November 10, 1886; A. E. Reynolds to Mary J. Weiglein, Denver, July 16, 1913; A. E. Reynolds to Rose Van Horn, Denver, April 30, 1914.

11. A. E. Reynolds to the President, Secretary, and Committee, Fourth New York Heavy Artillery Association, Denver, August 5, 1910; *Denver Republican*, May 27, 1910.

12. Biographical sketches of M. D. Thatcher are in Stone, *History of Colorado*, 3:16–18; and James D. Baker and LeRoy R. Hafen, eds., *History of Colorado*, 5 vols. (Denver: Linderman, 1927), 5:193–98.

13. Silver Quotations Note Book, 1883–1912. Reynolds kept a record of daily silver prices, the opening quotations on the New York and London markets.

14. *Daily Montrose (Colo.) Enterprise,* October 17, 1919; *Gunnison (Colo.) News-Champion,* October 17, 1919.

15. A. E. Reynolds to George R. Sheldon, October 26, 1889.

16. A. E. Reynolds to J. P. Sidwell, Denver, June 12, 1913. See also "Revenue Tunnel," *Ores and Metals* 10 (October 1901): 8; "Colorado's Greatest Mineral Bonanza," *Ores and Metals* 11 (December 1902): 6.

17. A. E. Reynolds to J. P. Sidwell, Denver, June 12, 1913. See also H. W. Reed to A. E. Reynolds, Ouray, March 14, 1895; "Tunneling in Colorado," *Mines and Minerals* 20 (July 1900): 547–48; "Colorado's Greatest Mineral Bonanza," *Ores and Metals* 11 (December 1902): 6; and *Mining World* 24 (January 20, 1906): 65.

18. H. W. Reed to A. E. Reynolds, Ouray, August 4, 1891, and June 1, 1895; A. E. Reynolds to Francis T. Freeland, June 18, 1901; A. E. Reynolds to C. F. Palmer, Denver, September 5, 1902; A. E. Reynolds to C. F. McKenney, New York City, May 28, 1903; A. E. Reynolds to D. W. Hartshorn Jr., Denver, April 21, 1904; A. E. Reynolds to Hartford Gold

Extraction Co., Denver, July 12, 1907; A. E. Reynolds to Gerald Hughes, Old Hickory, Tenn., February 8, 1921.

19. The legal contest between Hyman and Wheeler is treated in Malcolm J. Rohrbough, *Aspen: The History of a Silver-Mining Town, 1879–1893* (New York: Oxford University Press, 1986).

20. A. E. Reynolds to W. F. Havemeyer, Denver, September 18, 1908, September 21, 1908, and October 11, 1908; W. F. Havemeyer to A. E. Reynolds, New York City, September 25, 1908.

21. Starbuck's business career is in *New York Times,* May 30, 1925. For Starbuck's investment in Reynolds's mining enterprises, see Charles A. Starbuck in Account with A. E. Reynolds, 1899–1900; and Memorandum of Stock Purchases, 1899–1902.

22. D. M. Hyman to A. E. Reynolds, New York City, October 7, 1907.

23. Interview with Ben T. Poxson, Denver, August 5, 1984. Biographical data about Barnsdall are in *New York Times,* February 28, 1917. See also *Romance of American Petroleum and Gas* 2 vols. (New York: [J. J. Little and Ives, 1920]), 2:109–110, 274–75.

24. A. E. Reynolds to Francis Schell, Denver, February 7, 1910.

25. Reynolds was the exception to Joseph E. King's claim that Colorado mining promoters "mined" eastern investors; that is, they deliberately sold them securities for mines that were either worthless or of far less value than advertised. See King, *A Mine to Make a Mine: Financing the Colorado Mining Industry, 1859–1902* (College Station: Texas A&M University Press, 1977).

26. *Cripple Creek (Colo.) Citizen,* June 20, 1898.

27. Ibid.

28. "Tribute to A. E. Reynolds" (1921, typescript), 2 pp.; *Denver Post,* March 21, 1921. The origin and activities of the City Temple Institutional Society are discussed in Jerome C. Smiley, *History of Denver* (Denver: Denver Times, 1901), 777–78. See also "The Rescue Work of Dean and Mrs. Peck," *Denver Republican,* March 19, 1899; and "One Year's Work of the City Temple Society," *Denver Times,* January 19, 1903.

29. John F. Campion to A. E. Reynolds, Denver, January 1, 1898; Persifor M. Cook to A. E. Reynolds, Denver, May 11, 1905, and June 28, 1906; Colorado Museum of Natural History, Minutes of Trustees' Meetings, December 13, 1897–November 8, 1922, in Denver Museum of Natural History Archives, Denver.

30. A. E. Reynolds to H. M. Allison, Denver, May 28, 1904.

31. A. E. Reynolds to W. C. Wynkoop, Denver, November 25, 1892.

32. A. E. Reynolds to Frank Hall, Denver, November 20, 1902.

33. For the early history of the silver question, see Paul Studenski and Herman E. Kroos, *Financial History of the United States* (New York: McGraw Book, 1952), 187–91, 215–34.

34. W. J. Bryan to A. E. Reynolds, Washington, D.C., March 20, 1894, and March 31, 1894; A. E. Reynolds to W. J. Bryan, Denver, March 27, 1894.

35. A. E. Reynolds to George T. Bradley, Denver, November 5, 1892; Daniel J. Campau to A. E. Reynolds, Chicago, Ill., September 26, 1896, and January 7, 1897; Kimbrough Jones to A. E. Reynolds, Chicago, October 20, 1896; Milton Smith to Ernest Bacon, Denver, October 16, 1896; A. E. Reynolds to C. J. Hughes Jr., November 7, 1900.

36. A. E. Reynolds to H. W. Reed, Denver, April 2, 1902.

37. The role of successful mining entrepreneurs in banking, transportation, and manufacturing is treated in Geraldine B. Bean, *Charles Boettcher: A Study in Pioneer Western Enterprise* (Boulder, Colo.: Westview Press, 1976), chaps. 8–14. See also Stephen Frederick Mehls, *"David H. Moffat Jr.: Early Colorado Business Leader"* (Ph.D. diss., University of Colorado, Boulder, 1982); and King, *A Mine to Make a Mine*, 167–69.

38. Roger Henn, "Trials of an Indian Trader," *Chicago Westerner's Brand Book* 33 (March 1976): 1–3, 22–27.

39. B. P. Morse to Alice Reynolds, May 10, 1921; B. P. Morse to Anna Reynolds Morse, September 19, 1921.

40. A. E. Reynolds to Dora Earll, May 13, 1881, June 13, 1881, August 5, 1881, August 21, 1881, September 7, 1881, October 11, 1881, October 31, 1881, and November 7, 1881.

41. Obituary of Dr. Robert W. Earll in *Columbus (Wisc.) Republican*, October 31, 1914.

42. A. E. Reynolds to Dora Earll, June 16, 1882, and July 18, 1882; New York City, March 3, 1883.

43. Certificate of Marriage, Albert E. Reynolds and Dora Earll, April 25, 1883.

44. Bradish Morse to Anna Reynolds Morse, Old Hickory, Tenn., February 13. 1928.

45. Gail M. Beaton, "The Widening Sphere of Women's Lives: The Literary Study and Philanthropic Work of Six Women's Clubs in Denver, 1881–1945," *Essays in Colorado History* 13 (1992): 20, 60, 63; *Denver Post*, November 18, 1916.

46. The Reynolds' residences are listed in *Corbett's and Ballenger's Annual Denver City Directory*. Ballenger & Richards became the publisher in 1889. See also A. E. Reynolds to Denver Water Co., May 6, 1889; A. E. Reynolds to Mrs. General G. M. Dodge, Denver, April 1, 1892; A. E. Reynolds to C. L. Dodge, Denver, November 22, 1911, and October 10, 1913; A. E. Reynolds to Gen. G. M. Dodge, Denver, November 26, 1913; A. E. Reynolds to Simon Guggenheim, Denver, November 25, 1913, November 26, 1913, and December 23, 1913; Simon Guggenheim to A. E. Reynolds, New York City, March 19, 1920; and Contract, A. E. Reynolds with Simon Guggenheim for Purchase of Home at 1555 Sherman St., Denver, March 1, 1920. A description of the house at 1555 Sherman, originally built by Chester Morey, who sold it to Simon Guggenheim, is in Anna R. Garrey, "Notes on 1555 Sherman Street, Denver" (March 1975, typescript), 5 pp.

47. Helen C. Cole, "The Dobbs Curriculum: The First Fifty Years, 1877–1927," *Dobbs Alumnae Bulletin* (Fall-Winter 1968–1969): 9–10; Pamela Daly Vose, *The Masters School, 1877–1977: A Retrospective Portrait for the One-Hundredth Anniversary* (1977). There was no Daisy Lewis on the list of Smith graduates in 1907, but there was a Millicent Vaughan Lewis. Perhaps she was Daisy Lewis. See "Twenty-Ninth Commencement at Smith College, June 18, 1907."

48. "Descendants of Albert Eugene and Francis Eudorah Earll Reynolds," Albert E. Reynolds Collection.

49. Ibid.

50. *Silverite-Plaindealer* (Ouray, Colo.), August 19, 1898.

51. Trial Balances, December 31, 1890, and March 31, 1921.

2 Frontier Trader

1. The only study to examine the military post traders' contribution to the settlement of the American West is David Michael Delo, *Peddler and Post Traders: The Army Sutler on the Frontier* (Salt Lake City: University of Utah Press, 1992). Delo did not have access to the papers of Lee & Reynolds, whom he mentions only twice.

2. Daniel F. Schofield, *Indians, Cattle, Ships, and Oil: The Story of W. M. D. Lee* (Austin: University of Texas Press, 1985), 5–9.

3. U.S. House, Committee on Expenditures in the War Department, "The Management of the War Department," 44th Cong., 1st sess., *Report* no. 799 (Washington, D.C.: GPO, 1875), pp. 243–46.

4. Ibid., 246; Lee & Reynolds, Balance Sheet, December 31, 1879.

5. Schofield, *Indians, Cattle, Ships, and Oil,* 36, 38.

6. The most complete history of Camp (later Fort) Supply from its origin in 1868 until its abandonment in 1896 is Robert C. Carriker, *Fort Supply, Indian Territory: Frontier Outpost on the Plains* (Norman: University of Oklahoma Press, 1970). See also Susan Peterson, "Fort Supply: Isolated Outpost," in *Early Military Forts and Posts in Oklahoma,* ed. Odie B. Faulk, Kenny A. Franks, and Paul F. Lambert (Oklahoma City: Oklahoma Historical Society, 1978), 78–89.

7. Lee & Reynolds to W. A. Rose, February 17, 1874.

8. Among the correspondence with breweries in Lee & Reynolds letterpress books, see especially Lee & Reynolds to John B. Fleming & Co., July 18, 1871, and March 3, 1882; Lee & Reynolds to Brandon & Kirmeyer, February 9, 1874, December 30, 1874, and January 13, 22, 1875; C. F. McKenney to E. E. Polly, April 10, 1879; and Lee & Reynolds to Voechting Shope & Co., September 25, 1880. See also *Leavenworth (Kans.) Daily Times,* March 17, 1875.

9. Lee & Reynolds to John B. Fleming, July 18, 1871, March 7, 1872, March 14, 1873, and May 17, 1873; Lee & Reynolds to Brandon & Kirmeyer, February 9, 1874, December 30, 1874, January 13, 1875, January 22, 1875, March 17, 1875; Lee & Reynolds to J. H. Phillips, January 13, 1875; Lee & Reynolds to Voechting Shope & Company, September 25, 1880.

10. Lee & Reynolds to H. M. Gillette, September 4, 1873, March 26, 1874, and September 22, 1874; Lee & Reynolds to Capt. W. A. Rafferty, January 30, 1875.

11. C. F. McKenney to E. E. Polly, April 10, 1879.

12. Lee & Reynolds to Capt. E. M. Hays, May 30, 1877; Lee & Reynolds to Lt. O. W. Budd, July 27, 1878.

13. The relocation of the agency from Camp Supply to a new location is discussed in Donald J. Berthrong, *The Southern Cheyennes* (Norman: University of Oklahoma Press, 1963), 346–49; and Donald J. Berthrong, *The Cheyenne and Arapaho Ordeal: Reservation and Agency Life in Indian Territory, 1875–1907* (Norman: University of Oklahoma Press, 1976), 345–57.

14. A. E. Reynolds to W. N. Hubbell, January 5, 1873.

15. Lee & Reynolds letterpress books, 1870–1881.

16. Ibid. See also *Leavenworth (Kans.) Daily Times,* July 4, 1875, and July 31, 1875.

17. Lee & Reynolds letterpress books, 1870–1881.

18. Lee & Reynolds to S. R. Ainslee, April 3, 1870, and June 3, 1870; Lee & Reynolds to M. J. R. Treat, January 18, 1872, March 7, 1872, and April 3, 1872; Lee & Reynolds to W. H. Fanning, January 20, 1872, February 23, 1872, and April 13, 1872; Lee & Reynolds to A. Jard, March 3, 1872.

19. Lee & Reynolds to Work & Miller, December 7, 1872; Lee & Reynolds to J. H. Phillips, January 1, 1873, December 25, 1873, January 19, 1874, December 2, 1874, December 18, 1874, December 5, 1875, and October 29, 1876; Lee & Reynolds to Charles Rath & Company, April 23, 1874, September 25, 1874, October 16, 1874, and December 8, 1874. The roles of Dodge City merchants in the regional economy is treated at length in C. Robert Haywood, *Trails South: The Wagon-Road Economy in the Dodge City–Panhandle Region* (Norman: University of Oklahoma Press, 1986).

20. Lee & Reynolds to S. R. Ainslee, June 3, 1870; Lee & Reynolds to Samuel Morris, June 3, 1870; Lee & Reynolds to Will F. Wilson, August 23, 1871; Lee & Reynolds to W. A. Rose & Co., August 31, 1871; Lee & Reynolds to M. J. R. Treat, January 18, 1872.

21. Unidentified Fulton, Mo., newspaper clipping, December 20, 1904, attached to T. A. Russell to A. E. Reynolds, December 19, 1904; John L. Lillibridge, *The Red Fork Ranch and Its People* (Ocala, Fla.: Greene's Printing, 1990), 24, 133–35.

22. A. E. Reynolds to Maj. Gen. L. C. Easton, May 15, 1871; Lee & Reynolds to A. J. Anthony, August 21, 1874, and August 25, 1874.

23. Lee & Reynolds to L. C. Easton, September 2, 1870, September 30, 1870, September 12, 1871, September 24, 1871, and October 1, 1871; Lee & Reynolds to C. R. Morehead & Company, May 5, 1871, and May 17, 1871; Lee & Reynolds to W. A. Rose & Company, May 5, 1871; Lee & Reynolds to Chief Quarter Master, Fort Leavenworth, July 16, 1872, December 1, 1872, February 18, 1873, May 17, 1873, August 25, 1873, September 9, 1873, September 19, 1873, December 15, 1873, January 11, 1874, August 31, 1874, January 20, 1875, February 10, 1875, April 7, 1875, August 2, 1875, August 13, 1875, and August 30, 1875; Lee & Reynolds to Maj. Wirt Davis, August 13, 1875.

24. Wayne Gard, *The Great Buffalo Hunt* (New York: Alfred A. Knopf, 1960), 27, 37.

25. A. E. Reynolds Notebook, 1878–1880.

26. A. E. Reynolds to Ed Guerrier, March 4, 1873.

27. Personnel employed by the trader are listed in Lee & Reynolds to John D. Miles, December 18, 1873.

28. Lee & Reynolds to Buckley, Willing & Company, December 28, 1871, December 25, 1873, and January 30, 1874; Lee & Reynolds to Dodd, Brown & Company, March 25, 1873; Lee & Reynolds to E. H. Durfee, April 20, 1870, January 21, 1873, February 14, 1873, and February 26, 1873.

29. John C. Ewers, "Hair Pipes in Plains Indians Ornament," Anthropological Paper 50, *Smithsonian Institution Bureau of American Ethnology Bulletin* 164 (Washington, D.C.: GPO, 1957), 37, 42, 54–59; Thomas E. Mails, *The Mystic Warriors of the Plains* (Garden City, N.Y.: Doubleday, 1972), 359, 371; Lee & Reynolds to Buckley, Willing & Company, December 28, 1871.

30. Lee & Reynolds to Buckley, Willing & Company, August 11, 1871, and December 28, 1871; Lee & Reynolds to E. H. Durfee, April 20, 1870, and December 28, 1871.

31. Lee & Reynolds to Murray, June 17, 1870; Lee & Reynolds to B. S. Richards, January 3, 1872.

32. Lee & Reynolds to B. S. Richards, August 9, 1871, November 15, 1873, January 27, 1874, and January 31, 1874; Lee & Reynolds to Railroad Agent, Hays City, Kans., January 4, 1873.

33. Schofield, *Indians, Cattle, Ships, and Oil*, 26, 29–30; T. Lindsay Baker and Billy R. Harrison, *Adobe Walls: The History and Archeology of the 1874 Trading Post* (College Station: Texas A&M University Press, 1986), 43n. 11, 309.

34. Schofield, *Indians, Cattle, Ships, and Oil*, 39–40; Haywood, *Trails South*, p. 130.

35. Schofield, *Indians, Cattle, Ships, and Oil*, 39–40. See also Rex Strickland, ed., "The Recollections of W. S. Glenn, Buffalo Hunter," *Panhandle-Plains Historical Review* 22 (1949): 49–50; Gard, *The Great Buffalo Hunt*, 232–33, 237; Carl Coke Rister, *Fort Griffin on the Texas Frontier* (Norman: University of Oklahoma Press, 1956), 172–74. For the transporting of robes from the Panhandle to Darlington, Fort Supply, and Dodge City, see A. E. Reynolds & Company, Inventory, April 9, 1876; Lee and Reynolds to Charles Rath & Co., December 3, 1876, January 28, 1877, February 24, 1877, March 19, 1877, March 25, 1877, and April 14, 1877; Lee & Reynolds to Skinner, February 21, 1877; Lee & Reynolds to C. H. Lane, April 14, 1877, and April 28, 1877; A. E. Reynolds to Robert M. Wright, January 10, 1877, and April 1, 1877;

A. E. Reynolds to Hutton, February 24, 1877; A. E. Reynolds to C. H. Lane, February 24, 1877; George E. Reynolds to W. M. D. Lee, January 10, 1878.

36. Strickland, ed., "The Recollections of W. G. Glenn," 49–50; *Dodge City (Kans.) Times,* July 28, 1877.

37. Memorandum of Agreement, Lee & Reynolds with Charles Rath & Company, May 7, 1877.

38. Ibid.; John D. Miles to William Nicholson, August 31, 1877, in U.S. Commissioner of Indian Affairs, *Annual Report, 1878* (Washington, D.C.: GPO, 1879), 82. According to Philip McCusker, a part-time trader and interpreter, Miles, who was allegedly a silent partner in the firm of Lee & Reynolds, permitted the traders to overcharge the agency Indians. See Berthrong, *The Cheyenne and Arapaho Ordeal,* p. 32.

39. A. E. Reynolds to George, March 28, 1877.

40. Ibid.; John D. Miles to Commissioner of Indian Affairs, August 31, 1878, in U.S. Commissioner of Indian Affairs, *Annual Report, 1877–1878* (Washington, D.C.: GPO, 1879), 53. See also Berthrong, *The Cheyenne and Arapaho Ordeal,* 11, 16.

41. A. E. Reynolds bought 7,800 from Fisher, first name unknown, on August 28, 1877, and 5,320 from George A. Baker on August 29, 1877. See A. E. Reynolds Notebook, 1878–1880.

42. The shipment of robes by Lee & Reynolds from Camp Supply and Darlington is reported in correspondence in letterpress books, 1870–1879.

43. A. E. Reynolds to Friend Garbutt, February 11, 1877.

44. Business cards of Lee, Reynolds & Arnold, New York City, and Lee, Reynolds & Warren, Chicago.

45. Inventories and sales of robes by the Chicago and New York stores are reported in Lee & Reynolds, Memorandum of Transactions, September 10, 1877–March 1, 1879. For the Chicago sales in October 1877, see 1–17. See also Lee & Reynolds, Journal, vol. 13, 56, 70–72.

46. Contract, Lee & Reynolds with George E. Reynolds, December 8, 1878, Lee & Reynolds to Lyman Scott, February 13, 1879; Schofield, *Indians, Cattle, Ships, and Oil,* 58.

47. A. E. Reynolds to Commanding Officer, Fort Supply, December 31, 1879.

48. Lee & Reynolds to Chick Browne & Co., September 16, 1874, October 1, 1874, October 4, 1874, October 30, 1874, November 21, 1874, February 10, 1875, April 1, 1875, and April 4, 1875; Lee &

Reynolds to Charles Rath & Co., October 16, 1874; Lee & Reynolds to Capt. C. A. Reynolds, November 27, 1874; Lee & Reynolds to Chief Q. M., Department of Missouri, March 20, 1875.

49. See Lee & Reynolds Freighters, Dodge City, Kans., letterpress books, June 16, 1877–May 30, 1880, and December 27, 1878–August 23, 1879. For more information about Lee & Reynolds's freighting operations in the region south of Dodge City, Kans., see Haywood, *Trails South*, 125–26ff.

50. A. E. Reynolds Notebook, December 31, 1879.

51. Ibid.

52. Lee & Reynolds to Chief Signal Officer, War Department, July 28, 1879, and August 12, 1879; Lee & Reynolds to Lt. James A. Swift, August 21, 1879, September 20, 1879, and October 13, 1879; Lee & Reynolds to Lt. Thomas M. Wence, April 28, 1880; *Dodge City (Kans.) Times*, November 24, 1881.

53. Agreement, W. M. D. Lee with A. E. Reynolds, April 15, 1882.

54. A. E. Reynolds to Dodd, Brown & Co., June 9, 1883; A. E. Reynolds to Hubbell and Doty, July 21, 1883, and September 10, 1883; A. E. Reynolds to Bradstreets, [August 25, 1883].

55. D. W. Van Horn to A. E. Reynolds, July 23, 1882, July 8, 1889, November 11, 1889, January 3, 1890, July 11, 1890, October 10, 1890, October 22, 1890, November 2, 1890, December 24, 1890, and February 3, 1891; A. E. Reynolds to John A. Thatcher, July 12, 1899.

56. A. E. Reynolds to George E. Reynolds, August 8, 1885; A. E. Reynolds to Leavenworth National Bank, August 8, 1885; A. E. Reynolds to Bela M. Hughes, December 28, 1885; A. E. Reynolds to Robert M. Wright, February 15, 1886; A. E. Reynolds to Henry Moore Teller, January 11, 1886; Hemphill & Wey to A. E. Reynolds, January 2, 1886.

57. A. E. Reynolds to Robert M. Wright, February 15, 1886; A. E. Reynolds to Hubbell and Doty, March 16, 1886; C. F. McKenney to Hubbell and Doty, April 6, 1886; D. H. Doty to A. E. Reynolds, October 6, 1887.

58. D. H. Doty to A. E. Reynolds, October 16, 1887; A. E. Reynolds to Leavenworth National Bank, July 21, 1886.

59. Adna R. Chaffee to A. E. Reynolds, Manila, P.I., October 21, 1901; A. E. Reynolds to Charles J. Hughes Jr., Denver, December 18, 1909; A. E. Reynolds to H. M. Teller, Denver, January 3, 1910; A. E. Reynolds to Frank Baldwin, Denver, July 18, 1913; A. E. Reynolds to Edward T. Taylor, Denver, February 22, 1918.

60. *Denver Times,* November [5], 1905; Milo H. Slater to A. E. Reynolds, Denver, November 10, 1905; A. E. Reynolds to Milo H. Slater, Denver, November 11, 1905.

61. A. E. Reynolds to Jesse Smith, Denver, May 28, 1918, and June 15, 1918.

62. A. E. Reynolds to George Bent, June 7, 1912, September 1, 1913, November 27, 1914, November 10, 1915, November 24, 1916, December 29, 1916, and April 17, 1917; George Bent to A. E. Reynolds, January 13, 1897, December 13, 1903, November 12, 1904, September 13, 1905, November 6, 1906, April 8, 1911, June 23, 1911, and November 11, 1911.

63. Reynolds's assessment of his experiences in Indian Territory is in the biographical sketch he wrote for Wilbur Fisk Stone, *History of Colorado,* 4 vols. (Chicago: S. J. Clarke Publishing, 1918–1919), 3:244–47. See also Lee & Reynolds to John Miles, July 12, 1877; *Dodge City (Kans.) Times,* April 26, 1879; and Schofield, *Indians, Cattle, Ships, and Oil,* 43, 49.

64. The desperate plight of the Cheyenne and Arapahoe on the reservation is treated at length in Berthrong, *The Cheyenne and Arapaho Ordeal.*

3 Ranching on the High Plains

1. Lee & Reynolds to L. and R. Dickinson, October 26, 1873; W. M. D. Lee to Lewis Rinn, Fort Supply, Indian Territory, May 18, 1882.

2. John L. Lillibridge, *The Red Fork Ranch and Its People* (Ocala, Fla.: Greene's Printing, 1990), 24–25. See also A. E. Reynolds to Alvin H. Sanders, June 9, 1899; and A. E. Reynolds to John Clay, May 28, 1914.

3. Agreement, Lee & Reynolds with Captain Richard King, July 6, 1887; Lee & Reynolds to Henry Morris, April 21, 1874; Lee & Reynolds to Seth Ward, February 7, 1879; A. E. Reynolds to Alvin H. Sanders, June 9, 1899; A. E. Reynolds to John Clay, May 28, 1914.

4. Lee & Reynolds to Capt. J. H. Gilman, September 4, 1874, October 15, 1874, December 30, 1874, March 3, 1875, April 11, 1875, August 31, 1875, June 24, 1876, and June 22, 1877.

5. Lee & Reynolds to George M. Young, June 26, 1879; Volz & Kiesling to Chief Commissary Officer, Department of Missouri, July 3, 1879.

6. Donald F. Schofield, *Indians, Cattle, Ships, and Oil: The Story of W. M. D. Lee* (Austin: University of Texas Press, 1985), 54. See also W. M. D. Lee to Lewis Rinn, May 18, 1882.

7. The sheep-oriented society in the Canadian River valley in the 1870s is described in Pauline Durett Robertson and R. L. Robertson, *Tascosa: Historic Site in the Texas Panhandle* (Amarillo, Tex.: Paramount Publishing, 1977), 7, 18–19. An account of McAllister's selection of the future site of the Lee & Reynolds ranch is in Dulcie Sullivan, *The LS Brand: The Story of a Texas Panhandle Ranch* (Austin: University of Texas Press, 1968), 30.

8. See statement signed by Gunter & Munson, December 17, 1879.

9. Wages paid cattle herders, December 1–31, 1879, in Lee & Reynolds, Journal, vol. 14, 69.

10. A. E. Reynolds to Alvin H. Sanders, Denver, June 9, 1899; Agreement, Lee & Reynolds with George T. Reynolds, William Reynolds, and Joshua Matthews, February 14, 1881. See also Schofield, *Indians, Cattle, Ships, and Oil*, 53–54.

11. A. E. Reynolds to Alvin H. Sanders, Denver, June 9, 1899.

12. A. E. Reynolds to Charles F. McKenney, Alamosa, Colo., June 18, 1881.

13. Schofield, *Indians, Cattle, Ships, and Oil*, 58; Sullivan, *The LS Brand*, 32.

14. Agreement, A. E. Reynolds with W. M. D. Lee, April 15, 1882; Mortgage, A. E. Reynolds to W. M. D. Lee, April 15, 1882.

15. Schofield, *Indians, Cattle, Ships, and Oil*, 58. Schofield is in error on the distribution of assets. Lee acquired the partners' military store at Fort Supply and the freight terminals at Dodge City, Fort Supply, and Fort Elliott. The stores at Fort Elliott and Mobeetie were taken over by D. W. Van Horn & Co., in which Reynolds was an equal partner with his cousin. Schofield's biography of Lee treats at length his highly successful business career as a cattleman, a promoter of Houston as a deepwater port, and an oil entrepreneur after the breakup of Lee & Reynolds in 1881–1882.

16. Agreement, A. E. Reynolds with John H. Maugham, July 17, 1882.

17. Agreement, A. E. Reynolds and John H. Maugham with Julia Fletcher, October 16, 1882; Mortgage, A. E. Reynolds and John H. Maugham to Cornelius C. Cuyler, representative of the Dundee Mortgage and Trust Investment Co., Ltd., July 1, 1883.

18. See Reynolds family genealogy.

19. Reynolds Land & Cattle Company, Certificate of Incorporation, Secretary of State's Office, Albany, New York, June 8, 1892, in which is located the incorporation agreement of May 5, 1884; Reynolds Land & Cattle Company Minute Book, Board of Trustees' Meeting, May 26, 1884.

20. C. F. McKenney to George E. Reynolds, Denver, March 25, 1895; John L. McCarty, *Maverick Town: The Story of Old Tascosa* (Norman: University of Oklahoma Press, 1946), 47–48, refers to the Reynolds brothers as owners of the LE Ranch.

21. A. E. Reynolds to Alice Reynolds, January 15, 1889; A. E. Reynolds to George E. Reynolds, January 17, 1889; A. E. Reynolds to George W. Russell, August 6, 1889; A. E. Reynolds to George Law, December 4, 1890; C. F. Reynolds to C. F. McKenney, February 2, 1889.

22. C. F. Reynolds to C. F. McKenney, New York, February 14, 1887; J. H. Maugham to Chairman, Capitol Freehold Land & Investment Co., London, March 25, 1887; A. E. Reynolds to G. W. Russell, April 14, 1887.

23. A. E. Reynolds to J. H. Brady, April 13, 1887.

24. C. F. Reynolds to C. F. McKenney, October 15, 1889, June 29, 1890, and September 26, 1890.

25. C. F. McKenney to C. F. Reynolds, May 4, 1887; C. F. McKenney to George E. Reynolds, August 1, 1887; C. F. McKenney to J. H. Brady, August 1, 1887; A. E. Reynolds to J. H. Maugham, May 16, 1887; A. E. Reynolds to Springer (N.M.) Mercantile Co., May 18, 1887.

26. C. F. Reynolds to A. E. Reynolds, February 27, 1891, October 9, 1891, October 28, 1891, April 10, 1892, and December 10, 1897; C. F. Reynolds to C. F. McKenney, April 4, 1891.

27. C. F. Reynolds to A. E. Reynolds, August 18, 1889, and October 9, 1891; C. F. Reynolds to C. F. McKenney, July 6, 1890, August 11, 1890, July 25, 1891, April 17, 19, 1892.

28. A. E. Reynolds to John H. Maugham, July 10, 1884, and July 17, 1884. For the origin, evolution, and demise of the XIT, see J. Evetts Haley, *The XIT Ranch and the Early Days of the Llano Estacado* (Norman: University of Oklahoma Press, 1967).

29. A. E. Reynolds to John H. Maugham, April 12, 1885, February 26, 1887, and April 7, 1887; John H. Maugham to Reynolds, October 30, 1886, and December 3, 1886.

30. A. E. Reynolds to John H. Maugham, March 11, 1885, July 8, 1886, August 16, 1886, November 3, 1886, April 7, 1888, September 14,

1888, and November 13, 1888; A. E. Reynolds to Creswell Ranch and Cattle Co. (cable), November 2, 1886, and April 7, 1888; A. E. Reynolds to James Mackenzie, November 8, 1886; A. E. Reynolds to C. F. Reynolds, July 30, 1889; John H. Maugham to A. E. Reynolds, November 25, 1886.

31. A. E. Reynolds to C. F. McKenney, May 29, 1889; George E. Reynolds to A. E. Reynolds, Leavenworth, Kans., July 5, 1889.

32. Reynolds Land & Cattle Co., Minute Book, 58.

33. Ibid., 75.

34. A. E. Reynolds to John H. Maugham, June 17, 1886, and May 6, 1887; A. E. Reynolds to M. D. Thatcher, July 5, 1886, and July 7, 1886; M. D. Thatcher to A. E. Reynolds, December 12, 1887.

35. A. E. Reynolds to D. W. Van Horn, Denver, October 18, 1898.

36. John Paton & Co. to M. D. Thatcher, New York, July 2, 1890, and John Paton & Co. to A. E. Reynolds, New York, October 6, 1890; George Law to A. E. Reynolds, Kansas City, Mo., September 23, 1890.

37. William Mackenzie to A. E. Reynolds, Edinburgh, October 25, 1890; A. E. Reynolds to John Paton & Co., Denver, September 22, 1891. For the reaction of foreign investors to the declining value of American ranches, see W. G. Kerr, *Scottish Capital on the American Credit Frontier* (Austin: Texas State Historical Association, 1976), 45–46.

38. Reynolds Land & Cattle Co., Minute Book, 83, 85.

39. A. E. Reynolds to William Mackenzie, March 12, 1901, and April 23, 1901; Reynolds Land & Cattle Co., Payments on Note of July 1, 1896, January 19, 1901; Reynolds Land and Cattle Co., Mortgage with Alliance Trust Co., Ltd., July 1, 1986, stamped paid July 1, 1901.

40. A. E. Reynolds to James C. Johnson, Denver, March 14, 1902.

41. This description of the property is taken mainly from A. E. Reynolds to D. W. Van Horn, Denver, October 18, 1898.

42. K. L. Browne to Reynolds Land & Cattle Co., Kansas City, Kans., July 18, 1900; C. W. Browne to A. E. Reynolds, El Paso, Tex., May 27, 1902.

43. A. E. Reynolds to M. F. Beaumont, Denver, February 27, 1902; A. E. Reynolds to James C. Johnson, March 14, 1902.

44. Ibid.; Charles F. Reynolds to unidentified party, January 6, 1902; A. E. Reynolds to James C. Johnson, March 14, 1902.

45. A. E. Reynolds to M. F. Beaumont, February 27, 1902; A. E. Reynolds to James C. Johnson, March 14, 1902; James C. Johnson to A. E. Reynolds, Edinburgh, Scotland, April 3, 1902.

46. Edward Everett Dale, *The Range Cattle Industry: Ranching on the Great Plains from 1865 to 1925* (Norman: University of Oklahoma Press, 1960), 82; Kerr, *Scottish Capital,* 24, 49.

47. Reynolds Land & Cattle Co., Minute Book, 132.

48. A. E. Reynolds to William Boyce, Denver, September 5, 1902; Reynolds Land & Cattle Co., Minute Book, 134; W. M. Pearce, *The Matador Land and Cattle Company* (Norman: University of Oklahoma Press, 1982), 84–85.

49. Reynolds Land & Cattle Co., Journal, vol. 37, 345.

50. A. E. Reynolds to M. D. Thatcher, Denver, March 14, 1902.

51. Reynolds Land & Cattle Co., Journal, vol. 37, 343.

52. A. E. Reynolds to J. J. Hagerman, Denver, September 22, 1902, and November 10, 1902; J. J. Hagerman to A. E. Reynolds, Chicago, November 3, 1902.

53. A. E. Reynolds to J. J. Hagerman, December 5, 1902, and July 31, 1903; A. E. Reynolds to Percy Hagerman, January 7, 1916, and October 30, 1916; J. J. Hagerman to A. E. Reynolds, Roswell, N.M., August 25, 1903, December 10, 1903, and February 5, 1908; George P. Hovey to A. E. Reynolds, Kansas City, Kans., February 13, 1908.

54. A. E. Reynolds to H. L. Lubers, May 21, 1900, July 18, 1900, and August 3, 1900; A. E. Reynolds to J. H. Crosley, July 18, 1900, August 3, 1900, September 15, 1900, and October 26, 1900; A. E. Reynolds to G. F. Patrick, December 28, 1900; A. E. Reynolds to George H. Sly, December 28, 1900; A. E. Reynolds to C. F. Reynolds, November 30, 1902; A. E. Reynolds to William Mackenzie, December 10, 1907; A. E. Reynolds to John Clay, May 28, 1916. Mathews sold the EJM Ranch and herd in May 1916, at which time he paid Reynolds the balance of a note given for the purchase of cattle. See A. E. Reynolds to E. J. Mathews, May 5, 1916, and May 11, 1916.

55. Reynolds Land & Cattle Co., Journal, vol. 37, 302, 308, 314, 323, 325, 371, 372, 431, 434, 450, 451, 452, 453, 455, 456, 457, 561, 462, 463, 464, 468.

56. William Boyce to Reynolds Land & Cattle Co., Amarillo, Tex., June 6, 1907; William Boyce to A. E. Reynolds, Amarillo, Tex., October 7, 1907.

57. William Boyce to A. E. Reynolds, Amarillo, Tex., October 26, 1907, November 9, 1907, and January 28, 1908; A. E. Reynolds to William Boyce, Denver, April 7, 1908; A. E. Reynolds to M. D. Thatcher, Denver, February 15, 1908.

58. W. S. Mabry to A. E. Reynolds, Tascosa, Tex., April 2, 1887.

59. William Boyce to A. E. Reynolds, Amarillo, Tex., October 26, 1907, November 6, 1907, and January 28, 1908; A. E. Reynolds to William Boyce, Denver, April 7, 1908; A. E. Reynolds to M. D. Thatcher, Denver, February 15, 1908.

60. A. E. Reynolds to William Boyce, Denver, March 9, 1908; William Boyce to A. E. Reynolds, Amarillo, Tex., April 11, 1908; W. D. Twitchell to A. E. Reynolds, Amarillo, Tex., October 7, 1908; A. E. Reynolds to M. D. Thatcher, Denver, January 13, 1910, and January 24, 1912.

61. A. E. Reynolds to J. M. Rusk, Denver, June 8, 1917, and January 19, 1921; J. M. Rusk to A. E. Reynolds, Edinburgh, Scotland, April 7, 1920, November 16, 1920, and February 10, 1921.

62. A. E. Reynolds to Commissioner of Lands, State of Texas, August 9, 1917, September 26, 1918, and January 17, 1921; Fred A. Sabin to Anna R. Morse, La Junta, Colo., September 3, 1921; B. P. Morse to J. P. M. Humphrey, Old Hickory, Tenn., September 3, 1921; Berrien Hughes to B. P. Morse, Denver, August 16. 1921. In 1916 the Matador Land and Cattle Company leased from John M. Shelton the Romero pasture south of the Canadian River for three years. Later the same year it bought the 121,622 acres at a cost of $4.25 per acre. See Pearce, *The Matador Land and Cattle Company*, 147–48.

63. B. P. Morse to Edward S. Wiard, April 6, 1921.

4 Creating a Mining Empire

1. W. M. D. Lee to E. H. Garbutt, January 20, 1877; A. E. Reynolds to E. H. Garbutt, February 11, 1877, March 21, 1877, and March 24, 1877.

2. W. M. D. Lee to E. H. Garbutt, January 20, 1877; A. E. Reynolds Notebook, 1879–1880; Memorandum of Agreement Between H. P. De Graaf, C. W. Scofield, and W. M. D. Lee and A. E. Reynolds of the firm of Lee & Reynolds, October 15, 1879.

3. A. E. Reynolds Notebook, 1879–1880.

4. Donald B. Robertson, *Encyclopedia of Western Railroad History*, vol. 1, *The Desert States: Arizona, Nevada, New Mexico, Utah* (Caldwell, Idaho: Caxton Printers, 1986), 296.

5. A. E. Reynolds to C. F. McKenney, July 5, 1880, July 29, 1880, and August 31, 1880; W. M. D. Lee to C. F. McKenney, August 7, 1880, November 3, 1880, and April 30, 1881; W. M. D. Lee to L. E. Deger, May 1, 1881; J. H. Maugham to A. E. Reynolds, December 20, 1881.

6. A. E. Reynolds Notebook, 1879–1880.

7. See Henry C. Thatcher obituaries, *Pueblo (Colo.) Daily Chieftain,* March 21, 1884, and March 22, 1884.

8. *Silver World* (Lake City, Colo.), January 27, 1877, January 5, 1878, and April 10, 1880; *Ouray (Colo.) Times,* December 7, 1878.

9. *Silver World* (Lake City, Colo.), January 3, 1880.

10. *Silver World* (Lake City, Colo.), January 3, 1880, May 29, 1880, and June 5, 1880. See also John Duer Irving and Howland Bancroft, "Geology and Ore Deposits Near Lake City, Colorado," *United States Geological Survey Bulletin* 478 (1911): 13–14, 16–17.

11. *Silver World* (Lake City, Colo.), January 3, 1880; Irving and Bancroft, "Geology and Ore Deposits," 71–72.

12. *Silver World* (Lake City, Colo.), August 19, 1876, and June 12, 1880; *Ouray (Colo.) Times,* November 30, 1878.

13. *Silver World* (Lake City, Colo.), June 12, 1880, and May 27, 1882; *Ouray (Colo.) Times,* November 30, 1878.

14. *Silver World* (Lake City, Colo.), December 13, 1879, December 20, 1879, and July 10, 1880. See also Mark L. Gardner, "John Simpson Hough: Merchant on the Santa Fe Trail," *Wagon Tracks* 2 (February 1988): 10–12.

15. *Silver World* (Lake City, Colo.), January 13, 1877, September 9, 1877, December 22, 1877, May 18, 1878, August 24, 1878, and December 13, 1879.

16. *Silver World* (Lake City, Colo.), June 26, 1880; A. E. Reynolds to M. D. Thatcher, Denver, August 7, 1906.

17. *Silver World* (Lake City, Colo.), June 5, 1880.

18. *Silver World* (Lake City, Colo.), August 21, 1880, September 11, 1880, September 25, 1880, January 22, 1881, April 9, 1881, May 7, 1881, June 25, 1881, October 1, 1881, July 1, 1882, and August 5, 1882.

19. John C. Bell to M. C. Thatcher, Montrose, Colo., September 8, 1921.

20. A. E. Reynolds to Miller Crane, New York City, May 15, 1884.

21. Agreement, J. H. Maugham, A. E. Reynolds, H. C. Dickinson, and Linnaus C. Hill, to Organize the Belle of the West Consolidated Mining Co., April 7, 1880. See also *Silver World* (Lake City, Colo.), December 30, 1882.

22. A. E. Reynolds to J. H. Maugham, January 6, 1886, and August 12, 1886; C. F. McKenney to A. C. Mullen, March 10, 1887; A. E. Reynolds to M. D. Thatcher, Denver, August 7, 1906.

23. C. F. McKenney to Andy Jard, January 29, 1886, June 29, 1886, and March 30, 1887; John S. Hough to Gus Miller, July 4, 1886; C. F. McKenney to Gus Miller, July 8, 1886; A. E. Reynolds to Stoiber Bros., July 22, 1886.

24. A. E. Reynolds to Crooke Mining and Smelting Co., Ltd., October 1, 1886; A. E. Reynolds to J. H. Maugham, July 1, 1886.

25. A. E. Reynolds to Friend Hough, Leavenworth, Kans., June 16, 1884; A. E. Reynolds to C. F. McKenney, Chicago, November 12, 1884.

26. A. E. Reynolds to Friend Hough, June 19, 1884; A. E. Reynolds to J. H. Maugham, May 7, 1885; A. E. Reynolds to Angus Snedaker, October 15, 1890.

27. C. F. McKenney to H. W. Reed, September 30, 1885; A. E. Reynolds to Buddecke and Diehl, October 3, 1885; A. E. Reynolds to John C. Bell, October 4, 1885.

28. A. E. Reynolds to James H. Bradley, Denver, July 7, 1885.

29. Ibid.

30. Caleb Reed's death is reported in A. E. Reynolds to Friend Sheldon, January 7, 1886.

31. H. W. Reed to W. C. Sheldon, December 27, 1887; A. E. Reynolds to George H. Hyde, December 23, 1890.

32. David M. Hyman, "The Romance of a Mining Venture," the original 126-page typescript of which is in the American Jewish Archives, Hebrew Union College, Cincinnato, Ohio, explains how he acquired the mining claims and why he decided to press his claim to the apex of the principal vein on Aspen Mountain through the courts. The apex suit is treated at length by Malcolm Rohrbough, *Aspen: The History of a Silver-Mining Town, 1879–1893* (New York: Oxford University Press, 1986), chaps. 7–9.

33. Hyman, "The Romance of a Mining Venture," 41. See also A. E. Reynolds to B. M. and C. J. Hughes Jr., New York City, March 4, 1885; and A. E. Reynolds to Charles Robinson, March 13, 1886, and September 10, 1887.

34. Hyman, "The Romance of a Mining Venture," 48. See also A. E. Reynolds to Charles Robinson, March 31, 1885; and A. E. Reynolds to E. Senior, June 27, 1885. The record of Arms's and Robinson's accounts with as well as trial balances of the Aspen Pool are in A. E. Reynolds letterpress books, vol. 19, 170, 184; vol. 21, 113; vol. 22, 523; and vol. 23, 226, 265, 425.

35. Hyman, "The Romance of a Mining Venture," 43–44. 50; Rohrbough, *Aspen*, 101.

36. Hyman, "The Romance of a Mining Venture," 64; Rohrbough, *Aspen*, 106–17.

37. *Rocky Mountain Sun* (Aspen, Colo.), October 15, 1887, and April 28, 1888; Hyman, "The Romance of a Mining Venture," 64–65.

38. A. E. Reynolds to J. H. Bradley, June 17, 1888; A. E. Reynolds to George H. Hyde, October 11, 1888; Hyman, "The Romance of a Mining Venture," 67–68.

39. A. E. Reynolds to M. D. Thatcher, June 17, 1888; A. E. Reynolds to Robert McCurdy, October 17, 1888, and December 19, 1888; McCurdy to A. E. Reynolds, October 24, 1888.

40. A. E. Reynolds to Robert McCurdy, June 17, 1887; A. E. Reynolds to George H. Hyde, October 23, 1887.

41. A. E. Reynolds to Leavenworth National Bank, December 29, 1886; A. E. Reynolds to M. D. Thatcher, June 17, 1888; A. E. Reynolds to George H. Hyde, October 11, 1888. Subscribers to the Aspen Pool are listed in Trial Balance, October 3, 1887, letterpress book, vol. 22, 523.

42. A. E. Reynolds to Angus Snedeker, August 8, 1890.

43. Tabulated Statement Showing the Annual Product and Total Production of Metals and Money for the Years from 1881 to September n.d., 1895.

44. H. W. Reed to W. C. Sheldon, December 24, 1885.

45. Ibid.; A. E. Reynolds to H. W. Reed, January 5, 1888; A. E. Reynolds to W. C. Sheldon, January 5, 1888.

46. A. E. Reynolds to George R. Sheldon, October 26, 1889.

47. H. W. Reed to W. C. Sheldon, December 24, 1885.

48. H. W. Reed to W. C. Sheldon, August 9, 1888, August 29, 1888, and February 1, 1889; H. W. Reed to A. E. Reynolds, August 11, 1888; A. E. Reynolds to A. E. Wyeth, June 1, 1890.

49. A. E. Reynolds to H. W. Reed, June 1, 1886, June 4, 1886, and July 20, 1886.

50. A. E. Reynolds to H. W. Reed, July 20, 1886, and August 13, 1886; A. E. Reynolds to M. D. Thatcher, August 15, 1886; B. W. Lewis to A. E. Reynolds, July 24, 1886.

51. A. E. Reynolds to H. W. Reed, March 15, 1887; H. W. Reed to A. E. Reynolds, September 9, 1887, and September 12, 1887.

52. H. W. Reed to W. C. Sheldon, December 24, 1885.

53. H. W. Reed to W. C. Sheldon, Ouray, Colo., December 31, 1886.

54. A. E. Reynolds to H. W. Reed, March 15, 1887; H. W. Reed to A. E. Reynolds, September 12, 1887; H. W. Reed to W. C. Sheldon, December 27, 1887, and December 31, 1887; H. W. Reed to George M. King, January 24, 1888.

55. H. W. Reed to A. E. Reynolds, April 7, 1887. One historian has suggested that Jardine and Day sought only to force the citizens of Ouray to support the extension of the railway to that community. See Phyllis Flanders Dorset, *The New Eldorado: The Story of Colorado's Gold and Silver Rushes* (New York: Macmillan, 1970), 235.

56. A. E. Reynolds to President and Directors, Denver & Rio Grande Railroad Co., May 2, 1887; A. E. Reynolds to J. W. Gilluly, October 21, 1887; H. W. Reed to John H. Maugham, July 26, 1887; H. W. Reed to A. E. Reynolds, July 26, 1887; H. W. Reed to W. C. Sheldon, December 27, 1887. See also Marvin Gregory and P. David Smith, *Mountain Mysteries: The Ouray Odyssey,* 4th ed., rev. (Ouray, Colo.: Wayfinder Press, 1989), 156–57.

57. H. W. Reed to W. C. Sheldon, December 27, 1887, and February 1, 1889; A. E. Reynolds to H. Rogers, June 25, 1901. See also Frank A. Rice, "History of Ouray and Mines" (Ouray, Colo.: Ouray Public Library, unpublished manuscript).

58. David R. Reed to J. L. Hathaway, December 13, 1888. Ashenfelter, a native of Pennsylvania, had been a wagon master for Lee & Reynolds in Indian Territory before relocating to Ouray. He did virtually all freighting between Ouray and the mines on Mount Sneffels. He died in 1910, and his business was continued by his widow. See *Ouray (Colo.) Herald,* September 10, 1896; A. E. Reynolds to Mose Ashenfelter, Denver, August 20, 1910; and Frank Rice, "History of Ouray and Mines," 35.

59. H. W. Reed to A. H. Ward, October 1, 1888; H. W. Reed to W. C. Sheldon, [February 1, 1889]; A. E. Reynolds to George R. Sheldon, September 20, 1889.

60. H. W. Reed to A. E. Reynolds, November 8, 1888, and October 9, 1889; H. W. Reed to W. C. Sheldon, [February 1, 1889].

61. H. W. Reed to A. E. Reynolds, February 9, 1889, and March 8, 1889.

62. David R. Reed to M. D. Thatcher, July 29, 1887, and August 8, 1887; David R. Reed to J. H. Maugham, April 30, 1887; David R. Reed to J. L. Hathaway, December 3, 1888.

63. A. E. Reynolds to M. D. Thatcher, June 30, 1887, and March 26, 1891; A. E. Reynolds to William H. Emanuel, March 8, 1888, and April 8, 1892; L. C. Hill to A. E. Reynolds, April 20, 1888.

64. D. R. Reed to A. E. Reynolds, September 21, 1889, and March 4, 1890; A. J. Reynolds to A. E. Reynolds, December 27, 1890; A. E. Reynolds to J. B. Reynolds, November 9, 1887.

65. H. W. Reed to A. E. Reynolds, Ouray, Colo., June 29, 1892. See also Stocks Owned by A. E. Reynolds, Estate of A. E. Reynolds, Deceased, n.d.

66. Tabulated Statement Showing the Annual Product and the Total Production of Metals and Money for the Years from 1881 to September 1, 1895, n.d.

67. A. E. Reynolds to H. S. Le Roy, November 17, 1890 (two letters of the same date), [December 1, 1890].

68. H. W. Reed to A. E. Reynolds, November 8, 1886, and November 24, 1886; A. E. Reynolds to W. C. Sheldon, November 10, 1886, and July 28, 1888; George R. Sheldon to A. E. Reynolds, November 15, 1886; A. E. Reynolds to M. D. Thatcher, June 10, 1887.

69. A. E. Reynolds to Editor, *Mining Industry*, September 23, 1888; H. W. Reed to A. E. Reynolds, October 3, 1888.

70. A. E. Reynolds to Alvan Marble, Denver, January 10, 1890; A. E. Reynolds to George H. Hyde, December 3, 1890.

71. C. F. Reynolds to C. F. McKenney, February 6, 1889; H. W. Reed to A. E. Reynolds, August 8, 1889.

72. A. E. Reynolds to George R. Sheldon, October 26, 1889; A. E. Reynolds to George Hyde, December 23, 1890; H. W. Reed to A. E. Reynolds, March 14, 1895.

73. A. E. Reynolds to C. F. Reynolds, March 26, 1889; A. E. Reynolds to George H. Hyde, July 5, 1890; W. C. Sheldon to H. W. Reed, July 17, 1890; H. W. Reed to A. E. Reynolds, January 29, 1893; A. E. Reynolds to Herman S. Le Roy, January 30, 1893.

5 An Abundance of Silver

1. C. H. Hall, *Resources, Industries, and Natural Advantages of Ouray County: Mines, Mills, Manufacturing, Agriculture, Towns, Railroads, Etc.* (Ouray, Colo.: Humphrey Hulanski, 1894), 1–4.

2. A. E. Reynolds to Herman S. Le Roy, Denver, January 14, 30, 1893; A. E. Reynolds to George R. Sheldon, Denver, January 17, 1893.

3. H. W. Reed to A. E. Reynolds, October 10, 1892, January 29, 1893, and March 1, 1893.

4. A. E. Reynolds to Herman S. Le Roy, September 16, 1892; A. E. Reynolds to W. H. Faurell, Denver, November 5, 1892; H. W. Reed to A. E. Reynolds, January 29, 1893.

5. H. W. Reed to A. E. Reynolds, March 14, 1893, June 13, 1893, June 14, 1893, and June 16, 1893; A. E. Reynolds to George R. Sheldon, Denver, March 18, 1893; A. E. Reynolds to M. D. Thatcher, June 14, 1893; A. E. Reynolds to W. F. Havemeyer, June 19, 1893.

6. A. E. Reynolds to H. W. Reed, July 8, 1893, and July 21, 1893; H. W. Reed to A. E. Reynolds, Ouray, July 28, 1893, and September 11, 1893; A. E. Reynolds to George R. Sheldon, August 17, 1893; George R. Sheldon to A. E. Reynolds, New York City, September 23, 1893, and January 16, 1894.

7. A. E. Reynolds to C. H. Morse, January 17, 1893.

8. Hall, *Resources, Industries, and Natural Advantages*, 1–4.

9. Ibid.; H. W. Reed to A. E. Reynolds, Ouray, [January 24, 1896].

10. H. W. Reed to A. E. Reynolds, February 13, 1897; *Silverite-Plaindealer* (Ouray, Colo.), July 22, 1898, December 30, 1898, and December 8, 1899.

11. The Revenue Tunnel's power-generating plants are described in A. E. Reynolds to Harry A. Lee, December 21, 1900. See also *Silverite-Plaindealer* (Ouray, Colo.), July 22, 1898, and December 8, 1899.

12. H. W. Reed to A. E. Reynolds, March 1, 1893; *Silverite-Plaindealer* (Ouray, Colo.), December 8, 1899.

13. *Silverite-Plaindealer* (Ouray, Colo.), December 8, 1899.

14. A. E. Reynolds to Henry A. Wheeler, Denver, October 14, 1892.

15. H. W. Reed to A. E. Reynolds, Ouray, March 14, 1895.

16. H. W. Reed to A. E. Reynolds, Ouray, January 31, 1895, and March 14, 1895.

17. H. W. Reed to A. E. Reynolds, Ouray, March 14, 1895.

18. Ibid.

19. George C. Suggs Jr., *Colorado's War on Militant Unionism: James H. Peabody and the Western Federation of Miners* (Detroit: Wayne State University Press, 1972).

20. A. E. Reynolds to H. W. Reed, Denver, April 2, 1902.

21. Andrew J. Reynolds to A. E. Reynolds, Ouray, December 8, 1896; W. J. Benton to A. E. Reynolds, Ouray, December 11, 1896; A. E. Krisher to A. E. Reynolds, Ouray, December 11, 1896.

22. A. E. Reynolds to H. W. Reed, January 13, 1897; H. W. Reed to A. E. Reynolds, January 17, 1897, January 19, 1897, January 23, 1897, February 19, 1897, and March 5, 1897; A. E. Reynolds to George R. Sheldon, January 28, 1897.

23. A. E. Reynolds to Arthur Winslow, Denver, March 17, 1902.

24. A. E. Reynolds to John H. Bradley, July 6, 1890.

25. Agreement, A. E. Reynolds, H. W. Reed, John H. Bradley, and William F. Havemeyer to Purchase Cimarron Mining Claim, July, 1890; Hector Mining Co., Minute Book, 42; H. W. Reed to A. E. Reynolds, Ouray, May 19, 1891; A. E. Reynolds to W. F. Havemeyer, Denver, February 21, 1892.

26. H. W. Reed to A. E. Reynolds, December 7, 1892, and January 6, 1893.

27. A. E. Reynolds to H. W. Reed, Denver, November 18, 1892; W. F. Havemeyer to A. E. Reynolds, New York City, November 22, 1892, December 19, 1892, and December 23, 1892; A. E. Reynolds to John H. Bradley, Denver, December 2, 1892, and December 9, 1892; A. E. Reynolds to W. F. Havemeyer, Denver, December 10, 1892.

28. A. E. Reynolds to George R. Sheldon, May 29, 1896; W. F. Havemeyer to A. E. Reynolds, New York City, June 8, 1896; A. E. Reynolds to H. W. Reed, December 22, 1902.

29. A. E. Reynolds to H. S. Le Roy, January 17, 1898; A. E. Reynolds to M. D. Thatcher, January 17, 1898; Hector Tunnel Co., Minute Book, 3, 9.

30. "The Revenue Tunnel Mines Company" (typescript), 11 pp.

31. Ibid.

32. Ibid.

33. A. E. Reynolds to Stockholders of the Caroline Mining Co., Glacier Mining Co., Hector Mining Co., Hector Tunnel Co., and Revenue Tunnel Co., Denver, August 7, 1900.

34. Ibid.

35. Ibid.

36. Cumberland Mining Co., Articles of Incorporation, March 20, 1891; B. P. Morse to Floyd R. Thompson, April 3, 1923; B. P. Morse to George W. Potter, February 11, 1926.

37. Stock ownership records, 1899–1904.

38. A. E. Reynolds to Alvan Markel, Denver, January 10, 1900; A. E. Reynolds to Lawrence T. Gray, Denver, November 1, 1918; B. P. Morse to Floyd R. Thompson, April 3, 1923; B. P. Morse to George W. Potter, February 11, 1926; Wheel of Fortune Mining Co., Stock List, June 27, 1899–September 2, 1904.

39. A. E. Reynolds to Stockholders, Revenue Tunnel Mines Co., Denver, November 14, 1903.

40. A. E. Reynolds to H. W. Reed, August 14, 1901.

41. B. P. Morse to St. Louis Smelting & Refining Co., Old Hickory, Tenn., February 11, 1929.

42. Agreement, David M. Hyman with A. E. Reynolds, February 2, 1890, Establishing the Boundary Between the Gladstone and Parole Claims, Ute Mining District, Conejos County, Colo.

43. A. E. Reynolds to M. D. Thatcher, July 18, 1890; A. E. Reynolds to Theodore Rogers, August 8, 1890; A. E. Reynolds to C. P. Palmer, November 17, 1890; A. E. Reynolds to Stockholders, Forest King Mining Co., Denver, August 7, 1908.

44. See stockownership records for the Forest King Mining Co., Parole Mining Co., and Senate Gold and Silver Mining Co.

45. *Denver Times,* January 10, 1901.

46. A. E. Reynolds to M. D. Thatcher, Denver, December 3, 1891; A. E. Reynolds to Henry W. Magee, July 8, 1892; A. E. Reynolds to Theo. Rogers, July 9, 1894.

47. Agreement, A. E. Reynolds with Alexander Thornton and C. P. Palmer, August 15, 1893; A. E. Reynolds to Theo. Rogers, July 9, 1894; A. E. Reynolds to E. C. Campbell, Creede, February 6, 1898; A. E. Reynolds to T. N. Barnsdall, February 27, 1900.

48. C. P. Palmer to A. E. Reynolds, Del Norte, Colo., August 4, 1891; A. E. Reynolds to Thomas Bowen, December 1, 1893.

49. The deeds conveying these properties are in the Reynolds Collection.

50. William H. Emmons and Esper S. Larsen, "A Preliminary Report on the Geology and Ore Deposits of Creede, Colorado," *United States Geological Survey Bulletin* 530 (1913): 44, 54.

51. *Creede (Colo.) Candle,* February 4, 1892, and June 24, 1892.

52. *Creede (Colo.) Candle,* June 16, 1893.

53. *Creede (Colo.) Candle,* August 4, 1893; A. E. Reynolds to M. D. Thatcher, July 21, 1893; A. E. Reynolds to Alexander Thornton, July 31, 1893; A. Thornton to A. E. Reynolds, Creede, August 5, 1893.

54. *Creede (Colo.) Candle,* March 3, 1893.

55. *Denver Republican,* May 25, 1899.

56. A. E. Reynolds to M. D. Thatcher, December 15, 1893; *Creede (Colo.) Candle,* November 24, 1893; clipping from *Creede (Colo.) Miner,* March 1899, day unknown.

57. *Denver Republican,* May 25, 1899.

58. C. A. Hallam to A. E. Reynolds, Deadwood, S.D., May 28, 1899.

59. J. F. Vaile to A. E. Reynolds, Denver, November 21, 1893; A. E. Reynolds to Joel Vaile, Denver, November 23, 1893; A. E. Reynolds to C. J. Hughes Jr., December 19, 1893. Deeds conveying interest in the Commodore, I. L. Johnson to A. E. Reynolds and C. F. McKenney, are in the Reynolds Collection.

60. A. E. Reynolds to Byron E. Shear, Denver, March 19, 1892; A. E. Reynolds to Colin Timmons, Denver, April 19, 1892.

61. William H. Emmons and Esper S. Larsen, "Geology and Ore Deposits of the Creede District, Colorado," *United States Geological Survey Bulletin* 718 (1923): 5; Wilbur Fisk Stone, *History of Colorado*, 4 vols. (Chicago: S. J. Clarke Publishing, 1918–1919), 1:292.

62. Emmons and Larsen, "Geology and Ore Deposits," 5; *Engineering and Mining Journal* 53 (April 9, 1892): 407, and 67 (June 10, 1899): 688; *Creede (Colo.) Candle*, June 3, 1892.

63. A. E. Reynolds to B. E. Shear, I. L. Johnson, and O. E. Le Fevre, Denver, June 15, 1894; Byron E. Shear, C. F. McKenney, David George, I. L. Johnson, and O. E. Le Fevre to A. E. Reynolds, Denver, November 19, 1895; Emmons and Larsen, "Geology and Ore Deposits," 5; *Mining and Scientific Press* 79 (September 30, 1899); *Denver Republican*, January 1, 1900.

64. A. E. Reynolds to Owen E. Le Fevre, New York City, February 2, 1896; A. E. Reynolds to Theo. Rogers, May 20, 1896; W. H. Bogert to A. E. Reynolds, New York City, May 23, 1896; A. E. Reynolds to W. F. Havemeyer, May 6, 1896.

65. D. G. Miller to A. E. Reynolds, Creede, October 31, 1897; Commodore Mining Co., Memorandum of Output and Dividends, 1896–1915.

66. A. E. Reynolds to D. H. Moffat, July 21, 1896, August 15, 1896, August 16, 1896, and August 21, 1896; D. H. Moffat to A. E. Reynolds, August 13, 1896; A. E. Reynolds to W. F. Havemeyer, September 2, 1896, and February 4, 1897; A. E. Reynolds to H. M. Teller, January 2, 1897.

67. A. E. Reynolds to Frederick S. Stephen, May 22, 1899. See also George H. Garrey, "Report on the Mines Along the Amethyst Lode, Creede, Mineral Co., Colorado" (1916), 49 (pagination has been added for the pages beyond 48).

68. *Mining and Scientific Press* 80 (May 19, 1900): 554; *Rocky Mountain News (Denver)*, December 26, 1900; *Denver Times*, December 30, 1900.

69. A. E. Reynolds to New York and Chance Mining Co., Denver, March 20, 1902; A. E. Reynolds to Stockholders, Commodore Mining

Co., Denver, July 12, 1902, and August 15, 1902; *Rocky Mountain News (Denver)*, August 15, 1902; *Denver Times*, December 10, 1901.

6   Searching for New Bonanzas

1. *Gunnison (Colo.) Tribune*, June 6, 1902, and November 11, 1902.
2. A. E. Reynolds to M. D. Thatcher, May 29, 1891.
3. A. E. Reynolds to H. S. Le Roy, Denver, December 5, 1891; Agreement, A. E. Reynolds with Emile Vatable, for Purchase of 305,000 shares of Gold Cup Consolidated Mining Co. Stock; Gold Cup Mining Co., share ownership records, 1891–1892; A. E. Reynolds Estate, "Stocks Owned by A. E. Reynolds," 11.
4. A. E. Reynolds to M. D. Thatcher, December 28, 1891; A. E. Reynolds to B. E. Shear, April 1, 1892; A. E. Reynolds to A. Snedaker, May 19, 1892; A. E. Reynolds to Warren Emerson, August 30, 1894.
5. A. E. Reynolds to Theodore Rogers, Denver, February 21, 1892; A. E. Reynolds to A. Snedaker, February 27, 1893; A. E. Reynolds to Joseph Eastman, December 1, 1893, and May 25, 1905.
6. A. E. Reynolds to W. S. Morse, April 24, 1897; Reynolds Estate, "Stocks Owned by A. E. Reynolds," 11.
7. A. E. Reynolds to William O'Brien, Denver, December 10, 1904; A. E. Reynolds Estate, "Description of Pitkin Property," 1–2.
8. A. E. Reynolds to B. M. Baruch, Denver, December 8, 1913. See also unsigned and undated statement by A. E. Reynolds about his business relations with Fine, Eckbert, and Pearson (typescript), 2 pp.
9. A comprehensive description and analysis of the mines of the Pitkin–Ohio City area are in J. M. Hill, "Gold and Silver: Notes on the Economic Geology of Southeastern Gunnison County, Colorado," *United States Geological Survey Bulletin* 380 (1909): 28–35.
10. W. J. Fine to A. E. Reynolds, Denver, June 16, 1900.
11. See reports on Silver Basin drill hole, B. Sadtler to W. G. Smith, Denver, June 4, 1892, September 22, 1892, and December 10, 1892.
12. A. E. Reynolds to C. A. Starbuck, Denver, December 21, 1900; C. A. Starbuck to A. E. Reynolds, New York, June 26, 1909; A. E. Reynolds, "Suggestions of Requirements of the Colorado Smelting and Mining Company for Development," [1913, typescript], 3–4.
13. *Denver Republican*, January 18, 1901; *Denver Times*, January 18, 1901.
14. A. E. Reynolds to Burt Van Horn, Denver, May 15, 1902; A. E. Reynolds to S. F. Mallory, Denver, June 17, 1904.

15. Colorado Smelting & Mining Co., share ownership records, 1901–1906.

16. Ibid.

17. A. E. Reynolds to T. N. Barnsdall, Denver: May 14, 1906; Reynolds Estate, "Description of Pitkin Property," 2; *Gunnison (Colo.) Tribune,* October 5, 1900, and December 21, 1900; *Denver Times,* September 9, 1901; *Mining Reporter* 42 (September 27, 1900): 185, and 42 (October 18, 1900): 237.

18. *Gunnison (Colo.) Tribune,* December 21, 1900.

19. A. E. Reynolds to C. A. Starbuck, December 12, 1900; A. E. Reynolds to Robert Law, Denver, November 12, 1917; Reynolds Estate, "Description of Pitkin Property," 3; *Gunnison (Colo.) Tribune,* November 22, 1900, and December 21, 1900.

20. A. E. Reynolds to J. F. Pearson, December 23, 1901.

21. Ibid.

22. Reynolds, "Suggestions of Requirements of the Colorado Smelting and Refining Company for Development," 6–7; Reynolds Estate, "Description of Pitkin Property," 3; *Gunnison (Colo.) Republican,* June 2, 1904.

23. Reynolds Estate, "Description of Pitkin Property," 3–4; *Gunnison (Colo.) Tribune,* November 22, 1901; *Gunnison (Colo.) Republican,* June 2, 1904.

24. Reynolds, "Suggestions of Requirements of the Colorado Smelting and Mining Company for Development," 6–7; Reynolds Estate, "Description of Pitkin Property," 3.

25. Reynolds, "Suggestions of Requirements of the Colorado Smelting and Mining Company for Development," 5–6; Reynolds Estate, "Description of Pitkin Property," 3.

26. Reynolds, "Suggestions of Requirements of the Colorado Smelting and Mining Company for Development," 9–10; Reynolds Estate, "Description of Pitkin Property," 4.

27. Stephen Dunn, J. C. Bowerman, and A. E. Reynolds to First National Bank of Pueblo, Denver, January 11, 1904; A. E. Reynolds to W. F. Havemeyer, Denver, March 9, 1904; A. E. Reynolds to Mercantile National Bank of Pueblo, Denver, May 7, 1904; J. C. Bowerman to Mercantile National Bank, Denver, July 18, 1904; A. E. Reynolds to Millard Fairlamb, Denver, May 23, 1916; J. P. M. Humphrey to Carl J. Sigfrid, Denver, September 30, 1921.

28. A. E. Reynolds to George W. Morton and W. P. Rice, June 11, 1898.

29. F. H. Tobey to A. F. Adams and Horatio Dunton, June 14, 1898; Richard Keller to Creditors of Pactolus Mining Company, June 14, 1898; A. E. Reynolds to W. P. Rice, June 17, 1898; Contract, A. E. Reynolds with Richard Keller, April 5, 1899.

30. A. E. Reynolds to H. W. Fowler, December 24, 1898; A. E. Reynolds, Memorandum on Disposition of the Emma Mine, Denver, April 4, 1899.

31. A. E. Reynolds to Burt Van Horn, Denver, May 5, 1902.

32. *Mining Investor* 21 (February 25, 1901): 370; *Engineering and Mining Journal* 76 (October 10, 1903): 559, 76 (October 31, 1903): 673; *Mining and Scientific Press,* 89 (August 6, 1904): 94, and 89 (September 3, 1904): 161.

33. A. E. Reynolds to Richard Keller, Denver, December 19, 1902.

34. A. E. Reynolds to Horatio Dunton, Denver, May 15, 1909; Untitled and unsigned statement about the Emma Mine (ca. 1920, typescript), 6 pp.

35. A. E. Reynolds to Horatio Dunton, Denver, May 15, 1909.

36. *Gunnison (Colo.) Republican,* May 11, 1905.

37. *Gunnison (Colo.) News-Champion,* September 27, 1907.

38. A. E. Reynolds to J. F. Pearson, Denver, June 22, 1904; *Gunnison (Colo.) Republican,* July 7, 1904; *Gunnison (Colo.) News-Champion,* September 27, 1907.

39. *Gunnison (Colo.) Republican,* November 24, 1904, and June 8, 1905; *Gunnison (Colo.) News-Champion,* September 27, 1907.

40. Gold Links Mining Company, Minute Book, 1905–1923, 41, 43–45.

41. Ibid., 45–47.

42. Ibid.

43. Incorporation Certificate and Papers, Colorado Secretary of State, June 5, 1905; Gold Links Mining Company, share ownership records, 1905–1912.

44. A.E. Reynolds to T. N. Barnsdall, Denver, May 14, 1906.

45. A. E. Reynolds to James E. Lyon, Denver, September 8, 1906; A. E. Reynolds to T. N. Barnsdall, Denver, September 8, 1906; A. E. Reynolds to A. S. Hughes, Denver, September 15, 1906; A. E. Reynolds to J. C. Vaughn, Denver, October 10, 1906; A. E. Reynolds to Mrs. Addie J. Adams, October 11, 1906; *Gunnison (Colo.) News-Champion,* November 19, 1906.

46. A. E. Reynolds to J. F. Pearson, Denver, May 2, 1907; *Gunnison (Colo.) News-Champion,* September 16, 1910.

47. C. F. McKenney to Thomas S. Kelly, Denver, November 12, 1908; A. E. Reynolds to W. A. Garrett, Denver, August 14, 1909; *Gunnison (Colo.) News-Champion*, June 25, 1909, October 1, 1909, and November 26, 1909.

48. A. E. Reynolds to J. F. Pearson and W. A. Garrett, Denver, December 24, 1907; *Gunnison (Colo.) News-Champion*, January 17, 1908, and November 26, 1909.

49. Gold Links Mining Co., Receipts and Expenditures, 1908–1913; B. P. Morse to J. F. Robinson, Denver, November 2, 1923. These two sources vary on reports of profits from mining operations. See also A. E. Reynolds to J. F. Fine and W. H. Eckbert, Denver, November 11, 1910; A. E. Reynolds to T. N. Barnsdall, Denver, September 5, 1911.

50. A. E. Reynolds to Stockholders, Colorado Smelting and Mining Company, May 7, 1912; B. P. Morse to Hughes & Dorsey, October 31, 1922; J. P. M. Humphrey to B. P. Morse, Denver, November 7, 1922.

51. A. E. Reynolds to T. N. Barnsdall, Denver, December 24, 1912; A. E. Reynolds to T. H. Kelly, Denver, December 24, 1912; A. E. Reynolds to Stockholders, Colorado Smelting & Mining Co., March 14, 1913.

52. A. E. Reynolds to T. H. Kelly, December 24, 1912; A. E. Reynolds to T. N. Barnsdall, Denver, December 24, 1912; A. E. Reynolds to C. W. Winslow, Denver, [January 10, 1913]; B. P. Morse to Hughes & Dorsey, October 31, 1922.

53. A. E. Reynolds to Gerald Hughes, Denver, June 20, 1913; A. E. Reynolds to J. F. Pearson, Denver, March 5, 1914; B. P. Morse to Hughes & Dorsey, October 31, 1922. See also undated tenders by Reynolds to the Gunnison Bank & Trust Co., John Lupold, A. L. Pearson, and John McWilliams.

54. A. E. Reynolds to Robert Law Jr., Denver, May 27, 1914.

55. Reynolds, "Suggestions of Requirements of the Colorado Smelting and Mining Company for Development," 1–2.

56. A. E. Reynolds to Robert Law Jr., July 21, 1916; B. P. Morse to Gerald Hughes, September 26, 1922; *Gunnison (Colo.) News-Champion*, June 22, 1917.

57. A. E. Reynolds to T. N. Barnsdall, Denver, September 29, 1916.

58. *Gunnison (Colo.) News*, October 29, 1915, January 12, 1917, and August 31, 1917.

59. *Gunnison (Colo.) News*, October 5, 1917, October 26, 1917, and August 31, 1917.

60. *Gunnison (Colo.) News*, November 19, 1915, December 1, 1916, and December 15, 1916.

61. *Gunnison (Colo.) News,* June 2, 1916, and January 11, 1918.

62. *Gunnison (Colo.) News,* August 24, 1917, April 19, 1918, February 21, 1919, May 16, 1919, September 19, 1919, January 20, 1920, July 2, 1920, and September 3, 1920.

63. W. J. Sawyer to A. E. Reynolds, Pitkin, Colo., June 18, 1919; R. S. Bain to A. E. Reynolds, Ohio City, Colo., June 30, 1919.

64. James E. Dick to A. E. Reynolds, White Pine, June 20, 1919, and July 22, 1919; R. S. Bain to A. E. Reynolds, Ohio City, June 30, 1919, and July 23, 1919.

7 Decline of the Mining Industry

1. A. E. Reynolds to M. B. Brady, Denver, February 1, 1902; A. E. Reynolds to Stockholders, Revenue Tunnel Mines Co., Denver, June 28, 1902; A. E. Reynolds to Stockholders, Revenue Tunnel Mines Co., Denver, November 14, 1903.

2. A. E. Reynolds to Stockholders, Revenue Tunnel Mines Co., Denver, June 28, 1902; A. E. Reynolds to M. D. Thatcher, Glenwood Springs, Colo., August 28, 1902; H. Y. Russell to A. E. Reynolds, Ouray, October 26, 1902.

3. A. E. Reynolds to Stockholders, Revenue Tunnel Mines Co., Denver, June 28, 1902; A. E. Reynolds to W. S. Morse, Denver, September 1, 1902; W. S. Morse to A. E. Reynolds, TEL, Aguascalientes, Mex., September 6, 1902; E. M. Rogers to A. E. Reynolds, New York, October 16, 1902; A. E. Reynolds to Stockholders, Revenue Tunnel Mines Co., Denver, February 7, 1911.

4. A. E. Reynolds to Stockholders, Revenue Tunnel Mines Co., November 11, 1903, and June 10, 1904; A. E. Reynolds to John C. Montgomery, Denver, September 11, 1906; A. E. Reynolds to M. D. Thatcher, Denver, November 7, 1906.

5. A. E. Reynolds to Stockholders, Revenue Tunnel Mines Co., Denver, February 7, 1911.

6. Ibid.; E. H. Platt to A. E. Reynolds, Sneffels, Colo., April 2, 1910.

7. M. D. Thatcher to A. E. Reynolds, Pueblo, Colo., November 11, 1910; A. E. Reynolds to Board of Directors, Revenue Tunnel Mines Co., Denver, February 3, 1911.

8. A. E. Reynolds to W. E. Wheeler, Denver, February 25, 1910, and March 16, 1910; A. E. Reynolds to M. D. Thatcher, February 25, 1910; A. E. Reynolds to E. H. Platt, Denver, March 18, 1910; A. E. Reynolds to Stockholders, Revenue Tunnel Mines Co., May 4, 1910.

9. B. P. Morse to Floyd R. Thompson, Denver, September 3, 1923; *Engineering and Mining Journal* 72 (July 22, 1911): 179.

10. A. E. Reynolds to Stockholders, Wheel of Fortune Mining Co., Denver, May 14, 1913; A. E. Reynolds to H. W. Reed, Denver, May 9, 1913; A. E. Reynolds to E. H. Platt, Denver, August 5, 1913; A. E. Reynolds to E. H. Schultz, Denver, April 3, 1920.

11. A. E. Reynolds to H. W. Reed, Denver, June 18, 1915; A. E. Reynolds to Stockholders, Cumberland Mining Co., June 18, 1915; A. E. Reynolds to Stockholders, Wheel of Fortune Mining Co., June 19, 1915.

12. Agreement, A. E. Reynolds with First National Bank of Pueblo, First National Bank of Denver, and Denver National Bank, April 26, 1915.

13. A. E. Reynolds to H. A. Wheeler, Denver, July 21, 1915; A. E. Reynolds to H. W. Reed, Denver, January 23, 1917.

14. Agreement, A. E. Reynolds with St. John Mines (Colo.), Ltd., May 17, 1915; B. P. Morse to A. E. Reynolds, Denver, August 30, 1915.

15. A. E. Reynolds to James Clamp, March 15, 1917.

16. Commodore Mining Co., Memorandum on Dividends Paid, December 1, 1915.

17. A. E. Reynolds to Stockholders, Commodore Mining Co., June 15, 1906.

18. A. E. Reynolds to Stockholders, Commodore Mining Co., Denver, July 12, 1902, August 15, 1902, and September 20, 1902. On September 20 stockholders in a special meeting approved an increase in the capital stock from 2 to 3 million shares. One-half of the new shares could be used to purchase property; the rest were to remain for the time being in the company's treasury.

19. Arthur Ponsford to A. E. Reynolds, Denver, July 31, 1902; A. E. Reynolds to Stockholders, Commodore Mining Co., Denver, August 15, 1902; A. E. Reynolds to Charles J. Hughes Jr., Denver, December 27, 1902; A. E. Reynolds to H. M. Teller, Denver, January 27, 1903; D. G. Miller to President and Board of Directors, Commodore Mining Co., Denver, June 15, 1905.

20. A. E. Reynolds to Frederick S. Stephen, Denver, July 23, 1906; A. E. Reynolds to Stockholders, Commodore Mining Co., Denver, December 10, 1906. For the subsequent disposition of the property at Lawson, see A. E. Reynolds to Stockholders, Commodore Mining Co., Denver, December 10, 1906; A. E. Reynolds to H. E. Bonebrake, Denver, September 24, 1914; and A. E. Reynolds to R. B. Morton, Denver, September 24, 1914.

21. J. B. Ross to A. E. Reynolds, Denver, December 4, 1908, and January 2, 1909; A. E. Reynolds to H. Y. Russell, Denver, December 29, 1908; A. E. Reynolds to Stockholders, Commodore Mining Co., Denver, December 30, 1908; Frank L. Ross to A. E. Reynolds, Silverton, Colo., February 5, 1909; A. E. Reynolds to Frank L. Ross, Denver, November 15, 1912.

22. A. E. Reynolds to Sylvester T. Smith, Denver, June 18, 1906, and June 15, 1911; A. E. Reynolds to Frederick S. Stephen, Denver, July 23, 1906, and December 29, 1911; A. E. Reynolds to Joseph Wilson, Denver, December 5, 1910; A. E. Reynolds to Stockholders, Commodore Mining Co., Denver, July 16, 1913; A. E. Reynolds to S. W. Eccles, Denver, June 25, 1915.

23. A. E. Reynolds to Gerald Hughes, Denver, February 2, 1916, and March 22, 1916; A. E. Reynolds to Simon Guggenheim, Denver, June 9, 1916; A. E. Reynolds to Robert Le Roy, Denver, June 23, 1916; A. E. Reynolds to Frederick S. Stephen, April 25, 1917; A. E. Reynolds to Farmers' Loan & Trust Co., Denver, May 14, 1918; A. E. Reynolds to Stockholders, Commodore Mining Co., Denver, December 15, 1919.

24. A. E. Reynolds to Jefferson Groub, Denver, December 18, 1901.

25. *Ores and Metals* 11 (May 1902): 6.

26. A. E. Reynolds to American Concentrator Co., Denver, January 8, 1902; A. E. Reynolds to C. F. Palmer, Denver, September 5, 1902; Louis H. Schmidlapp to A. E. Reynolds, Cincinnati, Ohio, October 8, 1902; A. E. Reynolds to C. F. McKenney, New York City, May 28, 1903; A. E. Reynolds to John Pickens, Denver, August 6, 1903, and August 19, 1903; A. E. Reynolds to T. N. Barnsdall, Denver, March 12, 1904, and September 5, 1911; A. E. Reynolds to Hartford Gold Extraction Co., Denver, July 12, 1904.

27. A. E. Reynolds to D. M. Hyman, Denver, May 14, 1904, June 26, 1908, July 13, 1908, and September 14, 1908; A. E. Reynolds to Stockholders, Forest King Mining Co., March 3, 1908; A. E. Reynolds to Stockholders, Parole Mining Co., March 3, 1908.

28. A. E. Reynolds to C. E. McConnell, Denver, December 23, 1903.

29. May Day Gold Mining Co., Certificate of Incorporation, December 28, 1903; David G. Miller, "The May Day Gold Mining Company's Property" (n.d., typescript), 1–2; A. E. Reynolds, "The May Day Gold Mining Company" (n.d., typescript).

30. Miller, "The May Day Gold Mining Company's Property." 1–2.

31. Ibid., 3–5.

32. Reynolds, "The May Day Gold Mining Company"; A. E. Reynolds to W. F. Havemeyer, Denver, November 20, 1907.

33. Reynolds, "The May Day Gold Mining Company"; A. E. Reynolds to Robert Law and S. S. Mahard, August 29, 1918.

34. A. E. Reynolds to D. M. Hyman, Denver, May 24, 1912; A. E. Reynolds to George H. Derby, Denver, March 4, 1918; A. E. Reynolds to Stockholders, May Day Gold Mining Co., Denver, March 24, 1915, May 4, 1915, and January 6, 1920.

35. A. E. Reynolds to J. A. and M. D. Thatcher, Denver, April 29, 1907; J. A. and M. D. Thatcher to A. E. Reynolds, Pueblo, September 27, 1907; A. E. Reynolds to M. D. Thatcher, Denver, October 23, 1907; M. D. Thatcher to A. E. Reynolds, Pueblo, February 5, 1908, and February 25, 1908; J. P. M. Humphrey to R. P. Church, Denver, April 14, 1922.

36. A. E. Reynolds to Mrs. Rose Van Horn, Denver, May 30, 1914; "Frank Hough Group, Hinsdale County, Colorado" (n.d., typescript).

37. A. E. Reynolds to A. J. Reynolds, Denver, January 11, 1919.

38. Ibid.; A. E. Reynolds to Dear Sir (Stockholders, Ocean Wave Mining & Reduction Co.), Denver, September 8, 1916. See also Ocean Wave Mining & Reduction Co., Minute Book, 1–18.

39. A. E. Reynolds to Dear Sir, Denver, September 8, 1916; A. E. Reynolds to Frank Van Horn, Denver, August 23, 1918. See also Ocean Wave Mining & Reduction Co., Minute Book, 19–35.

40. Argenta Mining Co., Certificate of Incorporation, December 3, 1890; Minute Book, 306; *Prospectus* (1890), 1–2.

41. *Denver Times*, August 3. 1900.

42. Argenta Mining Co., Minute Book, 48; Golden Fleece Extension Mining Co., Minute Book, 22–23; Lake View Gold Mining & Milling Co., Minute Book, 21; A. E. Reynolds to Golden Fleece Consolidated Mining Co., Denver, February 18, 1905.

43. Argenta Mining Co., Minute Book, 52–55; Golden Fleece Extension Mining Co., Minute Book, 25–26, 29–30; Lake View Gold Mining & Milling Co., Minute Book, 32; Golden Fleece Consolidated Mining Co., *Prospectus* (Denver: 1905), 1–7.

44. Golden Fleece Mining & Milling Co., Prospectus (1919), 15 pp.

45. A. E. Reynolds to J. W. Robinson, January 3, 1890; A. E. Reynolds to Theo. Rogers, August 18, 1890, and February 21, 1893.

46. A. E. Reynolds to Francis Schell, Denver, February 7, 1910; A. E. Reynolds to J. W. Robinson, November 11, 1912, and May 23, 1916; B. P.

Morse to Gerald Hughes, Denver, May 12, 1921. See also "The Tarifa Mining Company," and "Etcetera Lode," descriptions of properties, A. E. Reynolds Estate, in B. P. Morse Notebook.

47. "Eastern Star Group," description of properties, A. E. Reynolds Estate, in B. P. Morse Notebook. Reynolds also owned the American lode, Eureka Mining District, San Juan County. He acquired an interest in it in 1881, charged it off to profit and loss in 1887, took it up again in 1906, and, after paying taxes on it for 1912, decided to abandon the claim. See "American Lode," description of properties, A. E. Reynolds Estate, in B. P. Morse Notebook.

48. Agreement, Mortimer F. Taylor with A. E. Reynolds, Denver, December 31, 1898; A. E. Reynolds to Adna Lawson, Denver, October 28, 1909.

49. J. P. M. Humphrey to Carl J. Sigfrid, Denver, October 23, 1922; A. E. Reynolds to Frederick H. Wickett, Denver, September 7, 1916; "Eagle Bird Group," description of properties, A. E. Reynolds Estate, in B. P. Morse Notebook.

50. A. E. Reynolds to Frederick S. Stephen, May 22, 1899; A. E. Reynolds to Colin Timmons, June 5, 1899; A. E. Reynolds to Francis Schell, Denver, February 7, 1910.

51. Mining Deed, S. & S. Mining Co. and Philip R. Stanhope to A. E. Reynolds, Big Four Group, June 2, 1902; Frederick S. Stephen to B. P. Morse, Dundee, Scotland, September 30, 1922; "Big Four Claims," description of properties, A. E. Reynolds Estate, in B. P. Morse Notebook.

52. Agreement, A. E. Reynolds, C. F. McKenney, J. A. Thatcher, and Charles J. Hughes Jr. with Newton J. Thatcher, 1898.

53. A. E. Reynolds to H. W. Reed, August 1, 1899; A. E. Reynolds to Daniel George, August 4, 1900; A. E. Reynolds to Daniel Harrington, October 10, 1900.

54. A. E. Reynolds to Daniel Harrington, November 15, 1900.

55. C. E. McConnell to Thomas H. Kelly, Denver, March 11, 1908; A. E. Reynolds to Frank Goudy, Denver, December 28, 1910; B. P. Morse to J. H. Eby, October 28, 1922. See also "Colorado Exploration & Mining Co.," a description of the property and A. E. Reynolds's interest in it, prepared by the Reynolds Estate in 1921.

56. H. A. Wheeler to A. E. Reynolds, Orchard Lake, Mich., December 27, 1905; Denton, Dunn & Bowltree to Myron H. Breach, Toronto, Canada, September 9, 1909; George L. English to Colorado Exploration

& Mining Co., Port Arthur, Canada, June 27, 1910; J. P. M. Humphrey to B. P. Morse, Denver, April 4, 1921. See also "The Ely-Revenue Copper Co.," a description of the property and A. E. Reynolds's interest in it, prepared by the Reynolds Estate, 1921.

57. J. P. M. Humphrey to B. P. Morse, Denver, April 4, 1921.

8   End of a Career

1. A. E. Reynolds to A. J. Reynolds, Denver, January 27, 1915; U.S. General Land Office, Patent for Indian Claim No. 12, issued to Armama, alias Aramama, Smith, September 20, 1870; John Francis Jr. to George Bent, Washington, D.C., May 10, 1911. See also James Earl Sherow, *Watering the Valley: Development of the High Plains Arkansas River, 1870–1950* (Lawrence: University Press of Kansas, 1990), 17.

2. Lee & Reynolds to Henry C. Thatcher, April 19, 1871; Lee & Reynolds to R. M. Moore, April 19, 1871; Lee & Reynolds to D. H. Van Horn, April 19, 1871; A. E. Reynolds to R. M. Moore, December 12, 1888.

3. Abstract, Indian Claim 12, 1870–1897. See also A. E. Reynolds to Paul Weiglein, Denver, November 19, 1892; and A. E. Reynolds to Ed Guerrier, Denver, November 1, 1892.

4. A. E. Reynolds to D. W. Van Horn, New York City, May 17, 1884; A. E. Reynolds to M. P. Dooley, New York City, May 17, 1884; A. E. Reynolds to Messrs. Hansbrough and Coulson, March 15, April 5, 1889; A. E. Reynolds to R. M. Moore, March 24, 1889.

5. Sherow, *Watering the Valley,* 17–20.

6. A. E. Reynolds to H. L. Lubers, March 27, 1900, and August 10, 1900; A. E. Reynolds to James H. Crosley, April 14, 1900, and May 14, 1900.

7. A. E. Reynolds to George Williams, [November 16, 1900].

8. Abstract of Title, Indian Claim 13, 1870–1901; A. E. Reynolds to Bent County Bank, December 31, 1900.

9. A. E. Reynolds to G. F. Patrick, December 28, 1900; A. E. Reynolds to George H. Sly, December 28, 1900; A. E. Reynolds to A. G. Boyce, Denver, March 20, 1902; A. E. Reynolds to C. F. McKenney, New York City, March 3, 1903; G. W. Williams to A. E. Reynolds, La Junta, October 21, 1905; A. E. Reynolds to William Mackenzie, Denver, December 10, 1907; A. E. Reynolds to T. P. Hamm, Denver, May 10, 1909.

10. A. E. Reynolds to John Clay, Denver, May 28, 1916; A. E. Reynolds to E. J. Matthews, Denver, May 5, 1916, and May 11, 1916; *Gunnison (Colo.) News-Champion,* March 17, 1916.

11. A. E. Reynolds to James H. Crosley, January 26, 1904; A. E. Reynolds to George W. Williams, Denver, March 10, 1904; A. E. Reynolds to H. L. Lubers, Denver, January 3, 1907; A. E. Reynolds to W. F. Havemeyer, Denver, September 18, 1908.

12. G. H. Bathrick to A. E. Reynolds, Des Moines, Iowa, February 15, 1905; A. E. Reynolds to Nichols & Shepard Co., Denver, March 8, 1906, and October 20, 1906; Lowell Steam Plow Co. to A. E. Reynolds, Kansas City, Mo., August 10, 1906; A. E. Reynolds to Lowell Steam Plow Co., Denver, February 1, 1908.

13. A. E. Reynolds to Bernard M. Baruch, Denver, November 30, 1909; Bernard M. Baruch, New York City, March 12, 1910.

14. A. E. Reynolds to M. D. Thatcher, Denver, November 12, 1913.

15. H. L. Lubers to A. E. Reynolds, Las Animas, Colo., December 14, 1906, and January 5, 1907; A. E. Reynolds to George A. Kilgore, Denver, January 28, 1908; A. E. Reynolds to J. A. Jackson, Denver, May 11, 1908; A. E. Reynolds C. F.Reynolds, May 12, 1908; A. E. Reynolds to Arkansas Valley Realty Co., Denver, October 26, 1909; Contract, A. E. Reynolds with A. J. Reynolds Jr., January 28, 1910.

16. A. J. Reynolds to A. E. Reynolds, La Junta, October 21, 1910.

17. A. J. Reynolds to A. E. Reynolds, Palmyra, Neb., October 2, 1911.

18. Conditions that prevented successful farming are discussed in A. E. Reynolds to W. F. Torbitt, Denver, September 17, 1913, and April 21, 1914.

19. A. J. Reynolds to A. E. Reynolds, La Junta, July 21, 1910.

20. A. E. Reynolds to First National Bank of Pueblo, Denver, January 2, 1915; A. E. Reynolds to Henry M. Atkinson, Denver, July 22, 1916.

21. A. E. Reynolds to Henry M. Atkinson, Denver, July 22, 1916. The Germans who immigrated from Russia have been known by various names, among them German Russians and Volga Germans. The correct name for them is Germans from Russia. See Sidney Heitman, ed., *Germans from Russia in Colorado* (N.p.: Western Social Science Association, 1978), 1.

22. See Kenneth W. Rock, "Colorado's Germans from Russia," in Heitman, ed., *Germans from Russia,* 70–80.

23. A. E. Reynolds to Henry M. Atkinson, Denver, July 22, 1916.

24. A. E. Reynolds to Holly Sugar Co., Denver, July 31, 1916; Records of Sales of La Junta Farms, June 15, 1918.

25. A. E. Reynolds to School District No. 2, Denver, August 25, 1915, and August 26, 1915; A. E. Reynolds to F. T. Lewis, Denver, September

23, 1918; A. E. Reynolds to W. J. Frederick, Denver, February 21, 1920; R. Phillips to J. P. M. Humphrey, La Junta, April 5, 1922; A. E. Reynolds Estate, "Otero Farms."

26. A. E. Reynolds to A. J. Reynolds, Denver, March 24, 1917; A. E. Reynolds to Colorado Land Co., G. W. Williams, E. N. Eveatt, J. G. Washburn, Mikeal Will, and others, Denver, March 29, 1917; A. E. Reynolds to Treasurer, Cornell University, Denver, May 25, 1917; A. E. Reynolds to A. A. Hausman & Co., Denver, August 12, 1920. See also Summary of Farm Sales, June 15, 1918.

27. A. E. Reynolds to C. E. McConnell, Denver, December 26, 1907; C. E. McConnell to A. E. Reynolds, Durango, December 29, 1907.

28. C. E. McConnell to A. E. Reynolds, Durango, October 19, 1908. In November 1975 Anna Reynolds Morse Garrey wrote a memoir in which she attributed Reynolds's intervention in behalf of his brother-in-law to family honor or pride. See A. Reynolds Morse, "Gold Links Tailings," *Gunnison (Colo.) Country Times,* June 28, 1979.

29. *Gunnison (Colo.) Country Times,* November 11, December 12, 1908, and February 24, 1909; A. E. Reynolds to Rowe N. Pingrey, Denver, February 20, 1909; Reese McCloskey to A. E. Reynolds, Durango, February 27, 1909.

30. A. E. Reynolds to C. E. McConnell, Denver, June 23, 1910; J. P. M. Humphrey to Berrian Hughes, Denver, September 20, 1921; Memorandum of Agreement, Richard Keller with A. E. Reynolds, September 24, 1913; Statement of Account of Mr. Charles E. McConnell with Mr. A. E. Reynolds, Denver, July 1, 1913; Statement of Account of Charles E. McConnell with A. E. Reynolds [Estate], Denver, January 31, 1927.

31. A. E. Reynolds to T. N. Barnsdall, Denver, February 21, 1914. For Barnsdall's role in the Gold Links property, see A. E. Reynolds to C. F. McKenney, French Lick, Ind., March 23, 1906; A. E. Reynolds to T. N. Barnsdall, Denver, May 14, 1906, September 8, 1906, and September 29, 1916; A. E. Reynolds to Robert Law Jr., Denver, July 21, 1916, and November 11, 1917.

32. A. E. Reynolds to C. F.McKenney, New York City, April 10, 1905; A. A. Hausman & Co. to A. E. Reynolds, New York City, May 2, 1905, and June 3, 1905; William C. Sheldon & Co. to A. E. Reynolds, New York City, March 5, 1907; M. D. Thatcher to A. E. Reynolds, Pueblo, December 17, 1907; D. M. Hyman to A. E. Reynolds, New York City, December 23, 1907.

33. A. E. Reynolds to Flower & Co., Denver, August 11, 1903; Flower & Co. to A. E. Reynolds, New York City, November 10, 1903;

D. M. Hyman to A. E. Reynolds, New York City, April 21, 1908; Record of New York Air Brake Shares Bought and Sold by A. E. Reynolds, 1891–1912.

34. William C. Sheldon to A. E. Reynolds, New York City, March 5, 1907; D. M. Hyman to A. E. Reynolds, New York City, October 18, 1907; M. D. Thatcher to A. E. Reynolds, Pueblo, December 17, 1907; Record of New York Air Brake Bought and Sold by A. E. Reynolds, 1891–1912. See also *Commercial and Financial Chronicle* 91 (July 3, 1910): 41, and 93 (October 28, 1911): 1192.

35. D. M. Hyman to A. E. Reynolds, New York City, April 21, 1908.

36. A. E. Reynolds to D. M. Hyman, Denver, October 31, 1912, April 16, 1915, April 24, 1915, April 30, 1915, May 5, and May 10, 1915.

37. A. E. Reynolds to D. M. Hyman, August 26, 1915, and August 27, 1915; A. E. Reynolds to A. A. Hausman & Co., Denver, September 20, 1915.

38. See New York Air Brake Co. Annual Report in *Commerical and Financial Chronicle* 108 (March 1, 1919): 873–74; Agreement, A. E. Reynolds with First National Bank of Pueblo, First National Bank of Denver, and Denver National Bank, April 26, 1915. For the sale of the Revenue Tunnel Mines Co. to the English company and its eventual default, see A. E. Reynolds to Henry F. Peters, Denver, May 26, 1914, and April 9, 1915; A. E. Reynolds to George A. Williamson, Denver, June 10, 1915; and A. E. Reynolds to Stockholders, Revenue Tunnel Mines Co., Cumberland Mining Co., and Wheel of Fortune Mining Co., Denver, January 23, 1917.

39. A. E. Reynolds to Denver National Bank, Denver, May 3, 1916; A. E. Reynolds to M. D. Thatcher, Denver, January 5, 1918; H. F. Bliss to A. E. Reynolds, New York City, January 7, 1920; A. A. Hausman & Co. to A. E. Reynolds, New York City, March 4, 1920, November 13, 1920, and November 19, 1920; Edward A. Pierce to A. E. Reynolds, New York City, December 30, 1920.

40. D. M. Hyman to A. E. Reynolds, New York City, October 18, 1907; M. D. Thatcher to A. E. Reynolds, Pueblo, October 23, 1907, and January 16, 1908; A. E. Reynolds to M. D. Thatcher, Denver, July 23, 1915, September 30, 1915, November 12, 1915, September 15, 1916, and February 21, 1918; A. E. Reynolds to Denver National Bank, Denver, May 3, 1916; H. F. Bliss to A. E. Reynolds, New York City, January 7, 1920; A. A. Hausman & Co. to A. E. Reynolds, August 17, 1920.

41. A. E. Reynolds to Colin Timmons, Denver, February 25, 1913.

42. Notice of Lease to Frank Stampfel, July 14, 1909; B. P. Morse to Gerald Hughes, May 12, 1921.

43. A. E. Reynolds to Tonopah-Belmont Development Co., Denver, March 24, 1917; A. E. Reynolds to George H. Garrey, January 8, 1919; A. E. Reynolds to Dolores Silver Mines Co., Denver, September 10, 1920; Agreement, Emma Gold Mining Co., A. E. Reynolds, and Tonopah-Belmont Development Co., April 19, 1916; Agreement, A. E. Reynolds with Frank Stampfel and Robert L. Pellet, October 1, 1919.

44. A. E. Reynolds to Frank Stampfel, Denver, September 4, 1920, and October 7, 1920; A. E. Reynolds to Gerald Hughes, Denver, February 8, 1921.

45. A. E. Reynolds to Frank Stampfel, Denver, September 4, 1920, and October 7, 1920; Frank Stampfel to A. E. Reynolds, Rico, Colo., September 30, 1921; James Clamp to A. E. Reynolds, Sneffels, Colo., January 8, 1921; B. P. Morse to George G. Morse, Old Hickory, Tenn., March 2, 1921.

46. A. E. Reynolds to A. J. Reynolds, Denver, December 13, 1920; A. E. Reynolds to Gerald Hughes, Old Hickory, Tenn., February 8, 1921, and February 14, 1921; M. D. Thatcher to A. E. Reynolds, Pueblo, February 11, 1921, and February 18, 1921; A. E. Reynolds to M. D. Thatcher, Denver, February 14, 1921; W. K. Dudley to J. P. M. Humphrey, Pueblo, February 17, 1921; Lime Shale Mining Co., Articles of Incorporation, January 1921, in Carl J. Sigfrid Collection, Ouray County Historical Society, Ouray, Colo.

47. James Clamp to A. E. Reynolds, Dunton, Colo., March 20, 1921.

48. A. E. Reynolds to Jim Clamp, Old Hickory, Tenn., February 8, 1921; A. E. Reynolds to George W. Williams, Old Hickory, February 8, 1921; J. P. M. Humphrey to A. E. Reynolds, Denver, February 17, 1921.

49. A. E. Reynolds to Gerald Hughes, Old Hickory, Tenn., February 8, 1921.

50. *Old Hickory (Tenn.) News*, March 27, 1929.

51. Ibid. See also J. P. M. Humphrey to B. P. Morse, Denver, March 7, 1921; *Denver Post*, October 13, 1920; and *Rocky Mountain News (Denver)*, October 14, 1920.

52. Anna R. Garrey, "Notes on 1555 Sherman Street, Denver" (1975, typescript), 3. The family frequently spent a portion of each summer at the "Bungalow," a log structure without buildings, at the Gold Links

Mine and Mill, near Ohio City, Gunnison County. See Option Agreement, Reynolds-Morse Corp. to Roy Cross, for the Gold Links Property, August 10, 1932.

53. A. E. Reynolds to B. P. Morse, Denver, October 23, 1920.

9 The Legacy

1. Hughes & Dorsey to B. P. Morse, Denver, February 25, 1922; J. P. M. Humphrey to B. P. Morse, Denver, November 19, 1923, and November 24, 1924; Anna R. Morse to Holly Sugar Co., September 13, 1926; B. P. Morse to Holly Sugar Co., February 15, 1926; W. H. Cary to B. P. Morse, Denver, February 9, 1927; Reynolds-Morse Corp., Circular Letter, August 15, 1927.

2. Reynolds Morse, "Gold Links Tailings," *Gunnison (Colo.) Country Times,* December 21, 1978, and April 9, 1979.

3. B. P. Morse to Edward S. Wiard, April 6, 1921; Anna Reynolds Morse Garrey, "Morse Brothers" (January 15, 1955, handwritten).

4. B. P. Morse to Alice Reynolds, April 7, 1921, and September 20, 1921; B. P. Morse to Gerald Hughes, April 14, 1921.

5. Ibid.; B. P. Morse to Gerald Hughes, April 14, 1921.

6. B. P. Morse to Gerald Hughes, January 1, 1923.

7. B. P. Morse to Willard S. Morse, Old Hickory, Tenn., August 5, 1921.

8. *Old Hickory (Tenn.) Times,* March 27, 1929.

9. Biographical data on Gerald Hughes are in Lyle W. Dorsett, *The Queen City: A History of Denver* (Boulder, Colo.: Pruett Publishing, 1977), 189, 191.

10. Carl J. Sigfrid to B. P. Morse, Ouray, Colo., September 9, 1923; *Portrait and Biographical Record of the State of Colorado* (Chicago: Chapman Publishing, 1899), 1290, 1293; *Silverite-Plaindealer* (Ouray, Colo.), September 3, 1897; *Ouray (Colo.) Herald,* June 2, 1899.

11. Gerald Hughes to B. P. Morse, Denver, May 19, 1921; Carl J. Sigfrid to B. P. Morse, Ouray, Colo., July 11, 1921; B. P. Morse to E. H. Platt, January 14, 1922.

12. Lawrence T. Gray to A. E. Reynolds, Colorado Springs, Colo., December 8, 1920.

13. Ibid. Radetsky was the proprietor of the Colorado Iron & Metal Co. and the Radetsky Iron & Metal Co. See *Annual Colorado State Business Directory, 1919* (Denver: Gazette Publishing & Printing, 1919), 410.

14. Gerald Hughes to Anna R. Morse, Denver, April 9, 1921, and April 21, 1921; B. P. Morse to Miss [Alice] Reynolds, September 20, 1922; B. P. Morse to C. A. Starbuck, April 11, 1922.

15. Carl J. Sigfrid to B. P. Morse, Ouray, December 20, 1921, May 26, 1922, May 31, 1922, and March 31, 1923; Carl J. Sigfrid to J. P. M. Humphrey, November 7, 1921.

16. B. P. Morse to Gerald Hughes, December 13, 1922; Carl J. Sigfrid to B. P. Morse, Ouray, Colo., December 28, 1922.

17. Carl J. Sigfrid to B. P. Morse, Ouray, July 22, September 6, October 11, 1921; Carl J. Sigfrid to J. P. M. Humphrey, Ouray, July 20, 1921.

18. B. P. Morse to Lewis & Grant, Attorneys, April 17, 1922.

19. B. P. Morse to Henry W. Toll, May 3, 1922; B. P. Morse to Floyd R. Thompson, Denver, April 3, 1923; B. P. Morse to J. C. Bradford, Jacksonville, Tenn., December 19, 1922; B. P. Morse to W. O. Palmer, January 8, 1923.

20. B. P. Morse to J. H. Skockley, July 24, 1923; B. P. Morse to Stockholders, Revenue Tunnel Mines Co., Old Hickory, Tenn., November 16, 1923.

21. Carl J. Sigfrid to B. P. Morse, Ouray, Colo., July 14, 1923; B. P. Morse to Carl J. Sigfrid, July 16, 1923; B. P. Morse to T. H. Woods, Jacksonville, Tenn., July 27, 1923.

22. B. P. Morse to Gerald Hughes, June 21, 1922; J. P. M. Humphrey to Carl J. Sigfrid, Denver, September 6, 1923.

23. James Clamp to J. P. M. Humphrey, Dunton, Colo., March 30, 1921; Gerald Hughes to B. P. Morse, Denver, May 19, 1921, and June 10, 1921; Carl J. Sigfrid to Gerald Hughes, Ouray, Colo., May 23, 1921.

24. Gerald Hughes to B. P. Morse, Denver, August 25, 1921; J. P. M. Humphrey to B. P. Morse, Denver, October 5, 1921; Robert L. Pellet to Emma Gold Mining Co., Dunton, Colo., November 29, 1921.

25. Gerald Hughes to B. P. Morse, Denver, April 17, 1922; B. P. Morse to Gerald Hughes, February 26, 1923.

26. Ben Sadtler's Reports to the Silver Basin Mining Co., June 14, 1892, and September 22, 1892; Ben Sadtler to W. G. Smith, Denver, September 22, 1892, and December 19, 1892; B. P. Morse to W. S. Keith, Old Hickory, Tenn., November 15, 1923.

27. B. P. Morse to Carl J. Sigfrid, March 3, 1923; Carl J. Sigfrid to B. P. Morse, Ouray, Colo., July 9, 1923; R. G. Dunn to B. P. Morse, Nashville, Tenn., July 9, 1923.

28. B. P. Morse to Gerald Hughes, April 14, 1921; B. P. Morse to Carl J. Sigfrid, Jacksonville, Tenn., August 26, 1921; B. P. Morse to J. P. M. Humphrey, March 29, 1923; B. P. Morse to W. G. Simmons, November 23, 1923; B. P. Morse to Harry D. Leech, November 27, 1923.

29. B. P. Morse to J. F. Robinson, November 28, 1923; B. P. Morse to J. F. Robinson, Old Hickory, Tenn., January 18, 1924.

30. B. P. Morse to J. F. Robinson, February 24, 1924; B. P. Morse to Carl J. Sigfrid, February 27, 1924.

31. B. P. Morse to J. F. Robinson, June 30, 1924; B. P. Morse to Malcolm Lindsey, July 7, 1924.

32. J. F. Robinson to B. P. Morse, Pitkin, Colo., July 25, 26, 1924; B. P. Morse to Carl J. Sigfrid, August 1, 1924.

33. B. P. Morse to Carl J. Sigfrid, August 1, 1924, and August 14, 1924; J. F. Robinson to B. P. Morse, Pitkin, Colo., August 10, 1924.

34. B. P. Morse to Anna R. Morse, September 8, 1924; W. G. Simmons to B. P. Morse, Nashville, Tenn., September 9, 1924; Bruce F. Shepherd, W. G. Simmons, and B. P. Morse to Stockholders, Tennessee-Colorado Development Co., Nashville, September 25, 1921; J. F. Robinson to B. P. Morse, Gunnison, Colo., November 25, 1924, and December 3, 1924; B. P. Morse to J. F. Robinson, Old Hickory, Tenn., November 26, 1924; F. A. Goodale to Bruce Shepherd and Associates, Grand Valley, Colo., December 5, 1924.

35. J. F. Robinson to B. P. Morse, Pitkin, Colo., December 3, 1924; B. P. Morse to Carl J. Sigfrid, December 5, 1924; B. P. Morse to J. F. Robinson, December 10, 1924.

36. J. F. Robinson to B. P. Morse, Pitkin, Colo., December 3, 1924; B. P. Morse to D. G. Miller, December 5, 1924; B. P. Morse to Carl J. Sigfrid, December 5, 1924; B. P. Morse to J. F. Robinson, December 10, 1924.

37. Carl J. Sigfrid to B. P. Morse, Ouray, Colo., December 15, 1924; B. P. Morse to Carl J. Sigfrid, December 24, 1924.

38. Gerald Hughes to B. P. Morse, Denver, May 19, 1921; J. P. M. Humphrey to George H. Derby, Denver, January 19, 1922; B. P. Morse to Cumberland Mines Co., Denver, October 18, 1923; C. O. Keiser to B. P. Morse, Canyon, Tex., November 12, 1925; B. P. Morse to J. P. M. Humphrey, Old Hickory, Tenn., November 18, 1925; B. P. Morse to George H. Derby, December 18, 1925.

39. B. P. Morse to Willard S. Morse, Old Hickory, Tenn., April 27,

1926; Gerald Hughes to B. P. Morse, Denver, October 6, 1926; Gerald Hughes to Carl J. Sigfrid, Denver, October 6, 1926; B. P. Morse to Gerald Hughes, October 12, 1926; Carl J. Sigfrid to Gerald Hughes, Ouray, Colo., October 12, 1926.

40. B. P. Morse to Stockholders, Commodore Mining Co., Denver, December 1, 1925, and December 15, 1926.

41. Carl J. Sigfrid to B. P. Morse, Ouray, Colo., October 6, 1926, and November 23, 1926; B. P. Morse to Carl J. Sigfrid, Old Hickory, Tenn., March 1, 1928; W. H. Cary to Stockholders, Commodore Mining Co., Denver, May 14, 1928; C. O. Withrow to B. P. Morse, Creede, Colo., August 28, 1928.

42. B. P. Morse to Carl J. Sigfrid, November 9, 1923, and March 24, 1925; B. P. Morse to J. F. Robinson, November 9, 1923; B. P. Morse to Gerald Hughes, December 7, 1923, and January 11, 1924; Carl J. Sigfrid to B. P. Morse, Ouray, Colo., December 28, 1923, March 18, 1925, and May 5, 1925.

43. Carl J. Sigfrid to B. P. Morse, Ouray, Colo., September 13, 1928, and October 22, 1928.

44. Ibid., March 18, 1930.

45. J. C. Wiley to B. P. Morse, Del Norte, Colo., August 4, 1925; B. P. Morse to J. C. Wiley, August 17, 1925; B. P. Morse to P. B. Butler, September 27, 1926; B. P. Morse to Anna Reynolds Morse, Tulsa, Okla., February 4, 1927; P. B. Butler to J. C. Wiley, February 5, 1927.

46. E. H. Platt to B. P. Morse, Denver, November 17, 1927.

47. W. H. Cary to B. P. Morse, Denver, January 6, 1929.

48. J. W. Pickens to B. P. Morse, Del Norte, TEL, September 5, 1930; *Pueblo (Colo.) Daily Chieftain*, September 5, 1930.

49. George H. Garrey to B. P. Morse, Salida, Colo., TEL, October 8, 1930.

50. Biographical data are taken from James B. Whiteside and Lee Scamehorn, "Inventory, George Henry Garrey (1875–1957) Collection, No. 1222" (Denver: Colorado Historical Society, 1985), ii–iv.

51. B. P. Morse to Directors, Commodore Mining Co., Denver, January 28, 1929; B. P. Morse to George H. Garrey, Denver, TEL, May 16, 1929.

52. W. H. Cary to B. P. Morse, Denver, January 25, 1930; B. T. Poxson to B. P. Morse, Golden, Colo., July 6, 1931; Carl J. Sigfrid to B. T. Poxson and George H. Garrey, Ouray, Colo., July 5, 1933; *Pueblo (Colo.) Daily Chieftain*, December 18, 1929.

53. B. T. Poxson to B. P. Morse, Denver, September 21, 1928; W. H. Cary to B. P. Morse, Denver, October 9, 1928; B. P. Morse to W. H. Cary, Old Hickory, Tenn., October 11, 1928; W. C. Sloan to B. P. Morse, Creede, Colo., October 14, 1928. See also B. T. Poxson, *A Reminiscence* (N.p.: Chronicle Publishing, 1988), 17–23.

54. W. H. Cary to B. P. Morse, Denver, January 25, 1930.

55. U.S. Bureau of Mines, *Mineral Resources of the United States, 1929,* 2 vols. (Washington, D.C.: GPO, 1932), 1:879.

56. W. H. Cary to Stockholders, Commodore Mining Co., Denver, January, 1931; W. H. Cary to B. P. Morse, Denver, May 5, 1931. See also U.S. Bureau of Mines, *Mineral Resources of the United States, 1920,* 2 vols. (Washington, D.C.: GPO, 1922), 1:513; U.S. Bureau of Mines, *Mineral Resources, 1929,* 1:879; U.S. Bureau of Mines, *Minerals Year Book, 1935* (Washington, D.C.: GPO, 1935), 39.

57. *Rocky Mountain News (Denver),* December 29, 1931.

58. "Reynolds Mines in Operation," *Mining Year Book* 25 (1937): 54, 57.

59. The impact of government policy on the prices of gold and silver is treated in John A. Brennan, *Silver and the First New Deal* (Reno: University of Nevada Press, 1969); and Dickson H. Leavens, *Silver Money* (Bloomington, Ind.: Principia Press, 1939), chaps. 25–27.

60. U.S. Bureau of Mines, *Minerals Yearbook, 1935,* 39; "Mineral County," *Mining Year Book* 25 (1937): 39.

61. Thomas A. Steven and James G. Ratte, "Geology and Ore Deposits of the Summitville District, San Juan Mountains, Colorado," *United States Geological Survey Professional Paper* 343 (1960): 6.

62. C. L. Ortloff to Marion Reynolds, Denver, March 12, 1937; Carl J. Sigfrid to Thomas P. Campbell, Denver, December 14, 1937; C. L. Ortloff to Dines, Dines & Holme, Denver, April 11, 1939; B. T. Poxson to George H. Garrey, Creede, Colo., March 14, 1940, and December 24, 1941.

63. Stevens and Ratte, "Geology and Ore Deposits," 6; F. M. Stanger to B. A. Brannock, Summitville, Colo., June 30, 1942; *Pueblo (Colo.) Daily Chieftain,* October 11, 1936, April 16, 1937, and July 10, 1942.

64. B. T. Poxson to George H. Garrey, Summitville, Colo., August 9, 1942, and August 15, 1942; E. B. Reeser to Anna R. Garrey, New York, August 11, 1942; Stevens and Ratte, "Geology and Ore Deposits," 6–7.

65. B. T. Poxson to George H. Poxson, Denver, October 20, 1942.

66. Poxson, *A Reminiscence,* 18; Interview with Ben Poxson, Denver, August 8, 1984.

67. Poxson, *A Reminiscence*, 20, 23.

68. U.S. Bureau of Mines, *Mineral Resources, 1929,* 1:879.

69. Interview with John H. Tippit, Boulder, Colo., October 12, 1993.

70. Ibid.

71. Stephen M. Voynick, *Colorado Gold: From the Pike's Peak Gold Rush to the Present* (Missoula: Mountain Press, 1992), 131–32; Robert H. Ramsey, *Men and Mines of Newmont: A Fifty-Year History* (New York: Octagon Books, 1973), 274–80; Timothy Green, *The New World of Gold: The Inside Story of the Mines, the Markets, the Politics, the Investors* (New York: Walker, 1981), 87–92.

72. U.S. Bureau of Mines, *Minerals Yearbook, 1987,* 3 vols. (Washington, D.C.: GPO, 1989), 1:404.

73. Voynick, *Colorado Gold,* p. 131; U.S. Bureau of Mines, *Minerals Yearbook, 1985,* 3 vols. (Washington, D.C.: GPO, 1987), 1:421, 2:112.

74. U.S. Bureau of Mines, *Minerals Yearbook, 1986,* 3 vols. (Washington, D.C.: GPO, 1988), 1:427; U.S. Bureau of Mines, *Minerals Yearbook, 1987,* 2:84; U.S. Bureau of Mines, *Minerals Yearbook, 1988,* 3 vols. (Washington, D.C.: GPO, 1990), 2:105.

75. U.S. Bureau of Mines, *Minerals Yearbook, 1989,* 3 vols. (Washington, D.C.: GPO, 1991), 2:105; U.S. Bureau of Mines, *Minerals Yearbook, 1990,* 3 vols. (Washington, D.C.: GPO, 1992), 1:506; *Denver Post,* April 24, 1992.

76. *Denver Post,* April 24, 1992, December 8, 1992, December 18, 1992, December 29, 1992, and February 21, 1993.

77. Interview with John H. Tippit, October 12, 1993.

78. Ibid.

Bibliography

Archives and Manuscript Collections

Denver Museum of Natural History, Denver
    Correspondence, 1897–1921
    Minutes of Meetings, 1897–1921
Colorado Historical Society, Denver
    Albert E. Reynolds Collection, No. 1220
    George H. Garrey Collection, No. 1222
Ouray County Historical Society, Ouray, Colorado
    Carl J. Sigfrid Collection
Hubbell W. Reed Correspondence
    Seven letterpress books, 1886–1896, of outgoing correspondence while Reed was superintendent of the Caroline Mining Company, the Revenue Tunnel Company, and related enterprises at Ouray, in possession of the author.

Public Documents

Emmons, William H., and Esper S. Larsen. "A Preliminary Report on the Geology and Ore Deposits of Creede, Colorado." *United States Geological Survey Bulletin* 530. Washington, D.C.: GPO, 1913, 42–65.

——. "Geology and Ore Deposits of the Creede District, Colorado." *United States Geological Survey Bulletin* 718. Washington, D.C.: GPO, 1923.

Ewers, John C. "Hair Pipes in Plains Indian Ornament." Anthropological Paper 50. *Smithsonian Institution Bureau of American Ethnology Bulletin* 164. Washington, D.C.: GPO, 1957, 29–85.

Hill, J. M. "Gold and Silver: Notes on the Economic Geology of Southeastern Gunnison County, Colorado." *United States Geological Survey Bulletin* 380. Washington, D.C.: GPO, 1909.

Irving, John Duer. "Ore Deposits in the Vicinity of Lake City, Colorado." *United States Geological Survey Bulletin* 260. Washington, D.C.: GPO, 1905, 78–84.

Irving, John Duer, and Howland Bancroft. "Geology and Ore Deposits near Lake City, Colorado." *United States Geological Survey Bulletin* 478. Washington, D.C.: GPO, 1911.

Steven, Thomas A., and James G. Ratte. "Geology and Ore Deposits of the Summitville District, San Juan Mountains, Colorado." *United States Geological Survey Professional Paper* 343. Washington, D.C.: GPO, 1960.

U.S. Geological Survey, *Mineral Resources of the United States, 1920–1923.* Washington, D.C.: GPO, 1922–1925.

U.S. Bureau of Mines, *Mineral Resources of the United States, 1924–1933.* Washington, D.C.: GPO, 1926–1935.

——. *Minerals Yearbooks, 1934–1991.* Washington, D.C.: GPO, 1936–1992.

U.S. Commissioner of Indian Affairs. "Annual Reports to the Secretary of State, 1871–1883." Washington, D.C.: GPO, 1872–1883.

U.S. House, Committee on Expenditures in the War Department. "The Management of the War Department." 44th Cong., 1st sess., *Report* no. 799. Washington, D.C.: GPO, 1875.

Books

Annual Colorado State Business Directory, 1919. Denver: Gazette Publishing & Printing, 1919.

Baker, James D., and LeRoy R. Hafen, eds. *History of Colorado.* 5 vols. Denver: Linderman, 1927.

Baker, T. Lindsay, and Billy R. Harrison. *Adobe Walls: The History and Archeology of the 1874 Trading Post.* College Station: Texas A&M Press, 1986.

Bean, Geraldine B. *Charles Boettcher: A Study in Pioneer Western Enterprise.* Boulder, Colo.: Westview Press, 1976.

Berthrong, Donald J. *The Cheyenne and Arapaho Ordeal: Reservation and Agency Life in Indian Territory, 1875–1907.* Norman: University of Oklahoma Press, 1976.

——. *The Southern Cheyennes.* Norman: University of Oklahoma Press, 1963.

Brennan, John A. *Silver and the First New Deal.* Reno: University of Nevada Press, 1969.

Brown, Robert L. *Silver: A History of the San Juan Silver Rush.* Caldwell, Idaho: Caxton Printers, 1965.

Carriker, Robert C. *Fort Supply, Indian Territory: Frontier Outpost of the Plains.* Norman: University of Oklahoma Press, 1970.

Corbetts and Ballinger's Annual City Directory, 1889–1913. Denver, 1889–1913.

Dale, Edward Everett. *The Range Cattle Industry: Ranching on the Great Plains from 1865 to 1925.* Norman: University of Oklahoma Press, 1960.

Delo, David Michael. *Peddlers and Post Traders: The Army Sutler on the Frontier.* Salt Lake City: University of Utah Press, 1992.

Dorset, Phyllis Flanders. *The New Eldorado: The Story of Colorado's Gold and Silver Rushes.* (New York: Macmillan, 1970.

Dorsett, Lyle W. *The Queen City: A History of Denver.* Boulder, Colo.: Pruett Publishing, 1977.

Fell, James E., Jr. *Ores to Metals: The Rocky Mountain Smelting Industry.* Lincoln: University of Nebraska Press, 1979.

Foster, Mark. *Henry M. Porter: Rocky Mountain Empire Builder.* Niwot: University Press of Colorado, 1991.

Frazer, Robert W. *Forts of the West: Military Forts and Presidios and Posts Commonly Called Forts West of the Mississippi River.* Norman: University of Oklahoma Press, 1965.

Gard, Wayne. *The Great Buffalo Hunt.* New York: Alfred A. Knopf, 1960.

Green, Timothy. *The New World of Gold: The Inside Story of the Mines, the Markets, the Politics, the Investors.* New York: Walker, 1981.

Gregory, Marvin, and P. David Smith. *Mountain Memories: The Ouray Odyssey.* 4th ed. Ouray, Colo.: Wayfinder Press, 1989.

Grinnell, George Bird. *The Cheyenne Indians: Their History and Ways of Life.* 2 vols. New Haven: Yale University Press, 1924.

———. *The Fighting Cheyennes.* Norman: University of Oklahoma Press, 1956.

Hafen, LeRoy R., ed. *Colorado and Its People.* 4 vols. New York: Lewis Publishing, 1948.

Haley, J. Evetts. *Charles Goodnight: Cowman & Plainsman.* Boston: Houghton Mifflin, 1936.

———. *The XIT Ranch and the Early Days of the Llano Estacado.* Norman: University of Oklahoma Press, 1967.

Haley, James L. *The Buffalo War: The History of the Red River Indian Uprising of 1874.* Norman: University of Oklahoma Press, 1985.

Hall, C. H. *Resources, Industries, and Natural Advantages of Ouray County: Mines, Mills, Manufacturing, Agriculture, Towns, Railroads, Etc.* Ouray, Colo.: Humphrey Hulanski, 1894.

Hall, Frank. *History of the State of Colorado.* 4 vols. Chicago: Blakely Printing, 1891–1895.

Haywood, C. Robert. *Trails South: The Wagon-Road Economy in the Dodge City–Panhandle Region.* Norman: University of Oklahoma Press, 1986.

Heitman, Sidney, ed. *Germans from Russia in Colorado.* N.p.: Western Social Science Association, 1978.

Kerr, W. G. *Scottish Capital on the American Credit Frontier.* Austin: Texas State Historical Association, 1976.

King, Joseph E. *A Mine to Make a Mine: Financing the Colorado Mining Industry, 1859–1902.* College Station: Texas A&M University Press, 1977.

Lamar, Howard R. *The Trader on the American Frontier: Myth's Victim.* College Station: Texas A&M University Press, 1977.

Leavens, Dickson H. *Silver Money.* Bloomington, Ind.: Principia Press, 1939.

Lillibridge, John L. *The Red Fork Ranch and Its People.* Ocala, Fla.: Greene's Printing, 1990.

Lingenfelter, Richard E. *The Hard Rock Miners: A History of Mining Labor Movement in the American West, 1863–1893.* Berkeley and Los Angeles: University of California Press, 1974.

Mails, Thomas E. *The Mystic Warriors of the Plains.* Garden City, N.Y.: Doubleday, 1972.

McCarty, John L. *Maverick Town: The Story of Old Tascosa.* Norman: University of Oklahoma Press, 1946.

Overton, Richard C. *Gulf to the Rockies: The Heritage of the Forth Worth and Denver—Colorado and Southern Railways, 1861–1898.* Austin: University of Texas Press, 1953.

Pearce, W. M. *The Matador Land and Cattle Company.* Norman: University of Oklahoma Press, 1982.

Portrait and Biographical Record of the State of Colorado. Chicago: Chapman Publishing, 1899.

Poxson, B. T. *A Reminiscence.* N.p.: Chronicle Publishing, 1988.

Ramsey, Robert H. *Men and Mines of Newmont: A Fifty-Year History.* New York: Octagon Books, 1973.

Rath, Ida Ellen. *Early Ford County.* North Newton, Kans.: Mennonite Press, 1964.

———. *The Rath Trail.* Wichita, Kans.: McCormick-Armstrong, 1961.

Rathjen, Frederick W. *The Texas Panhandle Frontier.* Austin: University of Texas Press, 1973.

Rister, Carl Coke. *Fort Griffin on the Texas Frontier.* Norman: University of Oklahoma Press, 1956.

———. *No Man's Land.* Norman: University of Oklahoma Press, 1948.

Robertson, Donald B. *Encyclopedia of Western Railroad History.* Vol. 1, *The Desert States: Arizona, Nevada, New Mexico, Utah.* Caldwell, Idaho: Caxton Printers, 1986.

Robertson, Pauline Durett, and R. L. Robertson. *Tascosa: Historic Site in the Texas Panhandle.* (Amarillo, Tex.: Paramount Publishing, 1977.

Rohrbough, Malcolm J. *Aspen: The History of a Silver-Mining Town, 1879–1893.* New York: Oxford University Press, 1986.

Romance of Petroleum and Gas. Vol. 2. New York: [J. J. Little and Ives, 1920].

Sandoz, Marie. *The Buffalo Hunters: The Story of the Hide Men.* New York: Hastings House, 1954.

Schofield, Donald F. *Indians, Cattle, Ships, and Oil: The Story of W. M. D. Lee.* Austin: University of Texas Press, 1985.

Sherow, James Earl. *Watering the Valley: Development of the High Plains Arkansas River, 1870–1950.* Lawrence: University Press of Kansas, 1990.

Smiley, Jerome C. *History of Denver.* Denver: Denver Times, 1901.

Smith, Duane A. *Colorado Mining: A Photographic History.* Albuquerque: University of New Mexico Press, 1977.

———. *Song of Hammer and Drill: The Colorado San Juans, 1860–1914.* Golden: Colorado School of Mines Press, 1982.

Stone, Wilbur Fisk. *History of Colorado.* 4 vols. Chicago: S. J. Clarke Publishing, 1918–1919.

Studenski, Paul, and Herman E. Kroos. *Financial History of the United States.* New York: McGraw Book, 1952.

Suggs, George G., Jr. *Colorado's War on Militant Unionism: James H. Peabody and the Western Federation of Miners.* Detroit: Wayne State University Press, 1972.

Sullivan, Dulcie. *The LS Brand: The Story of a Texas Panhandle Ranch.* Austin: University of Texas Press, 1968.

Vose, Pamela Daly. *The Masters School, 1877–1977: A Retrospective Portrait for the One-Hundredth Anniversary* (1977).

Voynick, Stephen. *Colorado Gold: From the Pike's Peak Gold Rush to the Present.* Missoula: Mountain Press, 1992.

Walker, Henry Pickering. *The Wagonmasters: High Plains Freighting from the Earliest Days of the Santa Fe Trail to 1880.* Norman: University of Oklahoma Press, 1986.

Wright, Muriel H. *A Guide to the Indian Tribes of Oklahoma.* Norman: University of Oklahoma Press, 1951.

Articles

Archambeau, Earnest R., ed. "Old Tascosa: Selected News Items from the *Tascosa Pioneer*, 1886–1887." *Panhandle-Plains Historical Review* 39 (1966): 1–183.

Bartlett, Robert F. "Aspen: The Mining Community, 1879–1893." *Denver Westerners' Brand Book* 5 (1950): 131–60.

Beaton, Gail M. "The Widening Sphere of Women's Lives: The Literary Study and Philanthropic Work of Six Women's Clubs in Denver, 1881–1945." *Essays in Colorado History* 13 (1992): 1–68.

Cole, Helen C. "The Dobbs Curriculum: The First Fifty Years, 1877–1927." *Dobbs Alumnae Bulletin* (Fall-Winter 1968–1969): 9–10.

Crimmins, M. L. "Notes on the Establishment of Fort Elliott and the Buffalo Wallow Fight." *Panhandle-Plains Historical Review* 25 (1952): 45–69.

Flores, Dan "Bison Ecology and Bison Diplomacy: The Southern Plains from 1800 to 1850." *Journal of American History* 78 (September 1991): 465–85.

Gardner, Mark L., "John Simpson Hough: Merchant on the Santa Fe Trail," *Wagon Track* 2 (February 1988): 10–12.

Harrison, Lowell H. "Damage Suits for Indian Depredations in the Adobe Walls Area, 1874." *Panhandle-Plains Historical Review* 36 (1963): 37–60.

Henn, Roger E. "The Revenue Mine, 1896." *Ouray County Historical Society Magazine* 1 (1984): 21–33.

———. "Trials of an Indian Trader." *Chicago Westerner's Brand Book* 33 (March 1976): 1–3, 22–27.

Kerr, W. G. "Scotland and the Texas Mortgage Business." *Panhandle-Plains Historical Review* 38 (1965): 53–71.

Le Van, Sandra W. "The Quaker Agents at Darlington." *Chronicles of Oklahoma* 5l (Spring 1973): 92–99.

Leckie, William H. "The Red River War, 1874–1875." *Panhandle-Plains Historical Review* 29 (1956): 78–100.

Leonard, J. Joseph. "On the Trail of the Legendary Dave Day." *Denver Westerner's Brand Book* 9 (1953): 165–84.

Mabry, W. S. "Some Memories of W. S. Mabry." *Panhandle-Plains Historical Review* 11 (1938): 31–51.

Morse, A. Reynolds. "Gold Links Tailings." *Gunnison (Colo.) Country Times*, 1978–1980.

Oswald, James M. "History of Fort Elliott." *Panhandle-Plains Historical Review* 32 (1959): 1–59.

Peterson, Susans. "Fort Supply: Isolated Outpost." In *Early Military Forts and Posts in Oklahoma*, ed. Odie B. Faulk, Kenny A. Franks, and Paul F. Lambert. Oklahoma City: Oklahoma Historical Society, 1978.

Rathjen, Frederick W. "The Federal Role in Opening the Panhandle." *Panhandle-Plains Historical Review* 49 (1976): 1–24.

Rister, Carl Coke. "The Significance of the Destruction of the Buffalo in the Southwest." *Southwestern Historical Review* 33 (July 1929): 34–49.

Rudolph, Charles F., ed. "Selected News Items from the *Tascosa Pioneer*." *Panhandle-Plains Historical Review* 39 (1966): 1–183.

Schofield, Donald F. "W. M. D. Lee, Indian Trader." *Panhandle-Plains Historical Review* 54 (1981): 1–117.

Strickland, Rex, ed. "The Recollections of W. S. Glenn, Buffalo Hunter." *Panhandle-Plains Historical Review* 22 (1949): 21–64.

West, G. Dereck. "The Battle for Adobe Walls." *Panhandle-Plains Historical Review* 36 (1963): 1–36.

White, Lonnie J. "Indian Battles in the Texas Panhandle." *Journal of the West* 6 (April 1967): 278–309.

———, comp. "Texas Panhandle News Items, 1877–1885, from the *Dodge City Times*." *Panhandle-Plains Historical Review* 40 (1967): 1–162.

Whitely, Philip W. "Trade Beads Among the American Indians." *Denver Westerner's Brand Book* 7 (1951): 269–88.

———. "Traders and Tokens." *Denver Westerner's Brand Book* 9 (1953): 85–112.

Magazines and Journals
Commercial and Financial Chronicle
Engineering and Mining Journal
Mines and Minerals
Mining and Scientific Press
Mining Industry
Mining Investor
Mining Reporter
Mining World
Mining Year Book (Colorado)
Ores and Metals

Newspapers
Columbus (Wisc.) Republican
Commercial & Financial Chronicle
Creede (Colo.) Candle
Cripple Creek (Colo.) Citizen
Daily Enterprise (Montrose, Colo.)
Denver Post
Denver Republican
Denver Times
Dodge City (Kans.) Times
Gunnison (Colo.) Country Times
Gunnison (Colo.) News-Champion
Gunnison (Colo.) Republican
Gunnison (Colo.) Tribune
Leavenworth (Kans.) Daily Times
New York Times
Old Hickory (Tenn.) News
Ouray (Colo.) Herald
Ouray (Colo.) Silverite-Plaindealer
Ouray (Colo.) Times
Rocky Mountain News (Denver)
Rocky Mountain Sun (Aspen, Colo.)
Silver World (Lake City, Colo.)*Pueblo (Colo.) Daily Chieftan*

Unpublished Materials
Hyman, David M. "The Romance of a Mining Venture." Typescript, 126
       pp., in American Jewish Archives, Hebrew Union College,

Cincinnati, Ohio. A photocopy is in the A. E. Reynolds Collection.

Mehls, Stephen Frederick. "David H. Moffat Jr.: Early Colorado Business Leader." Ph.D. diss., University of Colorado, Boulder, 1982.

Montgomery, Mary S., comp. "Lesser Known or Extinct Towns of Kansas." 9 vols. Topeka: Kansas Historical Society, n.d.

Rice, Frank A. "History of Ouray and Mines." Ouray, Colo.: Ouray Public Library, typescript.

Scamehorn, Lee. "Inventory, Albert Eugene Reynolds Collection, No. 1220." Denver: Colorado Historical Society, 1988.

Whiteside James B., and Lee Scamehorn. "Inventory, George H. Garrey (1875–1957) Collection, No. 1222." Denver: Colorado Historical Society, 1985.

Index

A. A. Hausman and Co. (N.Y.),
201
Abbott, J. J., 178
Aberdeen Angus cattle, 67, 74
Adams, A. F., 148
Adits. *See* Tunnels
Adobe Walls, Tex., 50
A. E. Reynolds and Co.:
Mobeetie, Tex., 50; Lake
City, Colo., 89–91
Agricultural Adjustment Act,
226
Akron Mines Co. (White Pine,
Colo.), 160
Alamocitas Ranch (Tex.), 78
Alamosa, Colo., 66, 85, 88, 224
Alamosa River, 232
Albrecht Lanphier and Finch
Co. (St. Paul, Minn.), 54
Alexander II (czar of Russia),
195
Alfrey, Ike, 48
Alliance Trust Co. (Dundee,
Scotland), 74–75, 171
American Concentrator Co.
(Joplin, Mo.), 174
American Flag claim (Boulder
County, Colo.), 182
American Smelting and Re-

fining Co., 173, 199, 223,
230
Amethyst Mine (Creede, Colo.),
132, 135–36, 228
Amethyst Mining Co., 135, 137
Anaconda Minerals Corp., 230
Anadarko, I.T., 59
Annie Wood Mine (Lake City,
Colo.), 86
Anthony, A. J., 45
A. O. Smith Corp. (Milwaukee,
Wisc.), 227–28, 230
Apex suit (Aspen, Colo.), 15,
93–95, 131, 181
Arapahoe Indians, 8–9, 44, 59,
61, 187
Argenta Falls (Lake City, Colo.),
179
Argenta Falls Silver Mining Co.,
179
Argenta Mining Co., 179
Arkansas River Land Town and
Canal Co., 189
Arms, Charles D., 15, 93, 95–
96, 129, 184
Arms, Wilford, 185
Armstrong Gulch Tunnel (Gun-
nison County, Colo.), 147
Arnold, Seth J., 53

Ashenfelter, John, 56, 101
Aspen, Colo., 15, 93–94, 115, 131, 134, 165, 181
Aspen Mine (Aspen, Colo.), 94–95
Aspen Mining and Smelting Co., 94
Aspen Pool, 93–95, 129, 181
Assessments on unpatented mining claims, 158, 212
Atchison, Topeka and Santa Fe Railroad, 45–46, 70
Atkins, J. D., 58
Atlantic-Richfield Oil Co., 230
Atlas Mine (Sneffels, Colo.), 168
Atlas Mining and Milling Co., 168
Aztec Resources Co., 232

Babcock, A. C., 72
Bachelor Mine (Creede, Colo.), 132, 221, 228
Bachelor Mining Co., 136–37, 220, 224
Baldwin, Frank, 60
Barnsdall, Theodore N., 17, 130, 153, 157–58, 173, 175–76, 182, 198
Barnsdall Corp., 222, 228
Baruch, Bernard M., 191
Beach, Myron, 184
Beaumont, M. F., 77
Bechtel Engineering Co., 231
Belle Lennox Nursery (Denver, Colo.), 20
Belle of the East Mine (Lake City, Colo.), 86
Belle of the West Mine (Lake City, Colo.), 19, 86, 88
Belle Vernon Mine (Lake City, Colo.), 86
Belnap, William, 40

Belzora-Bassick Tunnel (Ohio City, Colo.), 151
Bent, George, 48, 60–61, 187
Bent, Julia, 60, 187
Bent, William, 48, 187
Bent's Fort, Colo., 187, 208–209
Bent's Fort Farm Loan Association (La Junta, Colo.), 196
Bent's Fort Land & Cattle Co. (La Junta, Colo.), 205, 209
Bent's Fort National Park (La Junta, Colo.), 209
Big Casino Mine (Lake City, Colo.), 86
Big Four Group (Prescott, Ariz.), 183
Bimetallism, 14–15, 22–23
Black Prince Group (Chloride, Ariz.), 182
Black Prince Mining Co., 182–83
Blanket theory of mineralization, 203–204, 207, 215–16
Blum, John, 196
Boettcher, Charles, 24
Bond, A. G., 68, 92
Bon Ton Group (Pitkin, Colo.), 159
Bon Ton Leasing Co. (Pitkin, Colo.), 159
Bowen, Thomas, 130–31
Bowerman, J. C., 147–48
Boyce, A. G., 81
Bradley, J. H., 16, 123–24
Bristol Head Mining Co. (Creede, Colo.), 137
Brooklyn Children's Aid Society, 68
Brown, D. R. C., 94
Browne and Manzanares Co. (N.M.), 81
Bryan, William Jennings, 22–23

Bryant, T. S., 56
Buckley, Willing and Co. (N.Y.),
   16, 48, 53, 123, 130–31
Buddecke & Diehl Co. (Mont-
   rose, Colo.), 91
Buffalo, slaughter of, 49, 62
Buffalo robe and hide trade,
   44, 47–54
Bull teams, 45, 56
Burdick, Kans., 189
Busch, Peter, 196
Bush, M. P., 92
Butler, Calvin P., 134

Cahill, Luke, 60
Caldwell, Kans., 59
C. A. Morehead Co. (Leaven-
   worth, Kans.), 44
Camp Bird Mine (Ouray Coun-
   ty, Colo.), 168
Campion, John F., 21, 24
Campling, Mary Bridget, 188
Camp Supply. See Fort Supply
Canadian Ranch. See Reynolds
   Ranch
Capitol City, Colo., 86, 180
Capitol Freehold Land and In-
   vestment Co. (Tex.), 72, 78
Carbonate Hill Mine (Leadville,
   Colo.), 93
Caribou, Colo., 182
Carleton Mill (Cripple Creek,
   Colo.), 231
Carlin Mine (Ely, Nev.), 230
Caroline Mining Co., 16, 92,
   100–105, 120, 123, 125–28
Carter Tunnel (Ohio City,
   Colo.), 151
Catholic Colonization Society
   (Chicago), 94
Cattle trails (I.T.), 45–46
Chafee, Adna R., 60

Chamberlain, W. A., 26
Charles Rath and Co. (Dodge
   City, Kans.), 45, 50
Chase, Charles A. L., 123
Cheesman, Walter S., 21
Cheyenne-Arapahoe Agency
   (I.T.), 39, 41, 43, 45–55, 57
Cheyenne Indians, 8–9, 44, 59,
   61, 187
Chicago, Rock Island and Mex-
   ico Railroad, 78
Chicago, Rock Island and Pacif-
   ic Railroad, 71
Chicago, University of, 223
Chicago Park (Gunnison Coun-
   ty, Colo.), 20, 143, 145, 147,
   217, 224–25, 229
Chick Browne and Co. (Gre-
   nada, Colo. Terr.), 55
Chief Mining Co. (Hesperus,
   Colo.), 176
Chihuahua Mine (Lake City,
   Colo.), 86
Chino Copper Co. (N. M.), 160
Chipeta, Colo., 100
Church, Ralph P., 79
Cimarron Mill (Telluride,
   Colo.), 16, 124
City Temple Institutional
   Church (Denver, Colo.), 20
City Temple Institutional Soci-
   ety (Denver, Colo.), 20
Clamp, James, 204–205, 215–16
Clarendon, Okla., 58
Cleopatra Mine (Pitkin, Colo.),
   143, 147
Cleveland, Grover, 116
Cleveland Cliffs, Inc., 229
Coal mines, Pleasant Valley,
   Utah, 83–84
Cochran, Bittmann and Taylor
   Co. (Leavenworth, Kans.), 44

Coeur d'Alene, Idaho, 122
Coffin, Mary A., 131, 133–35
Coffin, Samuel D., 131, 133–35
Cole, Omer V., 133
Colgate College, 6
Colorado Exploration and Min-
    ing Co. (Ontario, Canada),
    184
Colorado Fish and Game Com-
    mission, 153–54
Colorado Iron and Metal Co.
    (Denver, Colo.), 274n.13
Colorado Midland Railway, 94
Colorado Mining Association,
    226
Colorado Museum of Natural
    History. *See* Denver Museum
    of Natural History
Colorado Seminary (Denver,
    Colo.), 5
Colorado Smelting and Mining
    Co., 144–46, 151–58
Colorado State Home for De-
    pendent and Neglected Chil-
    dren (Denver, Colo.), 27
Columbus, Wisc., 25–26
Commanche Indians, 48, 50,
    52, 55
Commodore-Bachelor litiga-
    tion, 222, 224
Commodore-Bachelor Mines,
    Inc. (Creede, Colo.), 226–27
Commodore Mine (Creede,
    Colo.), 19–20, 131–32, 134–
    37, 164–65, 170, 178–79,
    200, 209–10, 220, 225–36
Commodore Mining Co., 135–
    37, 171–73, 200, 221, 224–25
Commodore Tunnel (Creede,
    Colo.), 171
Compromise Mining Co. (As-
    pen, Colo.), 94

Congress Gold and Copper Co.
    (Silverton, Colo.), 172
Connell, Charles T., 55
Consolidated Gold Mining Co.,
    17, 130, 173, 222
Cook, H. H., 92
Copper Hill Mining Co., 86
Cornell University, 192
Costilla Grant (Colo.), 70
Cox, William J., 168
Crawford, E. H., 133
Creede, Colo., 115, 130–35, 161,
    170–73, 175, 209, 220–21,
    224–25, 227
Creede, N.C., 130
Creede Exploration Co.,
    173
Creswell Land and Cattle Co.
    (Tex.), 72
Cripple Creek, Colo., 122, 230–
    31
Cripple Creek and Victor Min-
    ing Co., 231
Crocker, Jenny Lind, 187–88
Crooke, John J., 87
Crooke Bros. Co. (N.Y.), 87
Crooke Consolidated Mining
    and Smelting Co., 86–87, 91
Crooke Mining and Smelting
    Co., 87
Crooke's Falls (Lake City, Colo.),
    180
Crosley, James H., 189–91
Cudahy, Jack, 145
Cumberland Mines Co. (Dun-
    ton, Colo.), 220
Cumberland Mining Co.
    (Sneffels, Colo.), 114, 127,
    168–69
Cyanide reduction of ores, 14,
    174, 216, 228, 230–32; heap
    leaching, 230–32

Darlington, Brinton, 43
Darlington, I.T., 43, 48, 55, 58, 64
Daughters of the American Revolution, 209
Davis, T. M., 94
Day, David, 100
De Graaf, H. P., 83–84
Del Norte, Colo., 66, 88, 173, 221–22
Denver and Fort Worth Railroad, 70
Denver, University of, 5, 20
Denver and Rio Grande Railroad, 100, 137, 180
Denver and Rio Grande Railway, 66, 84, 87
Denver and Rio Grande Southern Railway, 176
Denver Fortnightly Club, 27
Denver Museum of Natural History, 5, 21
Denver National Bank, 201
Diamond drill core tests, 217–19
Dick, James E., 160
Dickerson, E. A., 92
Dickinson Bros. (Dodge City, Kans.), 63
Dickson, S. Z., 132–33
Dodd, Brown and Co. (St. Louis, Mo.), 48, 58
Dodge City, Kans., 8, 55–56
Dolores Silver Mines, Inc., 203, 216
Dore, A. C., 131
Dorsch, George, 196
Dorsey, Clayton C., 211
Doty, D. H, 57–59
Doty, W. H., 59
Downieville Mining District (Clear Creek County, Colo.), 171

Downing, Jacob, 60–61
Downing, J. W., 94
Drake, John A., 134
Driskill, J. L. and Sons (Austin, Tex.), 64
Dudley, W. K., 204
Dundee Mortgage and Trust Investment Co. (Scotland), 68, 74
Dunn, Stephen, 147–48
Dunton, Colo., 30, 148, 202, 207, 209, 213–15, 224, 229
Dunton, Horatio, 148
Du Pont Powder Co., 206
Durango, Colo., 197–98
Durant Mine (Aspen, Colo.), 19
Durant Mining Co., 15, 93–94, 130
Durfee, E. H., 44, 48, 53
Durham cattle. See Shorthorn cattle
D. W. Van Horn and Co. (Mobeetie, Tex.), 246n.15
Dyer Taylor and Co. (Chicago), 54

Eagle Bird Group (Boulder County), 182
Eames Vacuum Brake Co. (N.Y.), 17
Earll, Angeline Lawton (Mrs. Robert W. Earll), 25–26
Earll, Anna, 26
Earll, Coie, 26
Earll, Dr. Robert W., 25–26, 80
Earll, Frances Eudorah, 26
Earll, Hattie, 26
Eastern Star Group (San Juan County, Colo.), 182
E. B. Allen and Co. (Leavenworth, Kans.), 46
Eckbert, William H., 142, 145, 151–52, 155–57

E. H. Garbutt and Co. (N. Y.), 16
EJM Cattle Co. (Montrose, Colo.), 190
EJM Ranch (Delta, Colo.), 79, 190
Ely-Revenue Copper Co. (Ely, Nev.), 184, 197–98, 210
Emerald Isle Mine (Lake City, Colo.), 86
Emma Gold Mining Co., 30, 149–50, 204, 213
Emma Mill (Dunton, Colo.), 150, 230
Emma Mine (Dunton, Colo.), 14–15, 19, 31, 148–50, 202–205, 207, 209, 213, 215, 224, 229
Emperius, Herman, 224–25
Emperius Mining Co., 228
Emperor Mine (Lake City, Colo.), 86
Engelman, Henry, 196
Engelman, Philip, 196
Englewood, Kans., 70
Erlich, Jacob, 196
Etcetera Mine (Highlands, Colo.), 19, 181
Eveatt, E. N., 193
Excursion Mine (Lake City, Colo.), 86

Fairview-Cleopatra Mines, Inc. (Pitkin, Colo.), 225
Fairview Mine (Pitkin, Colo.), 143, 147
Farmington, N.M., 31, 198
Farwell, Charles B., 72
Farwell, John V., 72
Fay, Charles, 30
Fay, Hattie Earll (Mrs. Charles Fay), 30

Federal Farm Loan Bank (Wichita, Kans.), 196, 201
Ferguson, Joe, 67
Fine, William J., 142, 145, 152, 155–56, 158
Finney, Henry, 25
First Missouri Cavalry Regiment, 46
First National Bank of Denver (Colo.), 201
First National Bank of Leavenworth (Kans.), 44
First National Bank of Pueblo (Colo.), 73, 85, 169, 200
Forest King Mine (Platoro, Colo.), 19, 209
Forest King Mining Co., 129, 174
Fort Dodge, Kans., 8, 85
Fort Edward Collegiate Institute, 6
Fort Elliott, Tex., 10, 45, 50, 55–57, 64, 67, 83, 85
Fort Griffin, Tex., 50
Fort Lyon, Colorado Terr., 7–8, 85, 88, 186
Fort Lyon Canal (La Junta, Colo.), 29, 79, 189–90, 192, 205
Fort Reno, I.T., 64
Fort Supply, I.T., 8–10, 41–43, 55–57, 63–64, 67, 83, 85, 188
"Forty Years with the Cheyennes," 60
Fowler, F. W., 149
Frank Hough Mine (Lake City, Colo.), 29, 86, 88–90, 177–78, 180, 209
Frank Hough Mining Co., 177
Frank Hough Tunnel (Lake City, Colo.), 178

Fred Harvey Restaurant (St. Louis, Mo.), 206
Freidenberger, Fred, 196
Freighting operations, 45, 88
Fulton, Mo., 46

Galactic Resources (Vancouver, B.C.), 230–32
Garbutt, E. H., 16, 83
Garbutt, Griggs and Co. (N.Y.), 16
Garret, W. A., 128, 153
Garrey, Anna Reynolds Morse (Mrs. George H. Garrey), 229, 232
Garrey, George H., 203, 223–25, 227–30
Gast, Charles E., 85
Gates, John W., 134
General Minerals Co., 229–30
General Sherman Mine (Lake City, Colo.), 86
German settlements in southern Russia, 195
Germans from Russia, 30, 194–96, 205, 208
Gibbons, D. G., 193
Gibbs, William, 56
Gillette, William, 216
Glacier Mining Co., 114, 117, 120–21, 123, 125–28
Golconda-Consolidation mines merger, 198
Golconda Gold Mining Co., 17, 19, 130, 173–74, 202, 209, 222
Gold Belt (Gunnison County, Colo.), 144
Gold Brick Mining District (Gunnison County, Colo.), 143–44, 151
Gold Cup Consolidated Mining Co. (N.Y.), 140

Gold Cup Mine (Tin Cup, Colo.), 139–41, 159, 209, 226
Gold Cup Mining Co., 140
Golden Cycle Corp., 231
Golden Fleece Consolidated Mining Co., 180–81
Golden Fleece Extension Mining Co., 180
Golden Fleece Mine (Lake City, Colo.), 86
Golden Rule Placer (La Plata County, Colo.), 175
Gold Links Group (Gunnison County, Colo.), 151
Gold Links Mill (Ohio City, Colo.), 154–55, 160
Gold Links Mining Co. (Ohio City, Colo.), 152–56
Gold Links Mining Co. (Summitville, Colo.), 228
Gold Links Tunnel (Ohio City, Colo.), 17, 151–52, 157, 160, 192, 198, 209, 213, 216, 219, 228–29
Goodale, F. A., 218
Goodnight, Charles, 58
Gordon and Ferguson (St. Paul, Minn.), 54
Goss, George, 84
Grand Valley Irrigation and Development Co., 16
Granger, Ralph, 228
Grant, James B., 21
Gray Eagle Mining Co., 232
Gray Eagle Tunnel. See West Mountain Tunnel
Guggenheim, Daniel, 166
Guggenheim, Simon, 172, 239n.46
Guggenheim Exploration Co., 166, 223–24
Gunnison, Colo., 87–88

Gunnison Mine (Lake City, Colo.), 86
Gunter and Munson (Tascosa, Tex.), 65
Gunter and Summerfield (Tascosa, Tex.), 81
Gurrier, Ed, 48, 60, 187–88

Hagerman, Arthur, 79
Hagerman, James J., 78–79, 94
Hagerman, Percy, 79
Hair pipes, 44, 48
Hall, Frank, 22
Hallam, C. A., 134
Halls Gulch Tunnels, 146
Hansen's Empire Fur Factory (Chicago), 54
Happy Thought Mine (Creede, Colo.), 137, 228
Hartford Gold Extraction Co., 174
Haskell, Otis L., 188–89
Havemeyer, William F., 16, 123–25, 136, 140, 148
Haven. See Industrial school for girls
Hays City, Kans., 45
Hector Mining Co., 16, 123–26
Hector Tunnel Co. (Telluride, Colo.), 125
Hedrick, J. M., 40–41
Heller, Clyde A., 203
Henry, Lyman I., 212
Henry Wilcox and Son, 192
Herbst, Frederick, 127
Hereford cattle, 65–66, 74, 78–79, 189–90
Hergenrader, Henry, 196
Herman, Alex, 196
Hesperus, Colo., 115, 175, 203, 209

Hidetown. See Mobeetie, Tex.
Hill, L. C., 68
Hill, Samuel W., 87
Hinsdale Mining and Development Co., 180
H. K. and F. B. Thurber and Co. (Chicago), 54
Holden, Howard M., 178
Holy Moses Mine (Creede, Colo.), 130
Hotchkiss Mine (Lake City, Colo.), 86
Hough, John S., 88–91, 177
Hubbell, Weller N., 57–59
Hubbell and Doty (Caldwell, Kans.), 59
Hughes, Berrien, 211
Hughes, Charles J., Jr., 15, 93, 211
Hughes, Gerald, 173, 204, 211, 216, 220
Hughes and Dorsey (attorneys, Denver, Colo.), 211
Hulen, J. L., 181
Humphrey, J. P. M., 11, 103, 152
Hurricane Mining and Milling Co. (Aspen, Colo.), 182
Hyde, George, 60
Hydroelectric power, 13, 97–98, 119, 132, 137, 179–80
Hyman, David M., 15, 93–95, 129, 134, 174, 181, 183, 199–200

Iliff School of Theology (Denver, Colo.), 20
Immigrants as miners, Colo., 167
Independence Mill (Crestone, Colo.), 153
Independent Gold Mining Co. (Bowerman, Colo.), 148

Indian beads. *See* Trade beads
Indian claims, Arkansas Valley, Colo., 187–88, 190
Industrial mobilization, World War I, 206
Industrial school for girls (Denver, Colo.), 20
Iron Mask Mine (Colfax County, N.M.), 183
Irrigated farms, Arkansas Valley, Colo., 188

James, William H., 21
Jard, Andy, 56, 90
Jardine, Jack, 100
Jim Blaine Mine (Pitkin, Colo.), 143, 147
JJ Ranch (Colo.), 77
Johnson, Isaac L., 131, 133, 135, 140–42, 159, 183–84
Johnson, James C., 77
Josie Mansfield Placer (Boulder County, Colo.), 182
Junction, Kans., 7

Kansas Pacific Railroad, 45–46
Keiser, C. O., 220
Keller, Anna Earll (Mrs. Richard Keller), 30
Keller, Richard, 30–31, 148–49, 197–98
Kennedy, W. H., 145–46
Kindsvater, Peter, 196
King, Richard, 64
Kingsford, Tenn., 211
Kiowa and Wichita Agency (I.T.), 59
Kiowa Indians, 48, 50, 52, 55, 59
Krisher, Ed, 128, 165

Labor unrest, 22–23, 122, 167

La Junta, Colo., 29, 79, 186–90, 192, 205
La Junta and Lamar Canal Co. (Colo.), 189
La Junta farms, 189–94, 196, 201, 205, 208–209, 229
Lake City, Colo., 10, 26, 29, 59, 66, 83, 85–89, 129, 139, 161, 165, 178–80, 209, 225
Lake Fork of the Gunnison River, 86, 88, 179
Lake San Cristobal (Lake City, Colo.), 86, 180–81
Lake View Gold Mining and Milling Co., 180
La Plata County District Court, 198
Last Chance claim (Creede, Colo.), 131–33
Last Chance Mining and Milling Co., 135
Late Acquisition Mine (Aspen, Colo.), 95
Latimer, Edwin C., 40
Law, Robert, Jr., 158
Lawson Tunnel (Clear Creek County, Colo.), 171–72
Leadville, Colo., 122, 193
Leavenworth, Kans., 5, 7, 44, 48
Lee, Orlina Whitney (Mrs. W. M. D. Lee), 25
Lee, Reynolds and Arnold Co. (N.Y.), 53–54
Lee, Reynolds and Warren Co. (Chicago), 53–54
Lee and Reynolds Freighters (Dodge City, Kans.), 54–55
Lee and Reynolds (partnership): buffalo robe and hide traders, 44, 47–54; cattle raisers, 9–10, 63–66; freight-

ers, 9, 45–46, 55, 57; Indian
  traders, 5, 39–41, 43–54, 60,
  83–84, 101, 187; investors in
  mines and railroads, 10, 66–
  67, 83–86; military contractors, 9–10, 46–47, 56–57;
  military sutlers, 38–41, 186;
  role in the Red River War of
  1874–1875, 50; termination
  of partnership, 10, 26, 57,
  66–67
Lee-Scott Ranch (Tascosa,
  Tex.), 77
Lee, W. M. D., 8; division of
  partnership's assets, 67; end
  of partnership, 10, 57–58,
  66–67, 86; partner with
  A. E. Reynolds, 8–10, 39–57,
  63–67, 83–85. See also Lee
  and Reynolds partnership
LeFevre, Owen E., 135
LE Ranch. See Reynolds Ranch
Lewis, Daisy, 28, 239n.47
Liberal, Kans., 70–71
Liepard, T. M., 56
Lime Belt (Gunnison County,
  Colo.), 143–44, 146, 158
Lime Shale Mining Co. (Dun-
  ton, Colo.), 31, 204
Little, Hugh M., 216
Little Annie Mine (Summitville,
  Colo.), 173
Little Chief Mine (Lake City,
  Colo.), 86
Little Tycoon Mine (Gunnison
  County, Colo.), 143, 147
Lobenstein, W. C., 44
Lockport, N.Y., 6
London Exploration Co., 167
Lorenz, George, 196
Lowe, Henry R., 182
Lowell, Wisc., 25

Lowell Steam Plow Co. (Kansas
  City, Mo.), 191
Low-grade, processing of, 96,
  98
Loyal Mining Co., 169
LS Ranch. See Lee-Scott Ranch
Lyon, James E., 153, 158

Mabry, W. S., 81
McAllister, Jordan Edgar, 65
McClurg, James A., 137
McConnell, Charles E., 30–31,
  175, 184, 187, 198
McCracken, R. M., 214
McCusker, Philip, 243n.38
McGillilard, William P., 131
McKenney, Charles F., 11, 55,
  68–71, 73, 88, 135–36, 152
McKenney and Over Cattle Co.
  (Cline, Okla.), 69
Mackenzie, John C., 131
Mackenzie, William, 74, 171
Madison College. See Colgate
  College
Magee, H. A., 129
Maid of Athens Mine (Pitkin,
  Colo.), 143
Maier, Jacob, 196
Malter, Lind and Co. (San Fran-
  cisco, Calif.), 89
Mammoth Mine (Platoro,
  Colo.), 174
Matadore Land and Cattle Co.,
  78, 250n.62
Mathews, Edward J., 79, 190
Matthews, Joshua, 65
Maugham, John H., 66, 68, 72–
  73, 80, 85, 177
May Day Gold Mining Co., 175,
  177
May Day Mine (Hesperus,
  Colo.), 17, 19, 29–30, 153,

176–77, 198, 203, 209–10,
220, 226, 229
Mayer, David, 196
Mears, Otto, 101
Megaham, J. R., 193
Mexico Central Railway, 199
Michigan, University of, 212
Michigan Military Academy
(Orchard Lake, Mich.), 184
Michigan School of Mines
(Houghton, Mich.), 223
Midnight Group (La Plata
County, Colo.), 176
Miles, John D., 51, 243n.38
Miller, August ("Gus"), 56, 90
Miller, David G., 136, 172,
174–76, 183
Miners, imported into Colo.,
122
Mining Industry & Tradesman, 21
Misses Masters School (Dobbs
Ferry, N.Y.), 28
Mobeetie, Tex., 15, 50, 55, 57–
58, 68
Moffat, David H., 20–21, 24,
100, 131, 137
Molybdenite Mine (Pitkin,
Colo.), 159
Molybdenum, 159
Monarch Mine, 103
Monarch Mining Co., 102–103
Montgomery Ward and Co.
(Chicago), 54
Morey, Chester H., 239n.46
Morse, Albert Reynolds, 29,
232
Morse, Ann, 29, 232
Morse, Anna Reynolds (Mrs.
Bradish P. Morse): birth and
education, 26–28; inheri-
tance, 207–11; management
of Reynolds-Morse Corp.,

226–29; marriage to B. P.
Morse, and family, 28–29,
206; marriage to G. H. Gar-
rey, 229
Morse, Bradish P., career and
marriage, 28–29; death,
225–26; manager of wife's
inheritance, 210–26; Nash-
ville Industrial Corp., 206,
211
Morse, Charles F., 129
Morse, Eudorah Goodell, 29,
232
Morse, George, 206
Morse Bros. Machinery and
Supply Co. (Denver, Colo.),
29, 206
Mount Sneffels Terrible Mining
Co., 102
Mule teams, eight-hitch for
freighting, 45, 56
Myers, A. C., 45, 50

Nashville, Tenn., 217, 219
Nashville Industrial Corp. (Na-
shville, Tenn.), 206, 211
Nelson, A. D., 8
Nelson Tunnel (Creede, Colo.),
135, 137
Newfane, N.Y., 5–6
Newmont Mining Co., 229–30
New York Air Brake Co. (N.Y.),
16–17, 144, 199–202
New York and Chance Mine
(Creede, Colo.), 21, 131–33
New York and Chance Mining
Co., 132, 133–35

Ocean Wave Mine (Lake City,
Colo.), 86, 178–79, 209, 225
Ocean Wave Mining and Smelt-
ing Co., 87, 187

Ocean Wave Tunnel (Lake City, Colo.), 178–79
Ohio City, Colo., 20, 138–39, 142, 145, 150–51, 153, 158–60, 191, 198, 209, 213–14, 216, 228
Oil flotation method of ore reduction, 14–15, 216, 228, 230
Oklahoma Scrip, 70
Old Hickory, Tenn., 205–206, 211
Omaha and Grant Smelting Co. (Denver, Colo.), 99
Onandago, (N.Y.), 201
One Thousand and One Mine (Aspen, Colo.), 95
Ophir Tunnel (Telluride, Colo.), 124–25, 166–68
Otero County District Court (Colo.), 188
Ottumwa, Iowa, 40
Ouray, Colo., 10, 29, 91, 96, 114, 129, 138–39, 161, 165, 167, 170–71, 212–14, 229
Ouray and Mount Sneffels Toll Road Co. (Ouray, Colo.), 101–102
Over, John, 69–71

Pactolus Gold Mining and Milling Co. (Dunton, Colo.), 148
Palmer, Charles P., 11, 129–31, 149
Palmetto Mine (Lake City, Colo.), 19, 86, 88–90, 209
Pandora, Colo., 124
Panic of 1893, 117, 120, 159, 185
Panic of 1907, 197–98
Paonia Packing Co. (Paonia, Colo.), 190

Parole Mining Co., 129, 174
Patterson, J. G., 193
Patterson, Thomas M., 94
Pay Day Group (Hesperus, Colo.), 176
Pay Day Mining Co., 176–77
Pearson, John F., 142, 145, 151–52, 155–56, 158
Pellet, Robert L., 203, 216
Phoenix Mine (Lake City, Colo.), 86
Pickens, John, 222–23
Pitkin, Colo., 20, 115, 138–39, 142, 159–60, 209, 214, 216, 218
Pitkin Mining Co., 145
Pittman Act, 160
Platoro, Colo., 115, 131, 139, 161, 165, 173–74, 209
Platoro Mine (Platoro, Colo.), 19, 174, 209
Platt, Edwin H., 167–68, 170
Pleasant Valley, Utah, 83–84
Plewis, Al, 158
Plewis, M. O., 158
Plutarch Mine (Lake City, Colo.), 86
Poe, J. D., 193
Pope, J. Worden, 60
Porter, George R., 104, 120
Porter, John A., 124
Porter's. See Sneffels, Colo.
Portland Mine (Cripple Creek, Colo.), 231
Powers, John Wesley, 88
Poxson, Ben T., 222, 224–30
Prairie Cattle Co. (Edinburgh, Scotland), 77–78, 80, 82, 190
Pride of America Mine (Lake City, Colo.), 86
Prosser, David B., 84

Provo, Utah, 83–84
Pueblo, Colo., 204–205
Pueblo Saving and Trust Bank (Pueblo, Colo.), 204
Pueblo Smelting and Refining Co. (Pueblo, Colo.), 99

Quartz Creek Mining District (Gunnison County, Colo.), 143–144, 150–51

Railroad transportation, effect on mining, 13, 140
Rapalje, John, 127
Rath, Charles, 45, 50
Rath City, Tex., 50
Raymond Consolidated Mining Co., 151
Raymond Mill (Ohio City, Colo.), 153
Raymond Tunnel (Ohio City, Colo.), 151, 153, 160
Red Elephant Mountain (Clear Creek County, Colo.), 138, 171
Redetsky Iron and Metal Co. (Denver, Colo.), 274n.13
Red River War (1874–75), 41, 50, 55
Reed, Caleb, 92
Reed, David R., 92, 102
Reed, Hubbell W., 11, 89, 92, 96, 99, 102, 104–105, 114, 122–24, 128–29, 140, 165, 183
Revenue Group (Ouray County, Colo.), 105
Revenue Mill (Sneffels, Colo.), 14, 120–23, 125, 127, 153, 166
Revenue Tunnel (Sneffels, Colo.), 10, 13–15, 19, 29, 104–106, 114–23, 125–29, 164–67, 171, 178, 204, 209, 213, 219, 224, 226, 229
Revenue Tunnel Co., 114, 120, 127
Revenue Tunnel Mines Co. (Colo.), 22, 126–28
Revenue Tunnel Mines Co. (Wyo.), 166–70, 210, 215
Reynolds, Abbie, 6, 80
Reynolds, Albert Eugene: cattle rancher, (Texas Panhandle) 67–82, (Colorado) 79–80; community leader, Denver, 20–21; death, 31, 206; estate, 207–14; farms at La Junta, Colo., 189–96, 205, 208–209; friendship with George Bent, 48, 60–61, 187; marriage and family, 25–29, 205–206; merchant, 7–8, 57–60, 88, 90–91, 120; military contractor, 5; military sutler, 5, 7–8; mining entrepreneur, 10–20, 30–32, (Arizona) 182–83, (Aspen, Colo.) 92–96, 181–82, (Boulder County, Colo.) 182, (Bowerman, Colo.) 147–48, (Canada) 184–85, (Creede, Colo.) 130–38, 170–73, (Dunton, Colo.) 148–50, 202–205, 207, (Ely, Nev.) 184, (Hesperus, Colo.) 165, 175–77, (Lake City, Colo.) 86–91, 165, 177–88, (Lawson, Colo.) 171–72, (New Mexico) 183, (Ohio City, Colo.) 150–60, (Ouray, Colo.) 91–92, 96–106, 114–23, 125–29, 165–70, (Pitkin, Colo.) 139, 142–47, (Platoro, Colo.) 129, 174–75, (Summitville,

Colo.) 130, 173–74, (Tell-
uride, Colo.) 123–25, (Tin
Cup, Colo.) 139–42, 159
(Utah) 183–84; speculation
in corporate securities and
silver futures, 199–202. *See
also* Lee and Reynolds
partnership
Reynolds, Alice M., 6, 80
Reynolds, Andrew J. (brother),
6, 7, 24–25, 59, 80, 122
Reynolds, Andrew J. (nephew),
196
Reynolds, Anna Earll, 26, 28
Reynolds, Caroline Van Horn,
5, 6
Reynolds, Charles F., 6, 24–25,
68–69, 75, 79–80, 86, 176
Reynolds City, Tex., 51
Reynolds, Elizabeth, 6, 80
Reynolds, Ellen C., 6, 80
Reynolds, Fanny, 6, 80
Reynolds, Frances Eudorah
Earll (Mrs. A. E. Reynolds),
26–28
Reynolds, George E., 6, 24, 51–
52, 54, 68, 80
Reynolds, George T., 65
Reynolds, Harriet, 6
Reynolds, Henry A., 5–7
Reynolds, Joe B., 103
Reynolds, William, 65
Reynolds farms (La Junta,
Colo.), 189–91
Reynolds Land and Cattle Co.
(Channing, Tex.), 68–69, 71,
73, 75, 80
Reynolds Mining Co., 229,
232
Reynolds-Morse Corp., 220–21,
222, 224–25, 228
Reynolds Ranch (Channing,

Tex.), 57, 62, 67–68, 76–78,
86
Reynolds-Thatcher-Maugham
Pool, 88, 90–91
R. F. Richards and Co. (Leaven-
worth, Kans.), 44
Richard, B. S., 49
Richmond, Mo., 7
Rico, Colo., 115, 148
Riddle, F. E., 215
Ridge Mine (Creede, Colo.), 131
Robinson, Charles, 15, 93, 96,
129
Robinson, James F., 217–19
Robinson, J. W., 181
Robinson, Phoebe, 145
Rob Roy Tunnel (Bingham
Canyon, Utah), 183
Rocky Ford, Colo., 30, 190,
194–95
Rogers, Theodore, 127, 129,
145
Romona, Colo. *See* Chipeta,
Colo.
Roosevelt, Franklin D., 226
Rose, William A., 44
Rose's Cabin (Hinsdale County,
Colo.), 86, 88
Ross, Frank L., 172
Ross, J. B., 172
Ruby Mountain Mining Co.
(Ouray County, Colo.), 105,
127
Rush Medical College (Chi-
cago), 25
Rusk, John M., 82
Russell, George W., 46, 56, 69,
141
Russell, H. Y., 165, 172
Rustler Mine (Lake City, Colo.),
86
Ryman, W. P., 127

INDEX   305

Sadtler, Ben, 143, 217–19
St. Elmo, Colo., 140
St. Johns Mines (Colo.), Ltd.,
    168–70
St. Paul's Evangelical Lutheran
    Church (La Junta, Colo.),
    196
S. and S. Mining Co., 171, 183
S. Brunswick Co. (St. Louis,
    Mo.), 43
Salt Lake City, Utah, 128
Sand Creek, Battle of, 60–61
Sandy Hook Tunnel (Ohio City,
    Colo.), 151
San Juan Country, Colo., 30, 85
San Juan Railroad and Tram-
    way Co., 86
San Luis Land & Mining Co.
    (Crestone, Colo.), 153
San Luis Valley, Colo., 70, 85,
    153
Schell, Francis, 127
Schell, Robert, 129
Schimpf, Henry, 196
Schmeltzer, J. F., 44
Schuch, John Philip, 174
Schwein, Henry, 196
Schwein, Jacob, 196
Schweitzer, Henry, 196
Scofield, C. W., 83–84
Scottish-American Mortgage
    Co., 77
Senate Gold and Silver Mining
    Co., 19, 129
Senate Mine (Platoro, Colo.), 19
Shear, Byron E., 131, 134–35,
    183–84
Sheepherders, Canadian River
    Valley, Tex., 65
Sheldon, William C., 16, 84, 92,
    104–105
Sheldon and Wadsworth Co., 84

Shelton, John M., 250n.62
Shelton, John T., 82
Sherman Silver Purchase Act,
    159–60
Shorthorn cattle, 66
Sidwell, J. P., 168
Sigfrid, Carl J., 211–14, 220–21,
    226
Silent Friend Group (Gunnison
    County, Colo.), 146–47
Silver, price of, 12–13, 116, 159–
    60, 185, 225–26
Silver Basin Mine (Pitkin,
    Colo.), 143, 145–46
Silver Basin Mining Co., 143
Silver Coin Mine (Lake City,
    Colo.), 86
Silver futures, speculation in,
    119
Silver Isle Mine (Pitkin, Colo.),
    143
Silver Purchase Act of 1934,
    226
Silverton, Colo., 172
Smelters, 87, 96–97, 99–100,
    174
Smelter State Bank (Durango,
    Colo.), 30–31, 197–98
Smith, Albert, 129
Smith, Armana (Aramana), 188
Smith, Eben, 24
Smith, George K., 133–34
Smith, John, 188
Smith, William Gilpin, 188
Smith College (North Hamp-
    ton, Mass.), 28
Smokeless power, manufacture
    of, 206
Smuggler Mine (Aspen, Colo.),
    19, 95
Smuggler Mining Co., 181
Smuggler-Union Mining Co., 124

Snedeker, Angus, 11, 140
Sneffels, Colo., 102, 119–20, 168, 209
Solid Muldoon (Ouray, Colo.), 100
Sonora Mine (Lake City, Colo.), 86
South Mountain Mining Co., 232
Southspring Ranch and Cattle Co. (N.M.), 79
Spurr, J. E., 223
Spurr & Cox (Philadelphia, Pa.), 224
Stampfel, Frank, 150, 203–204, 216
Stanhope, Philip R., 171, 183
Starbuck, Charles A., 16, 127, 144–45, 202
Steam power, cost of coal for, 13
Stearns, Thomas B., 180–81
Stephen, Frederick S., 171, 183
Stewart, Mrs. C. E., 87
Stoiber Bros. (Silverton, Colo.), 90
Stone, Frederick William, 64
Strickland, J. A. G., 193
Stryker, S. P., 193
Stuyvesant, A. V. H., 127, 129
Sugar beet factory, 190
Summitville, Colo., 17, 130–31, 139, 161, 165, 173, 198, 202, 209, 222–32
Summitville Consolidated Mines, Inc., 227
Summitville Consolidated Mining Co., 231–32
Summitville Gold Mines, Inc., 227
Summitville Mines Corp., 222
Sutton Tunnel, Chicago Park (Gunnison County, Colo.), 147

Sweetwater, Tex., 50
Swink, Colo., 190

Tailings, pollution of streams, 153–54
Tarifa Mine (Highlands, Colo.), 19, 181, 225
Tarifa Mining Co., 181
Tarifa Tunnel (Highland, Colo.), 181, 225
Tascosa, Tex., 59, 65
Tax sales of mining properties, 156–57, 212–14
Taylor, Abner, 72
Taylor, Babcock and Co., 72
Teller, Henry Moore, 15, 59–60, 93
Telluride, Colo., 23, 122–24, 166
Tennant, Robert, 68
Tennessee-Colorado Development Co., 217
Terrible Mine, 92, 102–103, 143
Texas Gulf Minerals and Metals Co., 231
Texas Land Commission, 82
Texas State Capitol, funding of, 72
Thatcher, Henry C., 66, 85, 177
Thatcher, John A., 8, 73, 85–86, 169, 177
Thatcher, Mahlon D.: gives Reynolds purchase option on Frank Hough Mine, 177; investments in Reynolds's mines, 85–86, 89, 104, 117, 125–26, 129, 140–42, 144, 166, 169, 179; Pueblo, Colo., banker, 11–12, 85; sells interest in Revenue Tunnel to Reynolds, 167–68; vice president of Reynolds

Land and Cattle Co., 73–74, 80, 82
Thatcher, Mahlon D. (son), 204, 216
Thatcher, Newton J., 183
Third Regiment, Colo. Volunteers, 60
Thomas, Charles S., 94
Thomas, Elmer, 226
Thornton, Edward, 131, 227
Timmons, Colin, 131, 133–35, 182–83
Tin Cup, Colo., 20, 115, 138–40, 159, 209
Tippit, Ann Morse (Mrs. John Tippit), 232
Tobey, F. B., 148–49
Tom Boy Gold Mining Co., 168
Tomichi Valley Smelting Co., 99–100
Tonopah-Belmont Development Co., 203–204
Topeka, Kans., 212
Towne homestead (La Plata County, Colo.), 176
Trade beads, 48
Trade tokens, 51–52
Treaty of Fort Wise, 187
Treaty of Medicine Lodge, 39
Trobett, W. F., 193
Tungsten mining, 159
Tunnels, 10, 13–15, 19, 29, 51, 104–106, 114–20, 121–23, 125–29, 135–37, 145–47, 151–54, 164, 167, 171, 175, 179, 181–83, 198, 209–10, 213, 215–16, 229
Two Johns Mining & Milling Co. (Deadwood, S.Dak.), 134

Underhill, Charles, 127
Unger, Bela A., 194

Union Pacific Resources Corp., 229
U.S. Department of War, 40
U.S. Environmental Protection Agency, 232–33
U. S. Geological Survey, 223
U. S. House of Representatives, 6
Utah and Pleasant Valley RR. Co., 83–84
Utah Coal and Coke Co., 83
Ute and Ulay (Ule) Mines (Lake City, Colo.), 86–87
Ute Mining Dist. (Conejos County, Colo.), 129

Valley View Consolidated Mining Co. (Hesperus, Colo.), 177
Van Gieson Lixiviation Works (Lake City, Colo.), 87
Van Horn, Burt, 6
Van Horn, D. W., 8, 57–58, 67
Van Horn, Frank, 179
Vatable, Emile, 140–41
Vidal, Henry C., 221–22
Virginius Mine (Ouray County, Colo.), 10, 13, 16, 19, 92, 96–98, 99–106, 114, 116–17, 120–21, 126, 164–65, 178, 204
Volz & Kiesling (Fort Elliott, Tex.), 64

Walsh, Thomas F., 32
W. A. Rose & Co. (Leavenworth, Kans.), 44
Warren, G. D., 53
Waskey, J. F., 88
Wave of the Ocean Mine (Lake City, Colo.), 86
Weiglin, Joe, 188

Western Federation of Miners, 23, 122

Western Oil, Coal & Investment Co. (Greeley, Col.), 213–14

West Mountain Tunnel (Pitkin, Colo.), 145–46

Wheeler, Harris A., 184

Wheeler, Jerome B., 15, 94, 181

Wheeler, W. E., 167

Wheel of Fortune Consolidated Mining Co., 128

Wheel of Fortune Mining Co., 114, 127, 168–69

White Mine (Downieville, Colo.), 171

Wiley, Jesse C., 221–23

Will, Henry, 196

Will, Mikael, 196

Willcox, William R., 16

Williams, George W., 189–91, 193, 205, 209

Withrow, Clarence O., 220, 227

Withrow-Commodore Lease, 221

Wolcott, Edward O., 132

Wolcott, Henry R., 21, 132

Woman's Club of Denver, 27

Wooster Tunnel (Creede, Colo.), 135

World War I, 206

Wright, Robert M., 45, 50, 59

W. S. Moore Co., 229

Wyandotte Mine (Lake City, Colo.), 86

Wyeth, E. A., 92

Wynkoop, William C., 21–22

XIT Ranch (Tex.), 71–72, 76–77, 80–82

Young Women's Friendly Club (Denver), 20

Zook, J. J., 193